St Marguerite Bourgeoys (1620–1700), canonized in 1982, founded the first school in Montreal and one of the first uncloistered religious communities of women. In this biography Patricia Simpson goes behind the mist of myth and hagiography. *Marguerite Bourgeoys and Montreal* documents her life both in France and in the struggling settlement of Ville-Marie (present-day Montreal), placing her experiences within the larger historical context of the time and highlighting the role of women in society and the church.

Born and raised in Troyes, France, in 1653 Marguerite Bourgeoys came to the tiny and beleaguered settlement of Ville-Marie, founded in 1642 as a Christian missionary society. These early years in New France marked a special period in her life. Committed to the belief that the world would be a better place if people learned to understand one another, she worked to build a better church and a better society, especially for women and children.

Marguerite Bourgeoys's life story is one of tolerance and compassion, ideals that are no less important now than three centuries ago.

PATRICIA SIMPSON, CND, is co-director of the Marguerite Bourgeoys Centre.

McGill-Queen's Studies in the History of Religion

Volumes in this series have been supported by the Jackman Foundation of Toronto.

SERIES ONE
G.A. Rawlyk, Editor

SERIES TWO   In memory of George Rawlyk
Donald Harman Akenson, Editor

Marguerite Bourgeoys and Montreal, 1640–1665
Patricia Simpson

Aspects of the Canadian Evangelical Experience
G.A. Rawlyk, editor

Marguerite Bourgeoys and Montreal, 1640–1665

Patricia Simpson

McGill-Queen's University Press
Montreal & Kingston • London • Buffalo

Legal deposit second quarter 1997
Bibliothèque nationale du Québec

Funds toward publication of this book have
been provided by Les Soeurs de la
Congrégation de Notre-Dame.

Printed in Canada on acid-free paper
Reprinted in paper 1998

Canadian Cataloguing in Publication Data

Simpson, Patricia, 1937-
Marguerite Bourgeoys and Montreal, 1640-1665
(McGill-Queen's studies in the history of religion,
ISSN 1181-7445)
Includes bibliographical references and index.
ISBN 0-7735-1607-7 (bound) -
ISBN 0-7735-1641-7 (pbk.)
1. Bourgeoys, Marguerite, Saint, 1620-1700.
2. Christian saints – Canada – Biography.   3. Nuns –
Quebec (Province) – Biography.   4. Canada – History – To
1663 (New France).   5. Montréal (Quebec) – History.
I. Title.   II. Series
BX4700.B76S54 1997   282'.092   C97-900090-4

To Sister Mary Eileen Scott CND,
who greatly loved both
Marguerite Bourgeoys and Montreal

Contents

Acknowledgments

The author wishes to express her gratitude to Joyce Roberts for assistance with research, for technical aid, and for reading and providing advice about the manuscript at every step of the way; to Danielle Dubois for reading and making suggestions about the manuscript and, with Rachel Gaudreau, for assistance with the selection and preparation of the illustrations; to Madeleine Huet and Judith Outerbridge for help with the final preparation of the manuscript; and to Starr Downing and Gisèle Laurin for technical assistance; also to Professor Malcolm M. Ross for reading the manuscript and for his advice and encouragement and to the members of the general administration of the Congrégation de Notre-Dame of Montreal for their confidence and support.

Note on Translation and Names Used

All the original sources and most of the secondary works relating to the life of Marguerite Bourgeoys are in French, and few of them have been translated into English. Where a suitable translation is available, it has been used and cited in the bibliography and notes. Since some of these translations were made many years ago, they employ terms that would not be used today, such as "savages" to translate the French *sauvages* (in the sense of "natural" or "uncultivated"), used to describe the Amerindians. Where no suitable English translation is available, the one provided is the author's own.

In the case of Marguerite Bourgeoys's contemporaries, the names of persons mentioned in the text appear in the form in which they are given in her own writings and those of such other frequently quoted writers as François Dollier de Casson and Sister Marie Morin: thus for example, "de Maisonneuve" for Paul de Chomedy de Maisonneuve, "Dollier" for Dollier de Casson, and so on. Other names are spelled as given in the *Dictionary of Canadian Biography*. As is the case in writings of the period, "Montreal" and "Canada" are used occasionally interchangeably with "Ville-Marie" and "New France." Marguerite Bourgeoys herself used the two earlier terms much more frequently. Because several different Congrégations de Notre-Dame and congregations are mentioned in this work, "the Congregation" (capitalized) always refers to the Congrégation de Notre-Dame of Montreal founded by Marguerite Bourgeoys. The Congrégation de Notre-Dame de Montreal, already "la Congrégation" to Montrealers of the 1660s, has been known among English-speaking residents of the city as "the Congregation" since soon after the community began to accept their daughters among its pupils at the end of the eighteenth century.

Portrait of Marguerite Bourgeoys painted by Pierre Le Ber at the time
of her death in 1700; subsequently overpainted and restored in 1962.
Marguerite Bourgeoys Centre, Montreal.

House in Troyes where Marguerite Bourgeoys was born, second from the left; demolished in 1976. In the background is Saint-Jean-au-Marché church, where she was baptized on 17 April 1620. Photo A. Landry, 1950.

Extract from the baptismal register of Saint-Jean-au-Marché church recording the baptism on 17 April 1620 of Marguerite, daughter of Abraham Bourgeoys and Guillemette Garnier, his wife; with godparents Nicolas Bertran and Marguerite Cantan, wife of Nicolas Garnier.

Stained-glass windows depicting events in the life of the Virgin Mary that were central to the spirituality of Marguerite Bourgeoys: the Visitation and Pentecost. Saint-Rémi church, Troyes, sixteenth century. Photo Rachel Gaudreau.

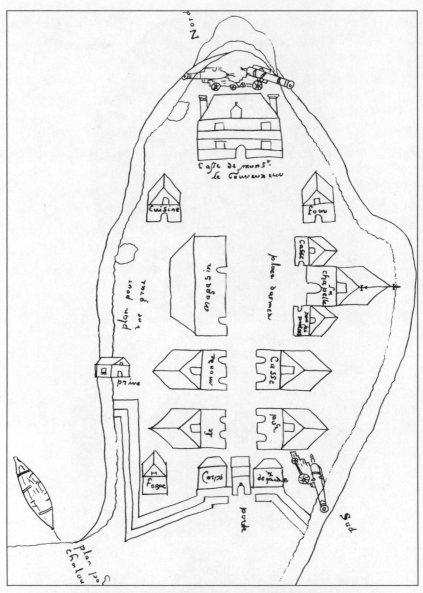

Drawing by Jean Bourdon, reputedly of the Montreal fort in 1647. Marguerite Bourgeoys lived in the fort from her arrival in 1653 until the opening of the first school in 1658. Department of Rare Books and Special Collections, McGill University.

Marguerite Bourgeoys, oil by Ozias Leduc.
Notre-Dame-de-Bon-Secours chapel,
Montreal.

Jeanne Mance, founder of Montreal's Hôtel-Dieu and co-founder of the city,
who worked closely with Marguerite Bourgeoys for many years. Sculpture
in Langres, France, her birthplace. Photo Rachel Gaudreau.

Paul de Chomedey de Maisonneuve, founder and first governor of Montreal, who recruited Marguerite Bourgeoys as the colony's first teacher in 1653. Oil by Ozias Leduc. Notre-Dame-de-Bon-Secours chapel, Montreal.

Artist's conception of the first school in Montreal, opened by Marguerite Bourgeoys on 30 April 1658; based on contemporary descriptions of the former stable. Françoise Delorme.

Angélique Faure, widow of Claude de
Bullion, treasurer of France. She was a leading member of the Société de Notre-Dame de
Montreal, endowed the Hôtel-Dieu, and
acted as one of Montreal's principal benefactors. Archives de l'Hôtel-Dieu de Montréal.

Members of the Société de Notre-Dame de Montréal sign, in Paris, the act
of foundation of Ville-Marie (Montreal). Detail of monument in Place
d'Armes, Montreal. Photo Rachel Gaudreau.

Monsieur

La facilité de vous escrire que vous m'offrites l'an
passé me donne la liberté de vous faire savoir les motifs
qui ont porté a faire l'establissement de la Congregation a
Montreal; et comme j'apprends que vous avez la charité de
travailler aux reglements qui y doivent servir, Je passe sur ma
Repugnance pour vous faire savoir les fins de Cet Institut...
Monsieur Gendret qui me voulut bien prendre sous sa direction, me dit
un jour, que Notre Seigneur avoit laissé 3 etats de filles pour suivre
et servir l'Eglise; que Celuy de Ste Madelaine estoit Rempli par les Carmelites
et autres Recluses, et Celuy de Ste Marthe par les Religieuses Cloitrées qui
servent le prochain; Mais que Celuy de la vie voyagere de la Ste vierge
ne l'estoit pas, et qu'il falloit l'honorer...... Je croys que pour honorer Cet etat de
la vie voyagere de la Ste vierge il faut que les soeurs soient filles de paroisse,
qu'elles soient gouvernées par les seminaires, que les derniers sacrements leur soyent
administrés par l'ordre de la paroisse, qu'elles y ayent leur sepulture et y soyent
enterrées, comme aussi une place pour y assister avec les ecoliers aux grand'-
Messes, Vespres et saluts, et y Communier quelquefois - qu'elles ne Chantent ny
grand' messes, ny Vespres, dans leur eglise, Mais seulement quelques Motets
aux messes basses et aux Jours qui seront Jugé a propos; que dans la
maison les soeurs soyent egales, en sorte que la Superieure a pris sa demission
put estre Cuisiniere, ou occupée a tout autre employ auquel elle sera
trouvée propre, et la Cuisiniere estre superieure, ou estre employée
aux gros ouvrages. le tout pour Imiter la vie et les vertus de la Ste
vierge. tout Cela ne m'empechera pas d'estre bien Contente de tout Ce
qui sera fait. C'est tout Moy desire que dieu soit servy dans Cette Communauté.
Je suis avec tout le Respect qui m'est possible

Monsieur

Votre plus obligée et obeissante
servante Marguerite Bourgeoys

Letter written in 1693 by Marguerite Bourgeoys to Louis Tronson, Superior
of the Sulpicians in Paris. She explains the motives which led to the founding of the Congrégation de Notre-Dame de Montréal.

Marguerite Bourgeoys and Montreal, 1640–1665

Introduction

When Marguerite Bourgeoys died in Montreal on 12 January 1700, the sisters of the Congrégation de Notre-Dame, which she had founded, commissioned the artist Pierre Le Ber to paint a likeness of her features before they disappeared forever.[1] The painting he executed that day, saved from the fires that were twice to destroy the mother house, was preserved as a treasure by the Congregation. In the middle of the twentieth century, however, concern was raised about the authenticity of the image displayed as the Le Ber portrait. The painting was submitted to Edward Korany, a distinguished art restorer in New York. His examination revealed that beneath the visible depiction of Marguerite Bourgeoys lay another quite different representation. The surface portrait, now believed to have been painted over the original in the mid-nineteenth century, was copied and then removed and for the first time in more that a hundred years, the face of Marguerite Bourgeoys as Pierre Le Ber had depicted her was revealed to the world. Sister M. Eileen Scott, who had brought the painting to the restorer, had told him as little as possible about the subject of the work; only that it represented a nun of the seventeenth century. When she asked him what the freshly revealed image said to him, he summed it up in one word, "compassion."[2] What manner of life had written this message on her features?

Marguerite Bourgeoys, a native of Troyes, the ancient capital of the province of Champagne, in 1653 came to a tiny and beleaguered Ville-Marie, still undergoing its birth pangs. The city that we now know as Montreal came into existence through the desire of a group of devout men and women in seventeenth-century France to share with the native people of the New World what they regarded as their most precious possession: their Christian faith. They hoped to achieve this goal through the establishment of a settlement on the island of Montreal in the colony of New France. The foundation was intended to embody the Christian ideal described in the Acts of the Apostles in such a way as to attract the Amerindians just as the communities of early Christians had drawn their first converts in the Mediterranean world of the first century. To attain this end, the Société de Notre-Dame de Montréal was formed in France in 1640, and Ville-Marie founded on the island of Montreal in May two years later.

Marguerite Bourgeoys's arrival eleven years after the initial foundation was to fulfil part of the original design for the colony, which included a plan to provide for the education of its children. She came with the recruitment known as the "hundred men," who were to prevent that first foundation from abandonment or extinction, the alternatives facing Ville-Marie by 1653. On the voyage between France and Canada, during which she had cared for the sick and consoled the dying, the prospective settlers with whom she journeyed had already begun to address her as "sister." From this beginning until her death in 1700, she was totally dedicated to the welfare of the people of Montreal. With the first settlers she shared the dangers and hardships, as well as the efforts and hopes, that marked life in the early colony. Like them, she was vulnerable to the threats posed by the environment, the enemy, and disease, as well as by sometimes hostile or incompetent authorities in both church and state. She consistently avoided and, whenever possible, refused all preferment or privilege that would remove her from the lot of ordinary people in New France, the poor and struggling settlers attempting to build a better life for themselves and their families in the New World. She also performed the task for which she had come to Montreal, opening the first school in an abandoned stable in the spring of 1658. To give permanence and stability to the work of educating children and women in New France, she founded a community of uncloistered women. Although civil and especially ecclesiastical approbation lay far in the future, this community came into existence on 2 July 1659 when Marguerite's first companions joined her on the ship carrying the last of the great recruitments undertaken by the Société de Notre-Dame de Montréal.

Like several of the other leaders in early Montreal, Marguerite Bourgeoys came from a region of France where women had played important public roles since at least the Middle Ages. In becoming part of the Montreal endeavour, she participated in an undertaking in which women played key roles, both behind the scenes in France and in the leadership of the early colony. The evidence of the time indicates that the relationship between these women and the men who were their partners was cooperative rather than confrontational. But Marguerite Bourgeoys was not just concerned with the prominent persons of Montreal, the men and women whose names history has recorded. She was convinced of the importance of the ordinary women of the colony: in their hands – the hands of those who were to be its wives and mothers – lay the future of Canada. Their education was of paramount importance to her. Marguerite's words, as well as the life work she undertook, reflect her belief that people, and therefore society, can be changed if only they can be enabled "to understand," an object of all true education.

The instruction that Marguerite Bourgeoys and her companions provided to the children (initially boys as well as girls) and women of New France was foremost an education in faith that sprang from a profound religious impulse. The faith, which found expression in her life as well as in the words of hers that have been handed down and was the foundation of all her teaching, was a belief in the primary and overriding importance of the double commandment at the heart of both the Old and New Testaments: You shall love the Lord your God with all your heart and soul and mind, and you shall love your neighbour as yourself. However, the school had, for Marguerite, other important functions than that of conveying religious instruction. Her first pupils were not the wealthy and powerful; they were the children of colonists in seventeenth-century Montreal, who had early faced the challenging tasks of earning a living for themselves and their families and of building a new country. To enable them to accomplish these tasks, she stressed the importance not only of "honourable work" but of the value and importance of their efforts.

Marguerite's educational efforts were not confined to the teaching of children in the schoolroom. She reached out to the young immigrant women who came as prospective brides to New France, going so far as to give them a home, where she lived with them while she helped them to adapt to their new country and situation. She also opened workshops where poor women could learn the crafts that would enable them to earn their living. The intimacy in which she and her companions lived with the other settlers in the early colony, as well as her genius for perceiving and responding to the needs around her, made possible a form of education that was truly relevant to the lives of those who received it.

Although Marguerite Bourgeoys spent most of her life on what her European contemporaries would have seen as a boundary of the world, she was at the centre of an important development taking place in the Roman Catholic Church of her time: the attempt to establish a different kind of consecrated life in community for women.

Until the seventeenth century, and until much later in the minds of many ecclesiastical authorities, women who lived in community and dedicated themselves to the service of the church were of necessity cloistered women, prohibited from leaving their convents and able to admit outsiders only into designated areas of those convents. The material security of these communities depended on endowments and dowries, thereby closing them to poor women unless they could find a sponsor. Marguerite was to be successful in establishing one of the first uncloistered religious communities of women in the Catholic Church, a community that was self-supporting and that, unlike most of its counterparts in France at the time, has survived until today. This community was to owe its character and its survival to her experience in the so-called heroic period of Montreal's history. Her inspiration in founding such a community was Mary the mother of Jesus, whom she saw as the first and most faithful disciple of the Lord, going about teaching and doing good in the primitive church. Her sense of identification with this figure grew with her own experience of the "primitive church" of Montreal's earliest years.

Marguerite Bourgeoys did not leave behind a wealth of autobiographical writing, such as is to be found in the letters of her older contemporary in New France, Marie de l'Incarnation, the great Ursuline mystic. She undoubtedly wrote more than is still extant; fires at the Congregation mother houses in Montreal in both the eighteenth and nineteenth centuries, as well as in Marguerite's own time, and the dispersal of some of her writings as relics have meant that almost nothing in her hand still exists. The small volume published as *Écrits autographes* was taken from two copies of what remained of her writings in the 1870s, one sent to the archives of the Vatican and the other intended to remain in the archives of the archdiocese of Montreal. These were prepared by different hands but contain identical material arranged in the same order. A third manuscript, also in Rome, has the contents in a different order and includes two passages not found elsewhere. Apart from these differences, the text is the same as in the official copies. These writings are fragmentary and contain many repetitions. They cover a range of subject matter that varies in importance, from a directive to the sisters not to spit in church – providing a startling glimpse of seventeenth-century manners – to statements about the central inspiration of the Congrégation de Notre-Dame. Given their present form, it is difficult, perhaps impossible, to know fair copy from foul or to distinguish a series of notes jotted down for a conference and given to the sisters from a résumé destined to be incorporated into a letter or a report to the bishop. A critical edition might help resolve some of these difficulties, but at present, none is available.

Several biographies of Marguerite Bourgeoys date from the eighteenth century. Her first chronicler was Charles de Glandelet, a priest attached to the seminary in Quebec from 1675, who had met her and possibly had served as her occasional spiritual director. He had in his possession letters that she had written and notes from the sisters who had known her, as well as other documents; all of which have since disappeared. Glandelet's biography was written in two parts: "Le vray esprit de l'Institut" in 1700–01, immediately after Marguerite's death, and "La vie de la Soeur Bourgeoys dite du Saint-Sacrement" in 1715. Research in the past half century has shown that many of the details Glandelet presents about her early life in Troyes are wrong, but in any case, he is not concerned primarily with the events of her life or with situating it in the context of the origins of Montreal and New France. Rather, his intention is to convey his understanding of her spirituality and sanctity. Glandelet knew that Marguerite Bourgeoys was generally regarded as a saint. Inevitably, then, he tended to some extent to impose upon her his own model of what a saint should be. Like many of his contemporaries, he looked for "signs and wonders": extraordinary visions and revelations, extraordinary penances. For him, as for some of her other earlier biographers, Marguerite was something of a disappointment in this respect.

Glandelet's work needs to be supplemented by the references to Marguerite Bourgeoys in other writings begun or completed in the seventeenth century. These are sometimes more helpful in bringing to life the woman who was known and loved in early Montreal. One such work is François Dollier de Casson's *Histoire de Montréal*; another is the *Annales de l'Hôtel-Dieu de Montréal, 1659–1725* by Sister Marie Morin. These two contemporaries of Marguerite wrote about her when she was still living and present her in a way in which she can be more fully understood as a human person; that is, in relationship with those among whom she lived her life. Both present the colourful panorama of life in early Montreal; both provide stories that bring their subject more vividly to life than abstract statements can. Their view of Marguerite is supported by the religious and legal records of the time: the baptisms, marriage contracts, burial records, account books, deeds, court cases, and wills that together tell their own story. Two lives of Marguerite Bourgeoys were written in the eighteenth century. In 1728 *La vie de la Soeur Marguerite Bourgeoys* by Michel-François Ransonet, a cleric of Liège and relative of the bishop of Quebec, was printed at Avignon. The author, who says he was selected for his task because the clergy of New France were too busy with apostolic ministry, had neither known Marguerite Bourgeoys nor visited the colony. His sources were documents sent him by the sisters of the Congrégation de Notre-Dame in Montreal and Glandelet's works. Étienne Montgolfier's *La vie de la vénérable Marguerite Bourgeoys*, though not published until 1818, was written in 1780. Montgolfier, a Sulpician who lived in Montreal from 1751 until his death in 1791, used as his sources Glandelet, the surviving writings of Marguerite Bourgeoys, and the reminiscences of sisters of the Congrégation de Notre-Dame who had known her.

Three important retellings of her life were published between the mid-nineteenth and the mid-twentieth centuries. The first scholarly biography was the two-volume *Vie de la Soeur Bourgeoys*, by Étienne Faillon, published in 1853. This work is scrupulously documented and forms an important part of the research that this Sulpician scholar contributed to the history of New France. The first volume of another work, the *Histoire de la Congrégation de Notre Dame*, is largely a biography of the founder. In its preparation the author, Sister Sainte-Henriette, made use of documents lost when the building known as the Mountain Mother House was totally destroyed by fire in 1893. The Benedictine Albert Jamet published his two-volume *Marguerite Bourgeoys, 1620–1700* fifty years later. He situated Marguerite's early life in the context of the Europe of her day and for the first time dealt at length with the dark events at the beginning of the last decade before her death, when her entire life's work was threatened and Montreal's religious communities were split by a supposed visionary and her supporters.[3]

Marguerite Bourgeoys's beatification in 1950 and canonization in 1982 have continued to stimulate interest in her in her native Troyes. The result has been the discovery of records and documents not known to previous biographers. These have shown that much of the information traditionally given about the size and make-up of Marguerite's family, for example, and the dates of her parents' deaths is in error. While some of these details are of minor importance, others affect our interpretation of her behaviour at significant moments in her life. Among the documents that have come to light are inventories made after the deaths of each of Marguerite's parents, which cast considerable light on the economic circumstances of the family. In addition to the discovery of these new facts, there have been other reasons for writing a new biography.

Each age puts its own questions to the past and does so in its own idiom. Both Faillon and Jamet wrote in the hagiographic style of their time, a style that tends to alienate today's reader. The questions of our own era are not those of the 1850s or even the early 1940s. The life of Marguerite Bourgeoys can tell us something about relationships between men and women in society and in the church, about contacts between North Americans of native and non-native origin, about the treatment of immigrants, and about the purposes of education. These are not aspects of her life on which earlier biographers focused their attention, but they are profoundly important for us today.

The task of writing a new biography of Marguerite Bourgeoys in English was originally entrusted by the Congrégation de Notre-Dame to Sister M. Eileen Scott, an indefatigable researcher, a considerable prose stylist and poet, a woman of wit, and a great lover of Marguerite Bourgeoys and Montreal, the city of her own birth. She was greatly assisted in the part of her research concerned with France, especially Troyes, by Alfred Morin, deputy librarian of the municipal library in that city, whose efforts over several years were responsible for the discovery of most of the new information about the Bourgeoys family. Sister Scott also wrote a significant number of papers, delivered to a variety of audiences, most of which were never published; as well, she acted as consultant for articles about Marguerite Bourgeoys and the Congrégation de Notre-Dame that appeared in magazines and newspapers and for radio and television programs dealing with those subjects. She was responsible for some of the articles relating to the Congregation in the *Dictionary of Canadian Biography*. To many of those who listened to her, it seemed as if Sister Scott achieved in words what Edward Korany had done in his restoration of the Le Ber portrait – stripped away the obscuring mask to reveal the true face of Marguerite Bourgeoys. Unfortunately, she had not completed her research to her satisfaction when the severe illness that led to her death in 1987 rendered her task forever impossible. The research done by Sister Scott and M. Alfred Morin has been particularly helpful in the preparation of this biography.

This biography is built around a series of statements that Marguerite Bourgeoys made about her own life in the belief that, as C.H. Dodd observed about the primitive church of the New Testament, "The interest and meaning which an event bore for those who felt its impact is part of the event."[4] The statements cited were generally written down in the last decade of Marguerite's life of nearly eighty years. They therefore represent her own understanding of the meaning and significance of the events of her long life as it drew to its close. Even though some of those events had taken place as much as fifty years before she wrote about them, they emerge in her reminiscences with a peculiar vividness and clarity.

In May 1990 an open-air musical celebration of another Montreal saint, Marguerite d'Youville, opened with a scene in which the poor of Montreal for whom she had cared in the eighteenth century demand to be allowed their place in the action. This study of the life of Marguerite Bourgeoys attempts to let the ordinary people of seventeenth-century Montreal onto the stage. From the moment that she first encountered them in the future settlers aboard the *Saint-Nicolas-de-Nantes*, they were the focus of her life and her activity. Any understanding of her life and rôle in early Montreal must be based, not just on a knowledge of her relationship to its leaders, such as de Maisonneuve and Jeanne Mance, but also on her contacts with the more humble and largely forgotten men and women who were the original Montrealers.

Hélène Bernier's article on Marguerite Bourgeoys in the *Dictionary of Canadian Biography* refers to the decade after 1672 as the golden age of her work in New France. Without doubt, it was the period of greatest expansion. But if Marguerite herself had been asked to choose an era of her life to designate as "golden," her writings imply that it would quite certainly have been the period with which this book is principally concerned: the years between 1653, when she arrived in Montreal, and 1665, when the departure of Paul de Chomedey de Maisonneuve and the arrival of the Carignan-Salières regiment signalled the end of an era in the city's history. These had been years of struggle, danger, deprivation, and hardship; they were also years of hope, friendship, and shared dreams. During these years, Marguerite knew every settler in Montreal, many of them intimately, and was as much a part of their lives as they were of hers. She worked closely with other leaders from her native Champagne; the first two chapters of this book deal with Troyes and Champagne, not just because of their significance in her life, but because almost all the leaders in early Montreal came from that province. During this period the original vision of the Société de Notre-Dame de Montréal – as a Christian missionary society – was still alive. The religious community of women that "God had not willed in Troyes" had its birth in an abandoned stable in Ville-Marie on the island of Montreal.

The life of Marguerite Bourgeoys did not finish with the departure of de Maisonneuve in 1665, the year with which this account closes. She was to win civil and then ecclesiastical recognition for one of the first uncloistered communities of women in the Roman Catholic Church. In her lifetime the members of that community were to include not just French but North American women of French, Amerindian, and even English ancestry. They were to extend their educational efforts beyond Montreal to Quebec and to the little settlements coming into being along the St Lawrence River. But that is another story. The Montreal that evolved after 1665 was not the settlement of which its founders had dreamed.

A study of Marguerite Bourgeoys can do more than help us understand the past. She was a pioneer, a leader in attempts to build a better church and a better society in a world where those two were not really separable. It was a world where she made the welfare of women and children her special concern, one that she believed could be improved if people could learn to understand one another. The worlds in which we lived only yesterday are as irrevocably lost to us as Europe was to the settlers of the seventeenth century who left it for the New World or as pre-Columbian America was to its native peoples once the Europeans had arrived. Though experienced so long ago, the life of Marguerite Bourgeoys in early Montreal can tell us something about meeting the challenges of the present, in which we are all pioneers, and about the need for understanding and compassion, which are no less important now than they were more than three centuries ago.

CHAPTER ONE

Beginnings, 1620–1640

In 1640 on Rosary Sunday, I went to the procession at the Dominican Church where there was so great a number of people that the cloister was not large enough. So we crossed the street and passed in front of the portal of Notre Dame [aux-Nonnains] where there was a statue in stone above the door. And glancing up to look at it, I found it very beautiful. At the same time, I found myself so moved and so changed that I no longer recognized myself. When I returned home, this was apparent to everyone.[1]

Marguerite Bourgeoys wrote these words in 1697, at the age of seventy-seven. She was reaching the end of a long life that had seen her cross the Atlantic Ocean seven times, participate in the beginnings of what would one day be the most important city in Canada, and found one of the first uncloistered religious communities for women in the Roman Catholic Church, the Congrégation de Notre-Dame de Montréal. Her words describe what she regarded as the transforming experience in which that congregation had its origin. Unlike some of her illustrious contemporaries, Marguerite was always extremely reticent about describing her intimate feelings or spiritual experiences. The two principal references in her autobiographical writings to the experience of Rosary Sunday in 1640 were both set down in the last decade of her life in situations that she perceived as crises in the life of her congregation. The earlier of the two was inspired by another of the many attempts by ecclesiastical authority to alter totally the nature of the congregation that she had founded by imposing cloister and dowry; the second by her fears that the ideals of simplicity, poverty, and service to the poor on which she had founded her community were in danger of being abandoned. In one of these statements, she makes explicit her repugnance for the task of describing her private religious experience. She does so only because, in this case, that experience had a public significance.[2] Precisely because such statements from Marguerite Bourgeoys are so rare and these two were produced in circumstances of some urgency, they are of inestimable importance in an attempt to understand her own perception of her vocation and that of the congregation she founded. Her description of the events of Rosary Sunday quoted above is an excellent starting point not only for her biography but also for any account of her role in the history of early Montreal.

In Marguerite Bourgeoys's view, the moment of her conversion in 1640 was not just a major turning point in her own life and the moment in which the Congrégation de Notre-Dame had its genesis; it was also intimately connected with the origins of Montreal. The earlier of the two accounts of what has come to be known as her conversion is found in the draft of a letter to Louis Tronson, the Sulpician superior in Paris, a letter he had solicited to help him in his efforts to prevent Bishop Jean-Baptiste de Saint-Vallier of Quebec from imposing unacceptable rules on the Congrégation de Notre-Dame. In her description of the event, Marguerite explicitly relates it to the history of Montreal. "During the procession on Rosary Sunday, in the year 1640 (which I have since learned was the year of the first arrival in Montreal), I was strongly moved when I looked up at a statue of the Blessed Virgin."[3] Later she adds, "At the same time [as her conversion], M. de Maisonneuve's sister ... gave to her brother a picture on which was written in letters of gold: 'Holy Mother of God, pure Virgin with a faithful heart, keep for us a place in your Montreal.'"[4] Elsewhere in her writings, Marguerite describes her first pilgrimage to the site of the cross on Mount Royal, erected by the early settlers on 6 January 1643 in thanksgiving for their preservation from a flood that had threatened the fort itself.[5] She found that the cross had been overthrown by the Iroquois, but that the picture Louise de Maisonneuve had given to her brother remained. "It was in poor condition. Written in gold letters around the picture were the words: 'Holy Mother of God, pure Virgin with a royal heart, keep us a place in your Montreal.' And that very year, I was deeply moved at the sight of a statue above the portal of Notre Dame in Troyes during the Rosary procession."[6]

The event that was not only to change the life of the twenty-year-old Marguerite Bourgeoys and the history of Montreal but also to help etablish a new form of religious life for women in the Catholic Church took place among the medieval religious houses of the ancient and beautiful city of Troyes, where Marguerite had been born on 17 April 1620. It is in this historic capital of Champagne that any study of her life must begin. Like all human beings, she was shaped by the time and place in which she lived. A knowledge of the context in which her life started makes possible an understanding not only of what in her derives from that background but also of what surpasses and transcends it.

Marguerite spent the first thirty-three years of her life in the city of her birth. Even given the greatly increased life expectancy of developed countries in the last years of the twentieth century, the first thirty-three years constitute a significant portion of anyone's life. In a century when 25 per cent of all children died before the age of one year and another 25 before they were twenty, and when 75 per cent of the population died before the age of forty-five,[7] Marguerite had already spent what constituted a lifetime for most of her contemporaries in her native city before she departed for Canada. Her life, her words, her attitudes, all strikingly demonstrate the lasting influence of the city and region of her origin. According to Dollier de Casson, it was as a fellow native of Champagne that de Maisonneuve enthusiastically announced her impending arrival in Montreal to Jeanne Mance. " Now let me tell you about an excellent woman I am bringing back with me called Marguerite Bourgeoys whose qualities are a treasure which will be a powerful help in Montreal. Besides, she is also a fruit of our Champagne which seems willing to give this place more than all the other provinces together."[8] In his survey of the population of early Montreal, Marcel Trudel has remarked that this statement seems somewhat excessive in view of how few early Montrealers originated in Champagne.[9] However, an examination of the leadership role played by de Maisonneuve himself and other natives of the province in Montreal's first decades shows that the statement has some justification in terms of the quality and influence of the first Montrealers from that region, if not their numbers, and is not simply an exaggeration reflecting regional prejudice.

Justified or not, de Maisonneuve's remark testifies to an attachment to a province that even today is characterized in the tourist literature as a region of merchants and poets. The phrase aptly describes the paradoxical combination of qualities that characterizes not only Champagne but also Marguerite Bourgeoys herself. The intensity and depth of her religious experience mark her as a mystic; at the same time, the events of her life reveal a practical woman endowed with great common sense and considerable administrative ability. The paradox is reflected in the title that one of her most perceptive twentieth-century biographers selected for his work: *Les dialogues de Marthe et de Marie*.[10] This combination of characteristics should not, perhaps, come as a surprise, for as Philip Toynbee has pointed out: "A very high proportion of the men and women who have laid claim to ... [mystical] experience were renowned in their daily lives for probity, charity and *good sense*."[11] So Governor de Maisonneuve enthusiastically heralded Marguerite's impending arrival in Montreal in 1653 by describing to Jeanne Mance not just a virtuous woman ("la vertu est un trésor") but also one endowed with good sense and intelligence ("bons sens et bon esprit)".[12]

Its days as a major centre are long passed, but Troyes continues one of the oldest cities in northern Europe. Situated on the banks of the Seine, it was already the principal settlement of the Tricassi tribe before the Romans arrived. There in 22–21 BC they established the town of Augustobona on the road linking Milan to Boulogne; the city was thus to develop much of its character from its situation on one of the main arteries of late classical and medieval Europe. The history of Troyes in Roman and medieval times might serve as a paradigm of Western history in those periods. The region was early converted to Christianity, and in the first half of the fourth century a bishopric was created at Troyes. The most famous and influential of the bishops was Loup, who occupied the see in the years 426–79. Not only did he exercise considerable influence in the Gallic church, but he is also credited with persuading Attila the Hun to spare the city from pillage. That legend recalls the fact that, as in many other areas of what had once been the Roman empire, ecclesiastical authority filled the vacuum created by the collapse of civil authority in the so-called Dark Ages. This situation continued in the region until the emergence of the counts of Troyes in the tenth century.

Of great interest to anyone studying the city as the birthplace of Marguerite Bourgeoys is the important role played by women throughout much of its known history. In the Middle Ages the influence of the monastery of men called Saint-Loup was quite overshadowed by that of an abbey of Benedictine women known as Notre-Dame-aux-Nonnains. Legend attributed the foundation of the latter to a group of vestal virgins in the third century;[13] a more plausible tradition credits its establishment to Bishop Leucon in the seventh century, but the destruction of all the early documents of the abbey in a fire in 1188 makes this story impossible to verify. The following, however, is undoubtedly true: "The privileges of the reigning abbess were no legend. She was virtually patroness of the city and head of the diocese. She could name parish priests to several cures and claim a share of the tithes and collections. Each succeeding bishop began his episcopate by swearing an oath of fealty, kneeling at her feet, his hands within hers in the old feudal gesture. She conferred on him his mitre, crozier, and cope. No bishop was ever allowed his rights of visitation. None, either, refused to recognize the abbess's privileges."[14]

One incident well illustrates the power of these Benedictine nuns in the thirteenth century, their sense of that power, and their will to preserve it. Jacques Pantaléon was elected pope in 1261 and took the name of Urban IV. He had been born in Troyes, the son of a shoemaker, and as pope, he bought the land where his father's shop had once stood with the intention of erecting a church there. Construction began in 1262, but the pope, it seems, had not obtained the permission of the abbess of Notre-Dame-aux-Nonnains for his building. Before it could be completed, she led her nuns, armed retainers, and other sympathizers to the unfinished church, where they utterly destroyed the marble sanctuary and the workmen's tools and removed the portals.[15] Though the church, the Gothic basilica of Saint-Urbain, is now one of the landmarks of Troyes, the main section was not completed until the sixteenth century and the tower not until 1630;[16] the church received its permanent stone roof only in 1905.[17] On a more constructive level, the abbey owned and administered large schools. It was at the gateway of Notre-Dame-aux-Nonnains that Marguerite Bourgeoys's conversion took place in 1640. A link between her and these great religious women of the medieval past exists, then, though she was to conduct her struggles with male ecclesiastical authority in a very different cause and in a strikingly different style from the women in this episode of the pope, his church, and the thirteenth-century Benedictines.

Under the rule of the counts of Troyes and of Champagne, the city became one of the great trading centres of medieval Europe; in the twelfth and thirteenth centuries, the fairs of Champagne drew merchants from all over the continent. The counts assured the success of these fairs by extending to the merchants who attended them the *conduit des foires*,[18] that is, protection for themselves and their merchandise for the length of their journeys. Other attractions were the use of standardized weights and measures (Troy weight), the regulation of taxes imposed on wares, and an exemption from certain excise duties. Six fairs were held in Champagne at different times of the year; the most important of these was the St John's Fair, or "warm fair," beginning on the feast of St John the Baptist on 24 June around the church of Saint-Jean, by Marguerite's time long known as Saint-Jean-au-Marché. This was the church in which she was baptized and the district of the city in which she was to grow up.

A consequence of the patronage accorded by the counts to the fairs was that Jews were assured of the counts' protection because they acted as their bankers. As a result, not only were several synagogues established in Troyes, but also, in the tenth century, a Jewish academy was founded, which produced Rabbi Salomon Rachi (1040–1105), a scholar so celebrated for his commentaries on the Bible and the Talmud that they are still the true starting point for the budding student. The rabbi, whose works were honoured in Christian as well as Jewish circles, felt so rooted in his city as habitually to sign his letters "Salomon de Troyes."[19]

The early importance of commerce in Champagne resulted in a blurring of some of the usual class distinctions. One historian remarks that the younger scions of noble families who became involved with commerce, rather than losing their noble status were considered as nobles living *marchandement*, in merchant style, while their elders remained nobles living *noblement*, in the noble manner.[20] But the counts of the High Middle Ages were not patrons of commerce only. The wife of Henri I (1152–81) was Marie de France, the daughter of Louis VII and Eleanor of Aquitaine, who brought to the court of Champagne a taste and enthusiasm for the literature of courtly love. At Troyes she set up the courts of love, and there she became the patron of one of the greatest poets of the Middle Ages, Chrétien de Troyes. He made a major contribution to the development of Arthurian romance, "the only complete and original myth to emerge from Western Christendom," as Rosemary Haughton has observed.[21] Marie's grandson, Thibault IV (1201–53), was himself the author of numerous poems of courtly love, so that he is known as Thibault "le Chansonnier." Champagne also included distinguished historians among its natives, for both Geoffrey de Villehardouin (c.1150–c.1213) and the great Jean de Joinville (c.1223–c.1317) came from this region.[22]

The works of these two men recall another important aspect of the history of Champagne, the participation of its warriors in the Crusades, especially the fourth, and in the organization of a new Latin empire in the east.[23] While its soldiers fought far away, the energy of other Champenois was finding a very different kind of outlet in the Cistercian monastery of Clairvaux, where the mystical traditions of the Holy Grail were developing in literature.[24] Home of merchants, poets, warriors, and mystics, medieval Champagne, at once commercial and artistic, practical and romantic, patriotic and cosmopolitan, was a fitting ancestral home for those who were to play important roles in the founding of Montreal: Paul de Chomedey de Maisonneuve, Jeanne Mance, Marguerite Bourgeoys, and Louis d'Ailleboust de Coulonge.

The fourteenth century brought great changes to Champagne. Jeanne de Navarre (1272–1305) became the last countess of Champagne on the death of her father in 1274. Ten years later she married the second son of Philip III, who would later accede to the throne of France as Philip the Fair. In 1285 Champagne and Navarre were attached to the French crown. However, Jeanne retained the administration of her property for her lifetime, and as in other cases where the French throne had acquired territories by marriage to an heiress, the transfer of power was not easily accepted by the local population. The effective union of Champagne to the realm of France did not take place until 1361. In the intervening years, the once-prosperous province was torn apart by warring nobles. The Hundred Years' War, in isolating Troyes from the rest of the kingdom, greatly diminished both commerce and industry, and the shifting of the trade routes to the Straits of Gibraltar forever put an end to the role of Troyes as a trading centre.

Yet the region showed remarkable powers of recovery. When all efforts to revive the old fairs that had once brought such prosperity failed, the inhabitants of Troyes in the fourteenth and fifteenth centuries turned to industry. In this, they were favoured by the existence of many streams around the town, a factor particularly conducive to the establishment of a large number of mills. The textile industry of Troyes was especially successful, but tanning and papermaking also flourished. It was perhaps the fact that the paper manufactured here had been famous since the time of the fairs that led to the early establishment of printing presses in the city. The first work printed here appears to have been *Le bréviaire de Troyes*, produced in 1483.[25] Numerous corporations existed in the city from the fourteenth century on, and the middle class became both wealthy and powerful. Troyes was to remain prosperous until the seventeenth century, and that prosperity was manifested in numerous buildings, public and private, religious and secular. A devastating fire in 1524 meant that large sections of the centre of the city were rebuilt at that time. It is largely as it was rebuilt in the sixteenth century that the city has, in part, been restored in the heart of modern Troyes.

Since it lies on the road between Geneva and Germany, the sixteenth century inevitably also brought the Reformation to Troyes. In Champagne the reform seems to have begun with an evangelical group in Meaux that included the bishop and several theologians. They attempted to change the church in an orthodox manner by purifying the cult and encouraging a simple and sincere piety through the reading of the gospels in French translation. This effort, however, soon became mingled in the popular mind with Lutheranism, and by the end of 1524 the more extreme were denouncing the pope as the Antichrist.[26] Lutheran and Calvinist ideas were introduced into Troyes as early as 1523, here they found a sympathetic reception in some of the leading families of the bourgeoisie. In 1551 Antonio

Caracciola, an Italian and a nephew of Pope Paul IV, became bishop of Troyes. Two historians of the region state, "Until the end [Caracciola] hoped to reunite in the same fold the faithful sheep and the dissident Calvinists despite the intractible elements on both sides who had daily confrontations in the streets."[27] However good his intentions, the bishop's perceived ambiguity was a source of considerable confusion and scandal. He was forced to resign the see in 1562 on the eve of the massacre of Vassy. Persecutions at Troyes later resulted in the emigration of some wealthy Calvinist families to Geneva and Lausanne. During the Wars of Religion the town was held first by one side and then by the other, and the fighting ended only with the triumphal entry of Henry IV into the city on 30 May 1595. Beginning with his reign, royal power was intensified and the role of the bourgeoisie gradually reduced in municipal affairs. Despite its distinguished history, the Troyes into which Marguerite was born was a city that had begun a long decline, a city from which many of its most talented offspring, particularly its artists, would tend to gravitate towards Paris rather than remain in the place of their birth.

Marguerite Bourgeoys was the seventh of the thirteen known children of Abraham Bourgeoys and his wife, Guillemette Garnier.[28] The records of their respective parishes indicate that Abraham was baptized in the church of Saint-Jean-au-Marché on 13 October 1579 and Guillemette in that of Saint-Rémi on 5 September 1593. The two were married at Saint-Rémi on 3 February 1609. Their marriage contract, signed on 15 January before Claude Bourgeoys, notary at Troyes, describes Abraham as the son of the late "honourable man Sadoch Bourgeoys, living merchant domiciled at Troyes, and Marguerite David" and Guillemette as the daughter of Claude Garnier, "merchant linen-weaver domiciled at Troyes, and Sirette Boutard his wife." The text of the contract is followed by the prescribed acknowledgment by the two newly-weds on 16 February of the payment of the bride's dowry of six hundred *livres*.[29] These documents indicate that both Marguerite's parents came from families of the artisan class, a class in which women worked alongside men in the small family businesses. Guillemette's family was engaged in the fashioning and selling of textiles, an industry for which Troyes had been well known for centuries. Abraham, as well as holding a master's licence for the making and selling of tallow or domestic candles, also held an honorary position in the treasury of Troyes: a document of January 1639 describes him as a merchant and official in the Troyes Mint.[30] The Bourgeoys family were property owners in the city of Troyes and not without prestige. They were among three prominent families that held important positions at the Mint over many years: six of the Bourgeoys line are recorded and several of the Maillet and Semilliard families. Intermarriage among them was not infrequent. Marguerite's eldest sister, Sirette, married Pierre Maillet, and Marie Bourgeoys married Orson Semilliard.[31] In his study of the family of Marguerite Bourgeoys, J.C. Niel cites a quotation which claims that office holders in the Mint had certain royal privileges and were considered somewhat above other members of their class, almost noble "presque nobles." He says of the privileges attaching to the office: "According to M. Anatole de Barthélemy, 'The Mint officials of Troyes, besides the liberties they possessed by royal concession, enjoyed in Champagne the privilege of not paying the jurée, the property tax owed the king by freemen called the *bourgeois du roi*. Finding themselves thus freed from a plebeian tax burden, the Mint officials considered themselves as almost noble, or at least as superior to the bourgeois.'"[32]

It is worthwhile quoting at length a comment on the importance of title, rank, and their prerogatives in seventeenth-century French society, not simply to throw light on Marguerite's family situation, but also because the attitudes these reflected were to have an often-unfortunate influence on the history of New France:

A title, however honorary, was worth a great deal in the eyes of public opinion. This society not only depended at every level on a rigorously ordered hierarchy, but held to giving to each person, as a function of his rank, conspicuous marks of his quality. A reserved place in church, a precise rank in processions, and the right to carry the canopy at the entry of the king into the town are examples of non-remunerative social prerogatives that codified daily life. They were deeply impressed on the mentality. Everyone conformed to them, and if they were transgressed, recriminations, even legal procedures, were multiplied to restore the right order of things.[33]

In later years, Marguerite's resolute rejection of marks of honour for herself and the congregation that she would found are in sharp contrast with the customs and outlook of her time and with the attitudes introduced by the French settlers even to the wilds of Canada, customs and outlook with which she would have been familiar from childhood.

Until the middle of the twentieth century, the tendency of Marguerite Bourgeoys's biographers was to exaggerate the economic position of the Bourgeoys family, characterizing its members as either very poor or very wealthy. Documents discovered since that time reveal that the family was neither. A study written at the time of her canonization compares their financial position with those of a late-sixteenth-century member of the haute bourgeoisie and a worker in a tannery to illustrate this point. It concludes, "Given ... that the nobility was little represented in Troyes and that in fact, the grande bourgeoisie ... dominated the town, the petite and moyenne bourgeoisie maintained a certain importance on the social ladder of the city."[34]

The house in which Abraham Bourgeoys lived with his family was a rented property; the occurrence of the name of the proprietor in the inventory of goods compiled in 1639 after the death of Marguerite's mother has made possible the discovery of its exact location from the tax records.[35] It was a three-storey building fronting on what was then called "la Grande Rue devant la Belle Croix" (now part of Place Alexandre Israel), opposite the city hall and the great Calvary, which the townspeople called "la Belle Croix." This cross, built first of stone in the thirteenth century and then replaced in bronze, was a celebrated monument of medieval Troyes destroyed during the Revolution. Part of the ground floor of the house was a candlemaker's shop for Abraham; to the rear beyond the shop was the family dwelling. As the house was not demolished until 1977, Niel was able to include a plan of the structure in his 1950 study.[36]

Of the thirteen children known to have been born to the Bourgeoys family, nine were living at the time of their mother's death in December 1638. Apart from the parish records of Saint-Jean-au-Marché, the most important source of information about the family at this time is the inventory of goods made on 5 January 1639.[37] From these sources we learn that the family consisted of Claude, born sometime between November 1609 and April 1610;[38] Sirette, baptized at Saint-Jean on 22 December 1610; Anne, born between September 1611 and January 1614; an unnamed child buried from Saint-Jean on 28 September 1617; Jérôme, baptized at Saint-Jean on 21 September 1618; Marie, born in June or July 1619; Marguerite born and baptized on 17 April 1620; Jeanne, baptized at Saint-Jean on 30 June 1623; Thomas, baptized at Saint-Jean on 7 November 1624; Nicolas, baptized at Saint-Jean on 26 November 1626; Edouard, baptized at Saint-Jean on 13 December 1628; Madeleine, baptized at Saint-Jean 13 September 1633; and Pierre, baptized at Saint-Jean 27 March 1637. For the most part, the godparents whose names appear in the register of baptism were relatives and family friends: Marguerite's godmother, for example, was Marguerite Coutant, wife of her maternal uncle, Nicolas Garnier; Sirette's godmother was her maternal grandmother, Sirette Boutard; and Claude, the first-born, was probably the godson of his maternal grandfather, Claude Garnier. Edouard Colbert, godfather of Edouard Bourgeoys, was distantly related to the great minister of Louis XIV.[39]

At first, Guillemette was fortunate in childbirth: as far as has been determined, she lost only one of her first seven children, six of whom were alive at the time of her death, a remarkable record in view of the seventeenth-century statistics already cited. However, of the next three children whose baptisms are recorded, Jeanne, Thomas, and Nicolas, none was living by the time the inventory was made after their mother's death. Nothing is known of the circumstances of their deaths – whether they came one by one or together as the result of some epidemic. There was an outbreak of the plague in Troyes in 1626, and another, which decimated the population of the city, broke out in October 1631 and raged until 1633.[40] That Marguerite survived the illnesses that may have carried off her younger brothers and sister is perhaps an early indication of the strength and resistance to disease which was to enable her to meet the physical demands of her long and laborious life. During her first years in Canada, she would frequently be called on to console the people of Ville-Marie on the deaths of their babies. She was to write, "There were about eight years when no one could bring up children; and this gave us great hope because God was taking the first fruits."[41] It is characteristic of her that at a time when there was a tendency to perceive such misfortunes as a punishment for sin,[42] she presents the deaths of these infants in so different a light. In her own family she had learned very early about parental grief.[43]

The death of Guillemette Garnier at the end of 1638 appears to have been sudden: intensive examination of the registers of Saint-Jean-au-Marché reveals that she took up the collection in the parish church on 12 December that year.[44] Her obituary is entered a week later. There is no hint in any known document of the cause of her death but it is not impossible that she died as the result of some complication in a late pregnancy. For the time, her death was not premature: however, then as now, it is doubtful that statistics provided much comfort to the family that she had left so suddenly, which included several young children.

Early biographers of Marguerite, incorrectly informed about the date of her mother's death and unaware of the existence of older brothers and sisters, claimed that she, the eldest, had to take charge of her family at the age of twelve. "She lost her mother when she was still very young," Glandelet wrote in 1715, "and since her father was devout, he was careful to see that his daughter received a Christian upbringing and was taught to read and write; she took complete charge of the household and the education of her sisters and brothers."[45] Records that have since come to light indicate not only that Marguerite was eighteen at the time of her mother's death but that two of her older sisters were still unmarried and living at home. Thus her contemplated entrance into the cloister at the age of twenty would not have involved the desertion of a father and young family who depended on her. This point is important: Marguerite was one day to teach that, for most people, the way to God lies not in the heroic gestures so popular in the dramatic literature of her time but through the fulfilment of the duties of each day.

However, what the early biographers may have sensed is that a very close bond of affection appears to have existed between Marguerite and her father. Among the exceedingly meagre references to her early life in her writings, we do find this passage, written many years later as instruction to the sisters who would one day be part of the Congrégation de Notre-Dame of Montreal:

The profit that these things [that is, small acts of generosity] gain for us when they are done for God reminds me of a present I gave my father, so small and trivial that it made those who saw it laugh – and my father, as well. But, seeing that I had [made it] with such great affection, he carried this present around with him and showed it to everyone ... The good God is pleased with little virtues which are practiced for love of Him and He ennobles them in the measure that they are exercised with greater love. I must do everything, therefore, for the greater love of God.[46]

It is difficult to capture, in translation, the warmth of Marguerite's words. She habitually referred to God as "notre bon Dieu," the French *bon* often having the sense not just of intrinsic worth but also of outgoing kindness. Perhaps Julian of Norwich's "our good Lord" is a suitable English equivalent. This passage not only casts light on the relationship between Abraham Bourgeoys and his young daughter, but it also shows explicitly that her lasting sense of a loving and merciful Father God, maintained in a century that saw the rise of Jansenism, had its roots in her early experience in her parents' home.

Of events in the first years of her life Marguerite tells us very little more in her autobiographical writings, except that she used to play at living in a community of women. "From early childhood, God had given me the inclination to gather little girls of my own age together to live and work together in some distant place to earn our living. I had never known any community of women, but only a few women who lived together. We imitated that as children."[47] This statement occurs in her writings in a context in which she is explaining the origins of the Congregation. When Marguerite's early biographies were written, it was conventional among hagiographers to seek in the childhood of the subject evidences of future sanctity. For example, we are told of Catherine de Saint-Augustin, a seventeenth-century sister of the Hôtel-Dieu in Quebec: "At the age of three she showed herself to be imbued with a desire for the heroic and the absolute, and asked how she might in all things do God's will. Her spiritual adviser ... explained this to her in the presence of a pauper covered with sores. Catherine concluded from his illustration that it is easier to find God in humiliation and suffering than in prosperity. The tiny tot then began, 'with unbelievable earnestness,' to wish for 'many maladies.'"[48] The incident, then, in which Marguerite sees a group of women gathering "to live and work together" and "to earn our living" has been given more pious overtones than the original statement possesses. Faillon comments:

Persons called by God for some particular purpose ordinarily give, from the earliest age, signs of their vocation, which are precocious fruits of the spirit that already animates and guides them. This can be observed in the young Marguerite Bourgeoys. She was scarcely ten years old when she could be seen gathering her little companions around her, inspiring them to virtue, proposing the plan that she had already conceived for the future. This was to assemble young women to live together in a remote place far from the business of the world, devoted in a holy manner to work and to regular prayer.[49]

In fact, Marguerite's point in the reminiscence quoted above and in similar passages where she is describing her preparation for her mission in Canada is that God was working in her in ways of which she was at the time completely unconscious. It is also probable that when she spoke of "some distant place," she had in mind the distance between Ville-Marie and France rather than a place removed from society, since her own life and that of her congregation was so thoroughly a part of the society around them. Her reference to girls working together to earn their living testifies to the great respect Marguerite always had for what she called "honourable work," another characteristic she shared with her native city and province. (To this day, in the Maison de l'Outil et de la Pensée Ouvrière, Troyes possesses the only museum in France dedicated to the display of tools of various trades and crafts.) She also foreshadows her later insistence that her community be self-supporting: she and her companions should never be a burden on the colony, but must earn their own living in such a way that they would be able to offer free education to the ordinary people of Montreal.

Marguerite's statement that as a child she had not known any religious communities of women raises the question of where she received her own education. Glandelet says only that she was educated at the wish of her father and that she then taught her younger brothers and sisters. But though he is the first of her biographers, he is particularly inaccurate about her early life.[50] Did Marguerite receive any of her early education from a religious community of women? The answers suggested by those of her later biographers who considered the question vary. Faillon says that the community of Pierre Fourier and Alix Le Clerc, the canonesses of St Augustine known as the Congrégation de Notre-Dame of Troyes, with which Marguerite Bourgeoys was eventually to be associated, established itself in her native city in 1628.[51] Jamet says that prior to 1628, none of the recently founded institutes dedicated to the education of women – the Ursulines, the Sisters of the Visitation, and Fourier's congregation – had yet made an appearance in Troyes; that until then there were only "humble spinsters or widows who, for a modest fee and often as pure charity, conducted elementary day schools or boarding schools where children learned the basics."[52] He therefore concludes that Marguerite Bourgeoys must have been educated in such a school.

Desrosiers, however, thought it possible that she had received some of her education from the Congrégation de Notre-Dame of Troyes; he mistakenly put their arrival in Troyes at 1625 instead of 1628.[53] Nevertheless, his reasoning stands on its own merits: he points to the desire of the sisters of that congregation to enrol Marguerite as a member of their extern congregation[54] even before her conversion in 1640 and deduces that the likeliest way in which they would have come to know and appreciate her would have been through her having been at some point their pupil. According to Marguerite, it was in *early* childhood that she had known no communities of women. That statement does not preclude her having received some education from the sisters at a later date. The course of studies at the Congrégation de Notre-Dame of Troyes in the seventeenth century envisaged some of their pupils remaining until the age of eighteen and in special cases even longer.[55] Roserot de Melin affirms that Marguerite Bourgeoys was a pupil of the Congrégation de Notre-Dame of Troyes when the convent was officially blessed in 1635, at which time she would have been fifteen years old; however, he identifies no source for this information.[56]

That there are no further references to her childhood in Marguerite's autobiographical writings is scarcely surprising since her accounts of the time before she came to Montreal were always written to explain the origins of the Congrégation de Notre-Dame of

Montreal. Apart from the two statements already quoted, her own accounts of her life begin on Rosary Sunday in 1640, when she was halfway through her twenty-first year. She describes herself at this time as *bien légère*, a term rendered "frivolous" in the English translation of the writings,[57] although "giddy" might also be a suitable English equivalent, and she tells us that this characteristic made her very popular with the other girls. Even so austere a commentator as Glandelet says that she was much loved and sought after by her friends because she was by nature "light-hearted, joyful, and kind,"[58] and Jamet echoes him when he writes, "She was naturally joyous and lovable."[59] Marguerite also implies that she liked to be chic; after her conversion, she tells us, "I gave up my pretty clothes."[60] The inventory of 1639 lists among the effects of the Bourgeoys household many objects of apparel and jewellery that might well have been pretty: an assortment of rings, one in the shape of a rose with opals set in it, some earrings decorated in enamel, belts of velvet embroidered in pearls or other stones, and metal cinctures with set-in jewels or gold motifs.[61]

Marguerite's assessment of her young self is not written in the same tone as the accounts that some of the saints have provided of their early imperfections, descriptions that sometimes shock the later reader with what appears to be their excessive severity. One can hear, rather, the tolerant voice of a woman who has had a great deal of experience dealing with the young and who can understand their pleasures and interests even as she challenges them to grow. Her views are a refreshing change from many of the contemporary clerical fulminations against female vanity that are extant. She has shown that to credit her with a premature piety is to contradict the little she really did say about her childhood and adolescence and to detract from the emphasis that she puts on her conversion of 1640 and her insistence on the completeness of the transformation wrought in her by that experience.

As stated at the beginning of this chapter, Marguerite Bourgeoys has left two accounts of the events of that Rosary Sunday in 1640. When she wrote the first, the draft of the 1695 letter to Louis Tronson in Paris, she was no longer superior of the Congregation; she had been replaced in September 1693 by Marie Barbier, the first Montrealer to enter the community. The Congregation was in crisis because Bishop Saint-Vallier, the second person to occupy the see of Quebec, was intent on imposing upon the fledgling community solemn vows, the payment of a dowry, and a special vow of obedience to the bishop, conditions that would have totally destroyed its identity. Marie Barbier had appealed to Father Tronson, and he had asked for the written opinion of Marguerite Bourgeoys on the matter. Hence this letter, in which she proposes to describe "the motives which led to the establishment of the Congregation in Montreal." She begins:

First, during the procession on Rosary Sunday, in the year 1640 (which I have since learned was the year of the first arrival in Montreal), I was strongly moved when I looked up at a statue of the Blessed Virgin. At the same time, M. de Maisonneuve's sister, who was a religious of the Congregation gave to her brother a picture on which was written in letters of gold: "Holy Mother of God, pure Virgin with a faithful heart, keep for us a place in your Montreal."[62]

The second account, that with which this chapter began, was written in 1697 and was once again set down by Marguerite in an attempt to save the Congregation from destruction by taking it back to its original inspiration, though in this case the danger she feared was corruption within, rather than attacks from ecclesiastical authority without. Although already quoted, this passage is worth examining in some detail. "In 1640 on Rosary Sunday," Marguerite wrote, "I went to the procession at the Dominican Church where there was so great a number of people that the cloister was not large enough." Religious processions were a very important part of the public celebrations of her time, and her own parish, Saint-Jean-au-Marché, as the oldest, richest, and most prominent in Troyes, was the site of many elaborate displays.[63] The Dominican monastery would have been the site of the place where the Rosary Procession was held because of the role played by the order in propagating devotion to the recitation of the rosary. Events such as this one would have enabled the participants to meet their friends and display their finery, as well as to express their devotion and nourish their piety.

The thirteenth-century Dominican church and cloister were built behind the gardens of the monastery of Notre-Dame-aux-Nonnains. The turnout for the procession seems to have been larger than anticipated, and Marguerite wrote of what happened next in these unconsciously prophetic words: "The cloister was not large enough." She was describing a simple physical fact about a given space, but it is difficult to avoid the latent symbolism of her words. In seventeenth-century France the cloister had indeed become "not large enough" to contain the Catholic women called to create a new form of religious life in answer to the needs of their time, women whose number she was one day to join. She continues: "So we crossed the street and passed in front of the portal of Notre Dame [aux-Nonnains] where

there was a statue in stone above the door. And glancing up to look
at it, I found it very beautiful. At the same time, I found myself so
moved and so changed that I no longer recognized myself." The procession passed over towards the historic monastery of Benedictine
nuns. Thus this great turning point in the life of a woman who was
to help establish a new form of religious life for women in the Roman
Catholic Church found its inspiration in a statue commissioned by
women who had created a religious life of their own in the church of
an earlier era. Marguerite's act of looking up at the statue was a delib-
erate one; the wording of her statement tells us this. She knew the
statue was there – had, then, seen it before and probably already
admired it. Yet what happened next was completely unanticipated.

Marguerite Bourgeoys did not claim to have had an apparition of
the Blessed Virgin, though later artists, attemping to capture the
inner meaning of that moment, have depicted the scene as if she had
done so. In fact, as she writes more than fifty years later about an
event that she had obviously often relived in prayer, she still conveys
a sense of the solid earthly reality of the statue: it was stone, she
says.[64] Then she adds quite simply, "I found it very beautiful." For
her, the truly amazing and important thing was what followed: her
own total transformation, confirmed by the perception of those
around her.[65] It is characteristic of Marguerite that she found confirmation of her personal experience in outside evidence; the observation of her family and friends. She was no sceptic, if a sceptic is one
who seeks reasons to withhold belief or deny the possibility of religious experience, but she was always aware of the danger of illusion.
In any case, the evidence she presents here is that suggested by Christ
himself in Matthew 7:20, that a tree is known by the fruit it bears.

Marguerite's account of this key moment in her life makes two
things clear: her experience of religious conversion was a Marian one
and it was an experience that came to her through an image. When it
happened, she would have been praying the rosary, where the repe-
tition of Gabriel's greeting to Mary at the Annunciation and the greeting of Elizabeth at the Visitation are accompanied by meditation on
events in the life of Mary. Marguerite's later years were to be spent
trying to lead the kind of life she believed that Mary had lived during her days on earth. That is one subject on which her surviving
writings are both extensive and definite, and they make it clear that
her vision of Mary developed in relation to her own life experience.
But in 1640, all that was in the future. What idea of Mary might she
have had at the age of twenty? What was the nature of the beauty that
so strongly attracted her on Rosary Sunday in 1640 that it was to
command her love and loyalty for the rest of her life?

In exploring this question, we are fortunate that many of the sources of Marguerite's ideas about Mary still exist to be examined. They are the statues, carvings, paintings, and stained-glass windows that surrounded her during her childhood and early adulthood in her native Troyes. That images "spoke" to Marguerite is apparent not only in the occurrence of Rosary Sunday but also in the other Marian experience that was to confirm her vocation to Canada in 1653.[66] In finding inspiration in images, she would not have been different from most of her contemporaries, for theirs was still a time when the image had not lost its power to the written word. For most Catholics, religious ideas were conveyed in the churches, not only by the sermons and instructions delivered there, but also by the images with which those churches were decorated. At its best, in places such as Chartres, the church was itself a Bible in stone and wood, marble and glass. The images in the churches had this advantage over the sermons: they were not ephemeral but permanent, and could be returned to again and again. In them, past generations had expressed their understanding of the faith, and through them, had conveyed that vision to future generations. And the images, more closely linked with popular piety and able to deliver a more integral message, sometimes suggest perspectives and insights that differ from those of the theologian-intellectuals whose words have been recorded.

The prosperity of Troyes in the centuries before Marguerite's time ensured that its churches and religious houses were rich in devotional art. Not only the wealthy had contributed to the beautification of the churches; for example, one of the loveliest pieces of religious art in Troyes is the statue of Martha in the parish church of Sainte-Marie-Madeleine sculpted by the gifted "Maître de Chaôrce" at the commission of the servant women of Troyes in the sixteenth century. The statue over the gateway at Notre-Dame-aux-Nonnains, like the whole monastery, did not survive the Revolution, a circumstance that is scarcely surprising since the monastery would have attracted the hostility of the revolutionaries both as a religious house and as a remnant of feudal power.[67] But many other statues of Mary from Marguerite's time still exist in the churches of Troyes, where they were returned after the Revolution.[68] These statues share an important characteristic with their counterparts in other areas of medieval and renaissance Europe: Mary is not depicted alone. The convention of showing her by herself did not arise in liturgical art until the nineteenth century.[69] Rather, she is always depicted in relationship, usually a loving one, with other figures.

Many of the scenes portraying Mary, not only in Troyes but across medieval and early modern Europe, were inspired not by the canonical gospels but by early apocryphal works on the life of the Virgin. The canonical scriptures say nothing about her life before the events surrounding the Annunciation. But interest in all that the New Testament did not reveal about her, especially her early life, led quite soon in the Christian era to a number of highly colourful accounts that attempted to fill in what the canonical gospels had omitted. From the beginning of the second century, that is, less than a hundred years after Mary's death, stories began to spread that, it was claimed, had originated in apostolic circles. This oral tradition took shape in the form of a "gospel"' attributed to the apostle James. The early manuscripts of this work are in Greek and are entitled "The Narrative of James on the Birth of the Holy Mother of God"; the work has twenty-five chapters and ends with the birth of Jesus. Later scholars have called this work the Protoevangelium of James or Pseudo-James. It dates from about 130–40 AD.[70] In the sixth century there appeared a work in Latin entitled "Book on the Birth of the Blessed Mary and of the Saviour's Infancy" with an introductory letter representing it as a supplement to the Gospel of Matthew. This second work is now recognized as a clever rearrangement of Pseudo-James, which it amplifies, embellishes, and adapts to the Latin West and to a later age in the church. These have been by far the most influential of the apocryphal works about Mary that appeared in the early Christian era. Their purpose was double: to fill in the gaps left in Mary's curriculum vitae by the canonical gospels and to prove to readers that she was, at the same time, virgin and mother.

Many of the events in the two works are based on stories in the canonical scriptures of both the Old and the New Testaments: the events that surround Mary's annunciation and birth draw upon not only the annunciations of Jesus and John the Baptist but also on the story of Samuel. According to the apocryphal works, Mary's parents were Joachim and Anne, a couple advanced in years and childless. Because of this disgrace, Joachim, though a man of great virtue, was cast out of the synagogue. After his expulsion, he went into the countryside to pray while Anne remained at home. Both received angelic messengers who promised them a child and uttered great predictions about her future. (None of the predictions about an unborn child's future in the canonical scriptures were made about a female child.) The couple were reunited with great joy at the Golden Gate of Jerusalem, and subsequently Anne conceived and gave birth to the promised child, a daughter whom the parents named Mary.

As the story continues, in fulfilment of a promise made before her birth, Mary took up residence in the Temple at the age of three. There she remained until she was twelve, at which time the high priest assembled all the widowers of Israel to select a husband for her from among them. Joseph was selected when his rod miraculously blossomed. However, he objected to marrying Mary on the grounds both of his advanced age and of the existence of his adult sons from a previous marriage.[71] Joseph was compelled to marry her by threats from the high priest, but did not live with her. Instead he placed her in one of his houses while he went off to pursue his trade as builder. When Mary was found to be pregnant, there was a sensational trial, though this development clearly contradicts the canonical Gospel of Matthew. The work reaches its climax with the birth of Jesus and the testimony of a doubting midwife to Mary's continued virginity in a scene reminiscent of the testimony by the doubting Thomas to the reality of the risen Christ. Both these apocryphal works are filled with miraculous and sensational elements, and the second one, appearing as it did just when monastic life for women was beginning to take form in the Western church, depicts Mary's mode of life both in the Temple and in the home of Joseph as very like that of a cloistered, contemplative religious.

The events described in these works are, of course, rejected by modern biblical scholars, not just in their more extravagant passages but also in their assertion that Mary lived in the Temple from the age of three until her marriage to Joseph, a claim still widely accepted by the scholars of Marguerite's time. At the end of the sixteenth century, in his *De Maria virgine incomparabili*, the Jesuit theologian Peter Canisius rejected Pseudo-James, but accepted the story of Mary's sojourn in the Temple from other sources without realizing that all of these ultimately derived from Pseudo-James. In the seventeenth century the symbolic and mystical interpretation of Mary's presentation in the Temple and her sojourn there was an important aspect of Sulpician spirituality.

One effect of the way in which theologians used these stories was to remove Mary from the domestic sphere of ordinary women, a sphere perceived as degrading to the mother of the Lord. But the images with which Marguerite grew up, which would have been familiar to people in the churches for several centuries, could convey a different impression. There is no medieval church in Troyes that does not contain a statue of Mary with her mother Anne. In all of these groups, Anne is instructing her daughter from either a book or a scroll;[72] in other words, every church contained an image of Mary being educated by her mother. To put it another way, in every church to which she went, the young Marguerite would have seen an image of the mother as educator and transmitter of the faith. (This theme is carried even further in a screen made up of a group of paintings, now in the museum in the Hôtel Vauluisant in Troyes; on one side Mary is depicted teaching his letters to a precocious baby Jesus as Joseph dreams of the flight into Egypt.)

Despite the legend that she was permanently separated from her parents at the age of three, these images show Mary with her mother, not as an infant, but as a child of eight or ten years. In fact, from among the elements of the legends, the images represent those universal life events to which ordinary women who prayed before them could relate intimately: betrothal, motherhood, bereavement. Although they end Mary's life with her assumption and crowning in heaven, they also show a young girl tenderly greeting her elderly and pregnant cousin Elizabeth, marrying her fiancé, Joseph, as a young mother supporting her baby on her hip or dangling a bunch of grapes before him, as an aging and grieving woman holding the broken body of her Son, and as a woman on her deathbed surrounded by the apostles. Several of the statues owe much of their charm to the humanity of their portrayal: the young Virgin with Anne, currently to be seen on the wall behind the main altar in Marguerite's old parish church of Saint-Jean-au-Marché is an exceptionally lovely depiction of affection between mother and daughter. In her instructions to the Congregation in later years, Marguerite was to suggest that Mary went to a kind of school in the Temple,[73] demonstrating that all women did not necessarily interpret the texts as setting Mary apart from the activities of ordinary women.

Devotion to Mary the mother of Jesus, once attacked as idolatrous by Protestant reformers, has more recently been targeted as a device to keep Catholic women humble, passive, and subservient, a claim that has not always been without foundation. That the Marian devotion of Marguerite Bourgeoys was positive, dynamic, and life-giving was demonstrated in the course of her own life. But in 1640 much of what was to constitute her vision of Mary was still inchoate. She wanted to give herself to God but did not yet know what form the gift was to take. Her first inclination was to do the conventional thing, to enter one of the existing religious communities, all of which were, of course, cloistered. Refused admission to the Carmelites and perhaps one other religious community, she was to embark on a long, and surely at times discouraging, process of discovering the true significance of that call of Rosary Sunday 1640.

Initially, at least, all the difficulties were offset by the immense sense of joy that was the immediate, felt effect of her conversion. Marguerite sensed herself both encompassed by and on fire with God's love.[74] Perhaps it was of these early days that she was thinking when she wrote many years later: "But true love is the love of a lover.

It is rarely found, for nothing touches it, neither good nor evil. The lover gives his life gladly for the beloved. He does not know his own interests or even his needs. Sickness and health are alike to him; prosperity and adversity, life and death; consolation and desolation are the same to him."[75] The challenge of the next few years would be to find a fitting way to embody that love.

CHAPTER TWO

Searching for the Way,
1640–1653

M. Jendret ... told me one day that Our Lord had left three states of women to follow Him and to serve the Church: the role of Magdalen was filled by the Carmelites and other recluses; that of Martha, by cloistered religious who serve their neighbour: but the state of life of the journeying Virgin Mary, which also must be honoured, was not yet filled. Even without veil or wimple, one could be a true religious ... About 12 years after his first voyage to Canada, M. de Maisonneuve came [to Troyes] and ... would accept only me without a single companion.

M. Jendret told me that what God had not willed in Troyes, He would perhaps bring to pass in Montreal.[1]

Even at the age of twenty, Marguerite Bourgeoys was a woman for whom inspiration flowed immediately into action; in the aftermath of her conversion, she at once sought and found a concrete form in which she might begin to make the gift of self. Describing the action that she took in response to her conversion, she wrote many years later: "I made my confession to Abbé Desguerrois, the grand penitentiary, and entered the Congregation."[2] Membership in the congregation to which Marguerite refers here was to play a role of incalculable importance in her life. It figures even in the brief remarks of Dollier de Casson and is mentioned by all her biographers.

The religious group of which the Congrégation de Notre-Dame of Troyes was a part had been founded in 1598[3] in Lorraine, still, at that time, an independent duchy, by Pierre Fourier, parish priest of Mattaincourt, and Alix Le Clerc, to whom he was spiritual director. This was the most avant-garde of several new communities that had come into existence in response to a growing awareness of the importance of mothers in the transmission of the faith.[4] Introduced into France at Châlons-sur-Marne in 1613, the community was established at Troyes in 1628 by a sister named Nicole Dominique. Because she was only twenty-eight years of age at the time, special arrangements had to be made to allow her appointment as superior, a position she was to occupy for thirty years, until her death in Troyes in 1663. The young superior faced severe problems during the early years of the foundation: the plague of 1633, which forced the sisters to abandon the city temporarily, and a debt of fifty thousand *livres*. The annals of her community were eventually to praise her in these terms: "Of extraordinary intelligence and ability, her administrative prowess enabled her to find the means to pay back all loans and debts and establish her house without founder or benefactor."[5] Above all, however, Nicole Dominique is praised for attracting to her convent women "who did it honour with their virtues." Among the subjects she admitted to the community was Louise de Chomedey de Maisonneuve, sister of the future founder of Montreal.

The main object of the Congrégation de Notre-Dame of Troyes, according to its constitutions, was to render the lives of its members as holy, fruitful, useful to the public and as agreeable to God as possible. Above all, the sisters were to employ themselves diligently and wholeheartedly in the instruction of little girls, freely and for the love of God, opening schools for this purpose in their houses. The constitutions further called on the sisters to teach all the children, poor and rich, who presented themselves for instruction and to do so themselves, not through others. The statements about membership and work in a lay or extern congregation found in the early accounts of the life of Marguerite Bourgeoys seem to indicate that, though the sisters themselves continued to teach the girls who came to the school in their convent, they had to make other arrangements for those to be instructed outside it. In its first days the women in Fourier's Congrégation de Notre-Dame were not cloistered, but cloister came with canonical approval of the institute. The desire of this and other new congregations for freedom from strict cloister for the sake of their apostolates brought them into conflict with attempts being made to reform the older contemplative orders by enforcing the rules of strict cloister.[6] To save his Congrégation de Notre-Dame from dissolution, Fourier was obliged to abandon attempts either to obtain a mitigation of the strict rule of cloister or to establish two kinds of house. One would have contained vowed members, been enclosed, and supported and guaranteed the existence of the other, which was to be unenclosed and occupied by secular women engaged in teaching, who observed the Rule but were not bound by vows.[7]

Glandelet, who wrote in the present tense of something still existing in his own time, implies that the extern congregation was founded to compensate for the restrictions imposed by the cloister: "There is, in the city of Troyes," he says, "an important convent of religious of the Congrégation de Notre-Dame ... [They] are cloistered, but their house serves as a centre for a large number of young secular women, who constitute a kind of extern congregation whose members live devoutly, teach school, and give religious instruction in various places, in mission style, going out two by two to their various destinations."[8] Jamet speculates that a condition of the establishment of Fourier's Congrégation de Notre-Dame in Troyes may have been a commitment to the city to provide education for the poor girls in the suburbs. Since the cloister made it impossible for the sisters to fulfil this commitment in their own persons, they carried it out by organizing the extern congregation.[9] Faillon adds certain other facts to our knowledge of this congregation: "It was a pious association of young women who, without binding themselves in conscience, met on feast days and Sundays for certain religious practice, and also undertook various works of charity and zeal."[10]

Taken together, the accounts suggest an association of young women who met regularly under the direction of a sister of the Congrégation de Notre-Dame (at the time of Marguerite Bourgeoys's membership, Louise de Chomedey, or Louise de Sainte-Marie, as she was known in religion), a spiritual director (Father Antoine de Gendret in 1640), and a prefect selected from among their own number. These women continued to live in their own homes and, without binding themselves by any vows or promises, undertook certain prayers and devotions, some of them in common, and certain work among the poor of the city, principally the teaching of little girls. They also appear to have had what might now be called a dress code; Faillon says that "they tried, in their appearance, to conform to the rules of the most austere simplicity."[11] They would, then, have been a highly visible group among the young women of Troyes. They were not, before 1640, a group to which Marguerite Bourgeoys felt any attraction.

The early accounts of her life make clear two things about her first relations with the members of the extern or secular congregation: that they very much wanted her to become a member of their group and that she was most reluctant to join them. Dollier de Casson says that she did not want to do so because she did not wish to be perceived as *bigotte*.[12] The general context would suggest that "sanctimonious" might be the best English translation of this term. His statement suggests that "peer pressure" among young people is nothing new; their fear of being perceived by their friends as ultra-pious or serious was strong even in the first half of the seventeenth century. Marguerite was also deterred, she implies, by a penchant for pretty clothes and ornaments. However, there may have been deeper reasons than these for her lack of enthusiasm for the secular congregation. To the end of her life, she had a profound distrust of conspicuous piety, of the desire to appear different.[13] All her biographers stress the great virtue of the secular congregation, but it would seem that the impression they made on their less pious contemporaries was not altogether positive. Faillon suggests that their exemplary behaviour might have inspired envy and guilt in more worldly young women,[14] and certainly this is an all-too-common human reaction. But it is also possible that something in their style of piety repelled the other girls. Glandelet's remarks imply that Marguerite's repugnance towards joining the group did not disappear on Rosary Sunday 1640, though he attributes her aversion to something in keeping with his own notion of how a future saint should act: "It was only by doing considerable violence to her feelings that she presented herself for reception into the extern congregation, because she was afraid of pretending to a devoutness she did not possess."[15] Dollier de Casson, who wrote about the living woman rather than the dead saint, tells us that Marguerite carefully investigated before she finally became a member of the extern congregation and that she only did so when she was satisfied about their sincerity and the value of the work they were doing.[16] As was to be her habit throughout life, she based her decision on the "fruits."

The extern congregation, however, showed no such reluctance about admitting Marguerite. Glandelet says that although the usual practice was to make a candidate apply twice for membership, she was received with alacrity and joy on her first application. Faillon tells us that their eagerness was in part founded on the hope that a girl so universally popular with her peers would attract many others into the group. Nor were they to regret their haste.[17] According to Dollier de Casson, Marguerite very soon became prefect of the group, a position that she held for twelve or fifteen years because the extern congregation made unprecedented progress under her leadership.[18] This expansion of the secular congregation is confirmed by the annals of the Congrégation de Notre-Dame of Troyes cited by Jamet and the letter written in 1701 by Mother Marie-Paule de Blaigny, the superior of that community at the time of Marguerite's death, cited by Glandelet. The former reveal that while Louise de Chomedey was the sister charged with the extern congregation, its numbers went from thirty to more than four hundred;[19] the latter source affirms that Marguerite had already been prefect for some years in 1647 and that she won the hearts of all with whom she came into contact.[20]

This early evidence of the nature and power of Marguerite's qualities of leadership suggests that she may have been instrumental in changing the impression made by the extern congregation on the world at large. Jamet writes in relation to her conversion, "Farewell to the laughter and merry meetings,"[21] but surely laughter did not entirely vanish from the life of someone who continued to exercise such an attraction on others. Perhaps what she now avoided was sarcastic and quasi-malicious laughter at the expense of others, the raillery against which she was to warn her sisters later in life.[22] Marguerite had an aptitude for wit, as is apparent in her later comments on the rule of human prudence or the external rule;[23] her reputation for unfailing kindness indicates that she curbed the temptation to express her sense of humour at the expense of others. Of all her biographers, Jamet has perhaps come closest to describing what he calls her *grâce personelle*, her special gift. He says that we tend involuntarily to retain from her early biographers an image of inflexibility (raideur) and sorrowful gravity (*gravité chagrine*), whereas in reality her most typical characteristics were what he calls *douceur* and *naturelle bonté*. These terms are both much richer than any single English equivalents can suggest, conveying as they do ideas of gentleness, kindness, goodness, and generosity. In fact, Marguerite seems to have been gifted with a natural temperament that reflected the qualities described as the fruit of the Holy Spirit in Galations 5:22–3.[24]

Whether or not Marguerite had ever been a pupil of the Congrégation de Notre-Dame of Troyes, she must now have come in contact with their theory and practice of teaching. In so doing, she was learning from one of the most advanced groups in France, for Pierre Fourier, their founder, had been a great innovator in the field of pedagogy. Many of the ideas about education that were later to inspire her apostolate in the New World and to animate the instructions that she was to present to her community find expression earlier in the constitutions of the Congrégation de Notre-Dame of Pierre Fourier. These constitutions called on the sisters to perceive in the girls they taught persons who would one day wield incalculable influence as the mothers of families. "Although still small in years, they are not a small or paltry portion of the Church of God even in the present, and in a few years will be capable of great good. For this reason, it is very expedient to see that everything necessary is done for their own well-being and for that of their fathers and mothers, the families they will one day govern, and the state itself."[25]

Several of Marguerite's key ideas are expressed in this passage. The first is an insistence on the importance of the role of women in

the family, the Church, and the whole of society (elsewhere the constitutions insist on the then-revolutionary idea that women are best
qualified to educate other women).[26] The second is the perception
that education in the schools is an effort directed not only towards
future families but also towards the families of which the students
are already members. Cooperation with parents is stressed, and the
sisters are warned against usurping the parents' prerogatives. "The
teachers and the Mother Directress will not meddle with the punishment of those misdeeds of students that take place outside school nor
listen to taletelling. They will leave such things to the devotion and
duty of the fathers and mothers."[27] In their relations with their students the constitutions insist that the teachers display unfailing gentleness, amiability, and kindness, that they use reward rather than
punishment to inspire the girls to good behaviour and learning, and
above all, that they avoid punishment of any kind. In fact, punishment could be administered only in the most drastic of circumstances, never by the teachers, and only when all else had failed.
Even then, it could only be of a very mild nature. Verbal abuse was
also forbidden, and the constitutions proscribe the appellations
"asses, beasts, idiots," and even "bad girls."[28] The sisters were forbidden ever to use words of contempt, mockery, or ridicule against
others whether they were present or absent. Above all, they must
avoid anything that would antagonize either parents or children in
such a way as to cause the withdrawal of students from school.[29]

One other idea that was profoundly important to Marguerite
Bourgeoys appears in these constitutions. From his first days as a
parish priest, Pierre Fourier had worked to alleviate the social conditions of the poor and even to assist members of the middle class
when they fell on difficult times. He did not stop at the collection and
distribution of alms, but attempted to inaugurate social action that
would make the giving of alms unnecessary, all this to realize a vision
of society exemplified in the primitive church of the New
Testament.[30] The Congrégation de Notre-Dame of Troyes existed to
serve the poor as well as the rich, though the restrictions imposed by
the cloister seem to have been an obstacle to the fulfilment of this
goal.[31] The poor, besides receiving instruction in Christian doctrine
and conduct and being taught to read and write, were to learn those
skills necessary to enable them to earn a living ("propres pour en
gagner du pain").[32]

It was particularly with these poor that Marguerite would have
come into contact through her work with the extern congregation,
where it would seem that her involvement went beyond teaching the
children. The philosophy of the sisters of the Congrégation de Notre-

Dame of Troyes that their apostolate extended beyond the girls they taught to the families of those girls probably inspired the extern congregation as well. There is direct evidence of Marguerite's involvement with the poor of Troyes in the letter already cited written by the superior of the Congrégation de Notre-Dame in Troyes in answer to the news of her death. The superior reports, "Her eagerness to serve the poor was her great concern, which sometimes caused her little problems with her relatives; however, as they were devout, she knew how to find the words to win them over, so that they let her continue."[33] It would seem that the persuasive skills that Marguerite would display in later life were honed early. Certainly, in the Troyes of 1640–53 she would have found plenty of poverty and misery calling for her skill and devotion.

Economic conditions in Troyes were so bad in the seventeenth century that its citizens looked back on the earlier part of the previous century as a golden age. Evelyne Chabroux cites several kinds of documentary evidence of the misery during the period. Even if one rejects the picture presented in the *cahiers de doléances* as exaggerated – the aim of the petitioners, after all, was to attempt to obtain relief from the tax burden imposed by the king – there are plenty of other indicators about the conditions of the time. At the end of the seventeenth century the census sets the number of poor in Troyes at 6,679, or 30 per cent of a population that had fallen to 18,198. While such precise statistics are not available for the earlier part of the century, historians have estimated the number of poor in 1649 as about one-third of the population.

Actions taken by the authorities and the citizens to cope with the situation were both positive and negative. Municipal and ecclesiastical authorities moved to assist the destitute. Regulations about the distribution of bread to the poor were set up, obligations of religious communities to assist the poor were specified, the tax for the Aumône Générale, an early version of relief or welfare, was drastically increased: at one time doubled and then tripled. The six hospitals of Troyes, which at that time had wider obligations than do hospitals today, including the succour of the poor, were reorganized so as to be able to use their resources more efficiently. Numerous individuals attempted to help the poor with gifts and legacies. If Jamet's suggestion is correct that the city of Troyes may have made instruction of the poor a condition for the establishment of the Congrégation de Notre-Dame there, such a requirement may have been part of an attempt by officials to enable the poor to support themselves.

On the other hand, harsh restrictions were passed against beggars, especially "foreign" ones, that is, those who were not natives of

Troyes. According to these laws, first enacted in 1602 and repeated in similar terms in 1651 and 1653, foreign beggars were ordered to leave within forty-eight hours on pain of being whipped or sent to the galleys, native beggars were forbidden to beg in the streets or churches and had to wear the insignia of their parish or risk being removed from the alms roll, porters were prohibited from admitting them to the city, and those who harboured them were liable to a fine. Penalties for transgressing these laws included shaving, imprisonment, flogging, and being set in the pillory. Anyone aiding a beggar directly, rather than through the institutions set up for this purpose, was liable to a fine of thirty *livres*, and anyone failing to drive mendicants away to a fine of one hundred *livres*. These regulations reflect the fear of the populace that beggars coming in from the countryside might include brigands and murderers or, in many cases, might be carriers of the dreaded plague.[34] They also arose from the fact that the city was often hard-pressed to feed its own population and frequently faced civil unrest as a result. In the circumstances, it is scarcely surprising that Marguerite's family was concerned about her work in situations where she might encounter disease and violence, as well as expose herself to some judicial penalty.

The issue of beggars from outside the city points to the major cause of unrest and poverty: the devastation of the surrounding countryside by war and the flight of the displaced population into the city in search of survival and safety, a situation that prevailed in Champagne from the end of the sixteenth century until about 1660. Even the Bourgeoys family, living in Troyes, knew at first hand the depradations of the military. They owned animals that were stabled outside the city. One of the documents settling the estate of Abraham Bourgeoys after his death records about one of the cows: "Taken by the soldiers and lost."[35] In the latter part of the sixteenth century, Champagne was disturbed by the Wars of Religion because some of the principals on both sides held lands in the province. In the early seventeenth century came the revolt of the nobles against Marie de Medici, widow of Henri IV and regent for her minor son; then, in Marguerite's time, the Thirty Years' War, beginning in 1635; and finally the Fronde, some of whose effects she would witness as she travelled across France on her journey to Canada.

The dilemma faced by the city during these conflicts was that, at the same time as it was increasingly strained by the influx of refugees rendered homeless and starving by the activities of native and foreign armies, it was crushed by the overwhelming increase in royal taxation to support the armies fighting on the side of the crown. Unable to pay these taxes, the city began to acquire massive and

unmanageable debts and eventually to alienate its assets in an
attempt to meet them. Marguerite could have seen concrete evidence
of the city's financial problems a few yards from her childhood home:
a new city hall projected for 1616 was not begun until 1624 and was
completed only in 1670, when the old city hall was literally falling
down. Individual citizens and corporations were overwhelmed with
taxation, direct and indirect, in an economy that was already suffering the effects of the shift in trade routes to the Atlantic and the problem of increased competition for traditional industries from foreign
competitors, such as English textile makers. Among the poor she
encountered, Marguerite would have found previously prosperous
merchants and artisans from her own class reduced to beggary. Even
the weather added to the misery of Champagne in the seventeenth
century, causing frequent crop failure and famine. The shortage of
grain in the years 1649–52 awakened in the authorities fears of civil
unrest such as had occurred in a previous famine in 1626.[36] These
were the problems with which Marguerite Bourgeoys would have
dealt first-hand in the course of her work among the poor of Troyes
over thirteen years.

Only one anecdote survives from this period in her life, and a version of it has found its way into her published writings. It is recounted in the letter from the superior of the Congrégation de Notre-Dame
of Troyes quoted by Glandelet.

Sister Bourgeoys learned that some young men had abducted a young
woman. She found out where they had taken her and went, crucifix in hand,
to beg these gentlemen to let her go. They confronted her with a pistol and
threatened to kill her. Fearlessly, she reminded them of their duty, that in
attacking a servant of Jesus Christ, they attacked Christ Himself, that sooner
or later they would be punished. She frightened them so much that they gave
up the poor girl, whom she is said to have kept with her and brought to
Canada.[37]

It must be remembered that this passage was written down more
than fifty years after it happened by someone who had never known
Marguerite, but who knew she was being called upon to say something edifying about Marguerite's life, something that conformed
with conventional ideas about saints' behaviour. That Marguerite
would set out to rescue a girl in the predicament described, that to do
so she would confront armed young men, that she would be successful in her attempt and would continue her concern for the girl after
the rescue – all these things are consistent with the Marguerite
Bourgeoys found in her writings and in the memories of her contem-

poraries in Ville-Marie. What is not characteristic is the style in which she is described as accomplishing this feat. Her own approach, which will be demonstrated later by an anecdote that she herself told about her first journey to the coast to take ship for Canada, was quite different. Tradition has identified the young woman rescued as Catherine Crolo,[38] a fellow member of the secular congregation, later to become one of Marguerite's first recruits to Ville-Marie, and it is generally safer to accept than to reject outright traditions that go back so far unless there is definite evidence to the contrary. However, this identification does raise some questions. Why had Catherine no protector in her own family? Was she molested as she performed her duties as a member of the extern congregation, or did Marguerite meet her first as a "client"? Why is the story never mentioned by Marie Morin, who writes at some length about Catherine, a woman she knew well? If Glandelet is right in placing the event after the death of Abraham Bourgeoys in 1651,[39] would Catherine, a year older than Marguerite and therefore in her thirties, be referred to as a young girl?

Membership in the extern congregation also brought Marguerite into contact with a priest whose influence on her future life can scarcely be overestimated. He was Father Antoine de Gendret, the spiritual director of the group. There might be some clerical bias and exaggeration, but there is undoubtedly a kernel of truth in Jamet's statement that "the meeting with Father Jendret was the principal event of the years of formation in Troyes, and, without exaggeration, of her whole existence." Certainly, he is right in the assertion, "No other priest played such an important role in her life."[40] Remarkably little has ever been discovered about this man who made so significant a contribution to Marguerite's spiritual development. Jamet believed that Gendret (he uses the spelling "Jendret") was associated with a movement of clerical reform and renewal led by Adrien Bourdoise and introduced into the diocese of Troyes by Bishop René de Breslay. Between 1623 and 1629 the priest was associated with the parish of Saint-Nizier, in the lower part of the city behind the cathedral, where his office was to instruct the altar boys of the cathedral in grammar. From about 1640 to at least 1653 he was chaplain of the Carmelites at the monastery of Notre-Dame-de-Pitié in the suburb of Croncels, and then in 1656 he was back at Saint-Nizier as priest-catechist.[41] These are the facts verified by Jamet. Although Alfred Morin continued to search for more information about Marguerite's director, he remains elusive.[42]

Her own words suggest that it was Father Gendret who first proposed to her the idea of religious life. The result was her attempt to enter the Carmelites and their rejection of her candidacy. "Some time later," she wrote, "this good Father spoke to me about religious life. But the Carmelites refused me even though I was strongly drawn to them."[43] The matter had apparently already been discussed in her family, and the comments of Dollier de Casson again suggest the warmth of the relationship between Marguerite and her father. "Wishing to be a nun, she hoped to become a Carmelite, and her father resolved to do all he could to provide her dowry, so that he might give her this happiness, because he could refuse her nothing."[44] This rejection by the Carmelites has puzzled all biographers of Marguerite Bourgeoys. Each acknowledges that it was providential, but none has been able to suggest with any confidence what motives might have led the community to turn her away. Glandelet did not even attempt an explanation, while Faillon observes: "We do not know the motives for her rejection; perhaps the sudden change remarked in the young prospective postulant, and of which the true cause was not known, raised the suspicion of a certain frivolity in the desire she expressed to enter such an austere order and a doubt as to whether such great fervour could be sustained."[45]

Jamet rejects this speculation, saying that surely such a change could only have been to the advantage of a proposed postulant. In fact, Faillon's explanation is unsatisfactory for many reasons. It is true that the time lapse between Marguerite's conversion and her attempt to enter Carmel could not have been a long one. She uses the indefinite term "later" – "later" she entered the extern congregation; "some time later" Father Gendret spoke to her of religious life – but certainly all these events took place before she was twenty-three years old, when Father Gendret allowed her to pronounce a private vow of chastity.[46] Had the Carmelites feared that her desire to join them was simply a passing impulse, they might rather have postponed her entrance than have given her what she seems to have regarded as a final answer. Nor had the change in her behaviour been from a life of depravity to one of sudden piety. Few religious communities in any era would accept many candidates if they rejected all those who had showed some frivolousness in their teens. In recent times, at least, communities are more likely to regard with suspicion aspirants who have failed ever to show evidence of such frivolity.

Another possible cause for the rejection is that Marguerite might not have been considered socially acceptable in Carmel.[47] The Carmelites, after their establishment in Paris by a group of Spanish nuns in 1601, became the fashionable order of the upper classes. Dollier de Casson's comment about the efforts that Marguerite's father was ready to undertake to raise her dowry implies that the amount would have been higher than the payments he made at the marriages of his other children and would have expected to make had she chosen to marry.[48] Marguerite's own lifelong insistence that economic and social position should never be a barrier to entry into her Congregation might have had its roots here. Certainly, when she was offered a place in Carmel on the eve of her departure for Canada, it was under the influence of ladies of higher social position than herself. Yet there are problems with the theory that her rejection was related to social rank. The Carmel of Croncels already contained a connection of the Bourgeoys family in the person of Marie Le Jeune, daughter of Claude Le Jeune, a merchant in silk sheets and the godfather of Madeleine Bourgeoys, Marguerite's youngest sister.

The most puzzling aspect of the situation is the fact that Marguerite was encouraged to seek entrance to Carmel by Father Gendret, who must have known something of the nuns who were his penitents and the atmosphere of their house, and who himself must surely have been much surprised by the refusal. If, as recent research seems to suggest, there was a policy not to accept aspirants in the Carmel of Croncels at this time, why was Father Gendret unaware of it?[49] Perhaps, in the end, we must emulate those biographers who, like Marguerite herself, attempt no other explanation of the Carmelites' rejection save the will of God. No doubt she was perplexed and hurt by the refusal. Her unfailing reticence about her own feelings would never allow her to expatiate on the subject, but for anyone who has become accustomed to her style, that wistful reference to the extent to which she had developed an attraction to Carmel is indication enough of the pain she must have felt. Yet one cannot help wondering whether life in Carmel would have brought complete expression for all of Marguerite's gifts. And that observation raises a final possibility about her rejection by Carmel: Did she encounter a prioress with sufficient wisdom and insight to recognize that her gifts were destined for development and service elsewhere? About Mother Marie-de-la-Trinité, prioress at the time, the archives of the convent state, "Her soul, always united to God, knew, almost at first glance, what there was of God in someone."[50]

Even more difficult to explain than Marguerite's exclusion from Carmel is the fact that her attempt to enter other religious communities also met with failure. It has always been assumed that these communities also refused her, but that is not exactly what she says. Rather, she records, "I went to others, but this did not succeed either."[51] She does not indicate clearly whether she was rejected or whether these communities did not meet her aspirations. Not all the older orders in seventeenth-century France were havens of austere fervour. Though the more gross disorders found in earlier periods had disappeared, the use of convents as refuges for the daughters of aristocratic families unable or unwilling to supply them with the dowries that would have enabled them to marry within their own class was still widespread in this era despite the reforms. In his study of French society during the reign of Louis XIV, W.H. Lewis provides abundant evidence of the continuance of this practice.[52] He remarks that though much sympathy has been directed towards such young women, it might perhaps be directed to a more fitting object. The convent was "by no means a miserable life, always providing that the girl did not by some plaguy mischance develop a genuine vocation after her profession; for then the struggle against the contented tepidity of her sisters could be heartbreaking."[53]

Marguerite does not specify which other communities she approached, though for many years it was taken for granted, on the authority of Glandelet,[54] that she attempted to enter the Poor Clares. Jamet, however, established that there was no foundation of this order in Troyes in her time, and he offers as alternatives the Sisters of the Visitation or, more probably, the Capuchin Sisters since as a Franciscan community they might more easily have been confused with the Poor Clares. Both of these communities had convents in Croncels not far from that of the Carmelites.[55]

Apparently, Marguerite did not fret over these failures. She continued her work with the secular congregation and perhaps began to develop an insight into the form of prayer proper to a religious working in the midst of the world. Of this, she was later to write to her sisters: "It seems to me that we do not pay enough attention to prayer, for unless it arises from the heart which ought to be its centre, it is no more than a fruitless dream. Prayer ought to carry over into our words, our thoughts and our actions."[56] Unable to pronounce public vows in a religious community, she sought permission from her confessor to make private ones while remaining in the world. Although Father Gendret is at first reported to have wanted her to delay taking this step until she reached the age of thirty, then twenty-five,[57] he permitted her to make a vow of chastity on the feast of St Thomas, 21 December 1643, when she was still four months short of her twenty-fourth birthday.[58] Some time later, he allowed her to make a vow of poverty. At an advanced age she was able to write about these acts with remarkable, yet characteristic, serenity and steadfastness. "I gave myself to God in 1640. A few years later, upon the advice of my confessor, I took the vow of chastity and some time later, the vow of poverty. I made both of these vows with all the zeal and all the perfection possible to me, together with the resolution to keep them all my life. I have never had a thought contrary to this.[59]

Now, at last, though still dimly, the shape of the future could begin to be discerned; she and Father Gendret started to share the dream of a different form of religious life for women than that sanctioned by the ecclesiastical authorities of their time. Marguerite's most complete acccunt of this new vision occurs in the draft of the letter to Father Tronson, quoted in the previous chapter, on the motives and purpose of the Congregation:

M. Jendret ... told me one day that Our Lord had left three states of women to follow Him and to serve the Church: the role of Magdalen was filled by the Carmelites and other recluses; that of Martha, by cloistered religious who serve their neighbour; but the state of life of the journeying Virgin Mary, which must also be honoured, was not yet filled. Even without veil or wimple, one could be a true religious. This was very acceptable to me because I had compassion on the young women who for lack of money could not enter the service of God.[60]

Marguerite makes it sound as if the idea for a new kind of community came completely from Father Gendret, and Glandelet says that this was a project whose inspiration Gendret had nourished for some time, presumably even before he met Marguerite Bourgeoys. It is difficult to believe, however, that there was not some form of reciprocal influence. In Marguerite, whose experience of conversion was so closely bound with her devotion to Mary the mother of the Lord and who spent her days working among the poor of Troyes, he found someone in whom he saw verified at first hand that one could be a religious without wimple or veil.

Of course, Father Gendret and Marguerite Bourgeoys were not the first to dream of uncloistered religious life for women, and certainly, in seventeenth-century France it was an idea whose time had come. Attempts had been made in the previous century to found communities of women who would pursue their apostolate unhampered by the restrictions of the cloister, one of the best known of these being the Ursulines, founded in Italy by St Angela Merici. Closer to home, St Francis de Sales had tried to keep his Sisters of the Visitation uncloistered, and in Paris, among the poor and wretched, St Vincent de Paul was attempting to establish in the Sisters of Charity a community of women whose veil was holy modesty and whose cloister was the street. Years later, on one of her trips back to France from Montreal, Marguerite was to stay with the Sisters of the Cross, founded by Madame de Villeneuve, and to consult them on the matter of a Rule for her community. There were, in addition, other, less-known attempts being made in France to move out of the cloister, many of them unrecorded, either because they were not successful or because they were destroyed at the time of the Revolution.

Jamet believed that Father Gendret's intentions might not have been as radical as they sound, that he might not have envisioned eventual ecclesiastical approval of a new kind of religious life, but have simply intended to form an elite group within the extern congregation whose members "would aspire to imitate the virtues of the cloister, and by the practice of private vows lead the life of religious."[61] This approach seems unlikely if Marguerite quotes Father Gendret with any accuracy. In her later writings, she was to express another idea about Mary and Martha besides the one that she attributes to her confessor; she saw them both as teaching in the early church alongside Mary the mother of Jesus. This belief strengthens the likelihood that in passages where she sees Mary the mother of Jesus, Mary Magdalen, and Martha as exemplifying three forms of religious life for women,[62] she reflects his ideas closely. His statement clearly parallels three forms of religious life: cloistered, contemplative religious life (Mary Magdalen); cloistered, apostolic religious life, where outsiders are received into restricted parts of the convent, such as the Hospitallers and the Congrégation de Notre-Dame of Troyes (Martha); and uncloistered, apostolic religious life, whose members are free to go out and move freely wherever they are needed (Mary the mother of the Lord). What is more, this new form of religious life envisages, not an imitation of the spirituality of the cloister practised in the midst of the world, except insofar as all Christian spirituality must share certain common elements, but rather, a new spirituality, which in Marguerite's case, at least, was to find its inspiration in the activity of women in the primitive church. Jamet has written that the originality of Father Gendret did not consist in an attempt to overturn received ideas about religious life or to establish an uncloistered community of women, but that he simply wanted to honour the life of the Blessed Virgin.[63] But it is difficult to see how the two can be separated.

When Marguerite talks about the "vie voyagère," or "journeying life," of Mary (the phrase is not one in the standard vocabulary of her day, and hence difficult to translate), she is pointing to an activity forbidden to religious women of her time. They could receive people into their houses, or at least into certain designated parts of those houses, but they could not go out to minister to the needs of others, a fact that cut them off from the very people whom many of their orders or congregations had been founded to serve, the poor. In her references to the "vie voyagère," Marguerite is alluding to Mary's whole life, especially to her life in the post-Resurrection church. She is looking for a term analogous to the "public life" of Jesus, for to have talked of "public life" for a woman would have suggested prostitution rather than going about teaching and doing good. Glandelet says that Father Gendret proposed to her "the plan he had to establish a community whose end was to honour the way of life of the Most Holy Virgin after the Resurrection of her Son and His Ascension into Heaven."[64] Marguerite herself wrote many years later, "This community was founded to honour the third state of women which Our Lord, Jesus Christ left on earth after His resurrection."[65] No subject can be better documented in her writings than her view of the role of Mary the mother of Jesus and other women disciples in the primitive church. Nor, perhaps, can anything bring her closer to the continuing struggle of women for their rightful place in the church. Whatever she may have received from Father Gendret, she would develop and mature in the course of a long life spent in the service of a church just coming into being in the New World.

In her study of the history of Marian doctrine and devotion in the Roman Catholic Church, Hilda Graef has noted that as early as the Council of Nicaea (325) Mary was portrayed, not as she appears in Scripture, but as the ideal of the fourth-century consecrated virgin always at prayer in her home, meticulously guarded against male society, whereas the Mary of the Gospels did not hesitate to visit her cousin Elizabeth, went up to the Temple for the feasts, and generally behaved like a normal Jewish woman of her time.[66] Mary was still depicted according to the cloistered ideal in the writings of many theologians of Marguerite's time. Her own vision is solidly based on the two New Testament books attributed to Luke, his Gospel and the Acts of the Apostles, where Mary is presented as the first believer and the first disciple of Jesus.[67]

In the first chapter of Luke's Gospel, when, immediately after the Annunciation, Mary goes to visit her cousin Elizabeth, she is greeted not just with praise of her physical motherhood ("Blessed is the fruit of your womb") but with an affirmation of her faith: "Blessed is she who believed." Luke has thus prepared for the incident in which a woman from the crowd calls out, "Happy the womb that bore you and the breasts you sucked," and Jesus replies, "Still happier those who hear the word of God and keep it!" Elizabeth had already affirmed that Mary was both physical mother and believer.[68] When Luke describes the origins of the church in Acts, it is not just the apostles who gather in the upper room to pray and await the descent of the Spirit. They are joined by Mary the mother of Jesus and several women.[69] Marguerite repeatedly made clear her belief that these women continued to play an active public role in the primitive church. Foremost among those whom she portrays as working actively and publicly with Mary the mother of Jesus in the early church are Mary and Martha, the sisters of Lazarus. "As the number of Christians increased, the apostles were not sufficient for all the instruction and the Blessed Virgin, Saint Madeline and Saint Martha helped in the instruction of their sex." Mary and Martha are thus no longer seen as prototypes of cloistered religious.[70]

Marguerite's final comment in the letter to Father Tronson quoted above calls attention to another characteristic of the projected community that departed from the norms of her time and was related to the existence of the cloister: "This [the third kind of religious life] was very acceptable to me because I had compassion on the young women who for lack of money could not enter the service of God." Since entrance into a traditional community demanded the payment of a dowry, the cloister was in effect closed to the poor. The community that Marguerite envisaged would support itself, not through dowries or the patronage of the wealthy, but through the daily labour of its members. Lack of cloister meant not simply that the new community would be able to reach out more easily to the poor; it meant that the poor themselves could become members. This was an essential part of the design from the beginning: "I always held to the purpose which we had hoped to realize in Troyes – that there would be a refuge for those girls who had all the qualities but who could not become religious for lack of money."[71]

The first step in the attempt to found the new community was the drawing up of a Rule. Marguerite states that this was done by Father Gendret and the theologian of Troyes, a canon of the cathedral chapter with the special office of teaching theology. Gendret seems then to have had the Rule examined by some acquaintance at the Sorbonne, who duly approved it. In the initial attempt to bring the new community into being, Marguerite took up residence with two other young women. The time references in her writings are too vague to enable us to know how old she was when this attempt was made or how long it lasted, though Glandelet says it was from 1644 to 1653.[72]

We do know, however, where the aspiring group took up residence. Glandelet says that Marguerite and her companions lived in an apartment belonging to Madame de Chevilly, sister of M. de Maisonneuve.[73] This was Jacqueline, the younger of de Maisonneuve's two sisters, who was married to François Bouvot, Sieur de Chevilly, and her involvement suggests that Sister Louise took an active interest in the establishment of the new community.[74] Prompted by Rumilly's identification of the house as "l'hôtel du Chaudron," Niel attempted to determine which of several houses designated with the *chaudron* (cauldron) was the house in question.[75] In 1950, when his monograph was published, he had not yet been able to determine which of these was the right dwelling. But using an inventory taken at the time of Jacqueline's death and discovered by Sister Scott in 1964, Alfred Morin was certain that the house bearing the sign of the cauldron was, in the seventeenth century, on the old street that bore that name.[76] The site is near the cathedral, almost opposite the present municipal library. Although the house has disappeared, a passageway has survived that Marguerite may have used to reach the rear section from the street now called Chrétien-de-Troyes. The house was owned by a neighbour of Madame de Chevilly in Neuville-sur-Vanne and must have been leased or lent to her, her main residence being the de Maisonneuve manor house at Neuville-sur-Vanne.[77]

The time for Marguerite's new community had not yet arrived, however. Of the three young women who were its members, one died and another left, possibly to marry, so that Marguerite remained alone. The experience must have taught her something about the difficulties and rewards of common life, and as she prayed in the cathedral that was now so near her dwelling, she perhaps acquired a deeper insight into an image that was to be very important in her writings and instructions to the Congregation she would later found. In the north aisle of the cathedral of Saint-Pierre et Saint-Paul in Troyes is a large stained-glass window by Linard Gontier, erected in 1625, depicting the *pressoir mystique*, the mystical winepress. The window represents the crucified and bleeding Christ, who lies prostrate and is approached by the apostles, one of them carrying a chalice in which to gather up the spilled drops of Christ's blood.

The image is rich and ancient. It has its roots in Isaiah 63:2–3: "Why then is your clothing red, and your garments like theirs who tread the winepress? I have trodden the winepress alone, and out of all the nations no one was with me." This passage, with its symbols of blood and grapes and wine, was early incorporated into the liturgy of Holy Week, where it came to be associated with both the passion of Christ and the Eucharist. Christ himself becomes not just the one who walks the winepress alone, but the grapes that are crushed in his passion to become the wine of the Eucharist. These symbols were still widely understood and invoked in seventeenth-century Europe, not just in Catholic France but also in English religious poetry of the period. George Herbert's poem "The Bunch of Grapes" concludes:

Blessed be God, who prosper'd *Noahs* vine,
And made it bring forth grapes good store,
But much more him I must adore,
Who of the Laws sowre juice sweet wine did make,
Ev'n God himself being pressed for my sake.

And later in the century, Henry Vaughan wrote in "The Passion":

Most blessed Vine!
Whose juice so good
I feel as Wine,
But thy faire branches felt as bloud.
How wert thou prest
To be my feast!
In what deep anguish
Didst thou languish,
What springs of Sweat, and bloud did drown thee!

In the thirteenth century, the legend of the Holy Grail had added new elements to this imagery: the Grail became a eucharistic symbol as the cup used by Christ at the Last Supper and then held up to the cross by Joseph of Arimathea to catch the blood of the dying Christ. The wine-growing area of Champagne was the place in which this legend developed. In his short pontificate the pope from Troyes, Urban IV, had extended the feast of Corpus Christi to the entire church.

In 1698, late in her life, Marguerite Bourgeoys was to choose a religious name. Her choice must have had a different significance from those names that, for centuries, most religious selected or were assigned at the outset of their lives in convents and monasteries. One might have expected her to choose a Marian name or title. Instead, she became "Marguerite du Saint-Sacrement," Marguerite of the Blessed Sacrament. In her surviving writings she twice uses the image of that eucharistic window in the cathedral of Troyes. About teaching in school she observed, "It is the work [most] suited to draw down the graces of God if it is done with purity of intention, without distinction between the poor and the rich, between relatives and friends and strangers, between the pretty and the ugly, the gentle and the grumblers, looking upon them all as drops of Our Lord's blood."[78] Elsewhere she addressed her sisters in a sentence that appeared on a painting which hung over the door of the Montreal novitiate of the Congrégation de Notre-Dame until after the mid-twentieth century: "Consider, dear, that when you go on mission, you go to gather up the drops of the blood of Jesus Christ which are being lost."[79] Seen in relation to that stained-glass window once so familiar to Marguerite, these statements associate the work of her Congregation with that of the apostles and with her vision of the primitive church, in which men and women both taught the word of God.[80]

The failure of the little community in Troyes did leave Marguerite free to perform one last duty towards her family, a duty that was obviously also a labour of love. "At this time, my father died and I had the consolation of caring for him in his illness and of burying him after his death."[81] This statement is more evidence not only of her deep love for her father, but also of her sense that God's call can come through duties within the family, through service to the people who are closest and to whom one is bound in love and duty. It was attitudes such as these that would help to bring Marguerite close to the ordinary people of Montreal. The documents relevant to the settlement of Abraham Bourgeoys's estate indicate that she signed a promissary note for thirty livres as part of the funeral expenses.[82] Glandelet sees in this final service to her father the first of the many occasions when Marguerite would be called to perform this work of mercy, whether for the prospective colonists who perished during her first voyage to Canada or for a child accidentally strangled in Lachine many decades later. Before the era of the professional undertaker, such service was important both to the dead and to the bereaved.

Abraham Bourgeoys died in October 1651. The inventory made after his death,[83] like the one compiled after the death of his wife, provides us with further information about the family. Abraham was no longer living in the house in which the children had grown up. Instead he occupied premises on rue de la Bourcerye; there was still a shop, however, so he apparently continued to pursue his old occupation of candlemaker. At his death, his estate was divided into eight parts:[84] Anne, the second daughter and third child, had died in the years since the death of Guillemette Garnier.[85] Of the rest of the family, Claude is described as a merchant at Sens; Sirette is the wife of Pierre Maillet, *marchand libraire* (bookseller) Hierosme or Jérôme is a surgeon at Évreux; Marie is the wife of Orson Semilliard, *sergent Roial* (royal sergeant); Edouard has apparently taken over his father's occupation, for he is described as *maître chandelier* (master candlemaker); and Madeleine, just eighteen, is not yet married. She and fourteen-year-old Pierre are still minors.[86]

Like the inventory made at the time of Guillemette Garnier's death, this one proceeds room by room in detail and assigns a value to each object.[87] Later documents indicate which articles were claimed by the various members of the family. An examination of those chosen by Marguerite implies that she had not abandoned the idea of establishing a community. Among them were a crucifix with two stone figures and some paintings of religious subjects such as St John, St Sebastian, and the sacrifice of Isaac, artefacts that suggested she may have had in mind the furnishing of a chapel. There were large cooking utensils such as would have been suitable for a group, and as late as April 1652 Marguerite chose, as part of her share of her father's estate, several cows, heifers, and sheep, all of which could have helped to sustain a small community. She herself says that she went back to live in the house of Madame de Chevilly at this time.[88]

In her letter of 1701, Mother de Blaigny makes one more statement about Marguerite's life after her father's death. She says that Marguerite redoubled her austerities, never, for example, sleeping in a bed but only on boards, to the extent that she became ill and was reproached by her confessor and in obedience to him she abandoned these excesses.[89] The practice of extraordinary penance was, for the hagiographers of Marguerite's time, one of the principal evidences of sanctity. In fact, some of them, by the emphasis they place upon asceticism, come perilously close to implying that such is the essence of holiness. This attitude inevitably affected Marguerite, as well as her first biographers and the companions who gave them information. But asceticism is a subject far less congenial or even comprehensible to a late-twentieth-century audience. Marguerite herself never mentions such penances and certainly never advises them to her community in her surviving writings. Instead, she recommends love of God and neighbour, fidelity to the duty of each moment, and the service that finds its happiness and inspiration in that love. She writes about poverty as a sharing of the insecurities and deprivations of ordinary people. Her extraordinary penances are mentioned by neither Dollier de Casson nor Marie Morin, both of whom knew her and wrote about the living woman rather than the dead saint.

But the question of what were, even then, regarded as extraordinary penances returns in some of the statements made about Marguerite's later life by Glandelet and Ransonet. It might be well to remember that she understood the traditional Catholic teaching and devotion regarding asceticism and penance – that they are, at once, liberating practices, setting the Christian free from the tyranny of impulse and desire, an atonement for personal sin, and a participation in the redeeming sacrifice of Christ for the redemption of the world. Marguerite Bourgeoys was a French Catholic of the seventeenth century, with attitudes towards physical penance very different from those that prevail today. An early practice of excessive penance perhaps taught her a valuable lesson. Voluntary deprivation would have prepared her to give away both blanket and bed on a cold night and to use a pile of rope as a bed during a month-long voyage from Canada to France. Her earlier acts of asceticism would thus have helped to set her free for the love and service to God and neighbour that undoubtedly were for her, the true essence of Christianity.

The year after her father's death, there arrived in Troyes an individual who was to alter completely the course of Marguerite Bourgeoys's life. In 1652 Paul de Chomedey de Maisonneuve came to the city to visit his sisters. He was the eldest in the family, whose estate lay at Neuville-sur-Vanne not far from Troyes. Marie Morin was at one point under the impression that he had known Marguerite since she was a child,[90] but she later admitted that she had been mistaken. De Maisonneuve had been born in February 1612 and was therefore eight years older than Marguerite. Evidence about his early life is scarce; Dollier de Casson says that in keeping with the custom of the time, he began his military career early and by the age of thirteen was fighting in Holland.[91] He did, however, visit Troyes before his departure for New France in 1641, and he probably returned in the autumn of 1645, when he was in the area to settle family business after the death of his father. He was again in France and may have visited Troyes in 1646–47. Through her connection with his two sisters, it is possible that Marguerite had seen him before 1652, although her writings indicate that she had not met him or known about his Montreal project before his first departure for New France. "M. de Maisonneuve ... had gone to Montreal as governor in 1640 as I was able to learn later."[92]

It is difficult to tell how seriously she had thought of Ville-Marie before 1652. Certainly, she had heard about the project. From the beginning, Louise de Chomedey had hoped to go with several of her fellow religious to establish a house of her community in Ville-Marie; in anticipation of that event, they had given de Maisonneuve the picture of the Blessed Virgin mentioned earlier, around which was inscribed a play on words: Sainte Mère de Dieu, pure Vierge au coeur royal, gardez-nous une place en votre Montroyal ("Holy Mother of God, pure Virgin with a royal heart, keep us a place in your Montreal").[93] As the years passed, the sisters continued to nourish the dream that they would one day be able to go to Canada, and they talked about it to members of the secular congregation. Many years later Marguerite wrote to Father Tronson: "I joined the lay Congregation where I learned that a settlement had been made in

Canada and that the religious hoped to go there. I promised to be one of the company."[94] But in 1652 Louise de Chomedey and her community were again to know disappointment: de Maisonneuve wanted a teacher for Ville-Marie, but the colony was not yet ready for a cloister of women.[95] So she suggested that he take Marguerite Bourgeoys.

When Marguerite committed herself to anything, she did so totally and permanently; however, before she made such an undertaking, she gave the matter serious and, if possible, long consideration. Just as she had investigated the secular congregation carefully before becoming a member, so she now sought and weighed advice on the Montreal project. Her own description of her behaviour at this time contrasts with the impression given in Glandelet's account of her meeting with de Maisonneuve in the parlour of his sister's convent:

It was at that time that she had the following dream. It seemed to her that she saw St Francis with a young man, beautiful as an angel, and another bald man, dressed simply like a priest going into the country, not an intellectual. The next day, she recounted her dream, and a few days later, she was asked to come to the parlour [of the convent of the Congrégation de Notre-Dame of Troyes], where she found Monsieur de Maisonneuve, of whose arrival she had not known. On entering she said, "Look, here is the priest I saw in my dream!"[96]

The account resembles the many "wonder" stories connected with the founding of Montreal, some of which will be told in the next chapter. Some of the details are supported by known facts about Marguerite Bourgeoys and de Maisonneuve. St Francis of Assisi is the only non-biblical (or apocryphal) saint to whom Marguerite ever refers in her surviving writings,[97] and Marie Morin stresses how unostentatious in dress de Maisonneuve always was. It is, of course, very likely that as Marguerite considered the great decision she had to make, she found it entering her dreams.

At this time, she no longer had family obligations; her father was dead, her older brothers and sisters were well established, and the younger ones were no longer children. The increase in numbers in the lay congregation meant that there were others to continue her work in Troyes. She turned first to Father Gendret, expressing hesitation because it seemed that this new enterprise would mean an abandonment of the dream of a community of women who would honour the life of the Blessed Virgin. Father Gendret replied that perhaps this was rather the opportunity to bring such a community into being, that the failure to do so in Troyes might have been providential. "M.

Jendret told me that what God had not willed in Troyes, He would perhaps bring to pass in Montreal."[98] When Marguerite objected that she alone hardly constituted a community, he told her that with his guardian angel and hers, there would be community of three. She then drew to his attention the problems likely to beset an unmarried woman who travelled alone with a man, for Marguerite was neither naive nor needlessly careless of convention. Father Gendret's answer is phrased in those terms of chivalric romance that de Maisonneuve seems so frequently to have inspired. "He told me to put myself in M. de Maisonneuve's hands as in the hands of one of the first Knights of the Chamber of the Queen of Angels."[99] At Gendret's suggestion, Marguerite then consulted Georges Proffit, grand penitentiary of the cathedral of Troyes and her occasional confessor, and afterwards, M. Rose, the vicar general of the diocese; she says she would have consulted the bishop, but he was away. Each man took three days to consider the matter, and each then counselled her to accept the invitation to Montreal.[100] Father Gendret now disappears from Marguerite's writings, perhaps from her life. He had guided, inspired, and encouraged her for nearly thirteen years. That he now willingly, even eagerly, sent her forward on her own is the last we know of her relationship with this truly remarkable priest. Marguerite communicated her decision to de Maisonneuve, who had left for Paris, and in early February 1653 she set out to join him there.[101]

Her account of her departure from Troyes implies that both she and de Maisonneuve anticipated objections to their plans and hatched some schemes to circumvent the obstacles. De Maisonneuve invited his sister, Madame de Chevilly, to come to Paris to bid him goodbye, bringing Marguerite Bourgeoys with her as companion. Marguerite's uncle[102] was also one of the party. She did not inform them of her intention to go to Canada until after the journey had begun and their initial reaction was one of disbelief.[103] "Both he and Madame de Chevilly thought I was joking," Marguerite says. One can only conjecture that, when they were finally convinced of her seriousness, their reaction was not encouraging since she remarks, after she reports their return to Troyes, "I no longer had any difficulty from that quarter."[104] Instead, problems were to arise from a wholly unexpected source.

The external circumstances of the journey from Troyes to Paris must have been uncomfortable, not to say harrowing. A coach trip of four or five days on seventeenth-century roads in the month of February would pose hazard and hardship, even in the most favourable circumstances. This journey took place through a country ravaged by the fighting of the Fronde. One of Marguerite's stories gives some idea of what such travel implied. She says that on Sunday morning they heard church bells ringing for mass in one of the settlements along the way, but their coachman refused to stop in order to allow them to attend. About noon one of the wheels broke, and they had to await a replacement from Paris. During the delay the passengers who were able to do so walked into the nearest village. "After dinner, a little bell rang, and a priest who appeared totally debilitated chanted Vespers with five or six sickly men. This priest told us about all the calamities of the war in this place: all the houses ruined, a large number of dead horses, and even [the corpses] of some men and a woman. We tried to cover them over with a little earth."[105] Jamet observes that such scenes were common in the area between Troyes and Paris at this time and that on the later journey to Orléans Marguerite would have seen still greater desolation. Many of St Vincent de Paul's workers became infected and died as they went to help with the burial of the rotting corpses that were spreading contagion in a countryside already devastated and depopulated by war.

Dollier de Casson, in writing about how Marguerite first came to be involved in the Montreal project, gives a different version of her failure to enter Carmel from that found in other early sources. After the remarks already quoted in which he describes her father's resolution to raise the dowry required by the Carmelites because "he could refuse her nothing," Dollier continues:

Meanwhile, however, a member of the Congregation who was keenly interested in Canada met her and told her forcibly that she must not become a nun, but that she must go with her to serve God in New France. With this she so shook her mind that in the end she caused her to mention the matter to the Superior of their Congregation, who was an excellent nun, with the charge of all the lay congregationists, of whom Marguerite Bourgeois ... was prefect. By God's will, however, this superior was own sister to M. de Maisonneuve, to whom she related all the anxieties of the prefect. No sooner had M. de Maisonneuve learnt this than he asked to meet her, and no sooner had he done so than he was anxious not to lose such a treasure, and did all he could to secure her for New France.[106]

This account, which contradicts Marguerite's own description of events, can scarcely be accurate and may perhaps be a confusion of her first attempt to enter Carmel with the opportunities given her once she had determined to go to New France. Certainly, the sudden inner doubt belongs to that experience, for now, on the eve of her departure for the New World, Marguerite, so long repulsed by

Carmel, was to be almost propelled through the doors that had previously been so determinedly barred against her.

In Paris, Marguerite stayed with a Madame de Bellevue, who was a cousin of Jeanne Mance, one of the leaders of the Montreal expedition.[107] Madame de Bellevue also had a brother who was provincial superior of the Carmelites and who now, Marguerite says, "sent word to me that if I wished to be a Carmelite, I could enter wherever I wished, since in Troyes I had asked to enter."[108] Glandelet adds another reason why Marguerite might have experienced disquiet about her plans. He says that while she was in Paris, someone tried to persuade her that de Maisonneuve "was not the kind of man she had been told he was";[109] she mentions nothing of this suggestion in her writings, perhaps in respect for the memory of the man who was to become so valued a friend. Certainly, the Montreal expedition had, at this point, many and vocal enemies, and so it is all too possible that an attempt was made to discourage the new recruit by casting suspicion on the governor of Montreal. Marguerite had been entrusted with de Maisonneuve's belongings and had already paid her deposit on the coach to Orléans, the first stage in her journey to the meeting place in Nantes. She delayed long enough now to lose that deposit. But again she received unexpected encouragement to remain firm in her commitment to Montreal. Glandelet says that she went to consult the Jesuits on the rue Saint-Antoine. She herself relates, "By chance, I spoke to a Jesuit who knew Canada. I left the next day."[110] Neither Marguerite nor Glandelet gives any clue as to the identity of this Jesuit, but Father Paul Le Jeune, another native of Champagne, was procurator of the Canadian mission in Paris after his return from New France in 1649 until 1662. Profoundly involved both in the inspiration and in the actual founding of Montreal,[111] he would have been able to speak of the project with personal knowledge and authority.

On the next lap of her journey, without the protection or consequence previously supplied by her uncle and de Maisonneuve's sister, Marguerite began for the first time to experience the plight of an obscure woman travelling alone. She wrote that once, at nightfall, the coach stopped at an inn where only men were staying. The old woman who ran the place refused to give her lodging, and the men began to taunt and jeer at her. In this nasty situation, however, someone whom Marguerite describes only as "a man dressed in black" intervened, and the woman allowed her to lie on her bed, fully dressed, for the night. At another inn on another night, she was again refused lodging, though several rooms were vacant and she had demonstrated her ability to pay. The owners were not willing even to let her spend the night in front of the fire for a fee. Then a cart driver from Champagne who had recognized her accent came forward. When he offered to pay her way, Marguerite was led to a room "very far away." She was not so unsophisticated as not to know what to anticipate. "I closed the door," she writes, "and barricaded it with everything I could find. I lay down on the bed fully dressed."

Sometime later there was a knock at the door and then an attempt to enter the room. Finally her erstwhile supporter called to her, "Mon pays, ouvrez-moi la porte," freely, "Let me in, my countrywoman."[112] When he persisted, she tells us, "I went to the door to see whether it was really he and I spoke to him as if I were a person of great importance; I said that I would bring charges against him and that I would know quite well how to have him found."[113] She must have been convincing because, she concludes, "He went away." This story is typical of her insight into people and situations, her common sense, her resourcefulness, and, in its telling, her sense of humour. It cannot but contrast with elements of the anecdote about her rescue of the abducted girl in Troyes, since the manner of proceeding was not the same. The story also had an epilogue. There was much noise during the night. When daylight came, Marguerite lifted what appeared to be a wall hanging to find that it alone separated her from "a whole crew of men, lying there asleep after having spent the night carousing." Her later biographers would use this material to moralize on the providential preservation of her chastity. Not so Marguerite. "It was said that since the war all these people were still aroused and fierce," she wrote.[114] Always ready to give others the benefit of the doubt and to seek reasons for their actions, she sought in the effects of war an explanation for the less-than-admirable behaviour of the people she had encountered.

At Orléans, Marguerite boarded a boat to continue the journey down the Loire to Nantes. If this was her first trip by boat, it was a mode of travel she would come to know very well. The journey would not have been the scenic tour of chateaux popular in more settled times; Jamet graphically describes the horror of a once-beautiful countryside become, at best, a wasteland and in many places a charnel house.[115] Glandelet reports that many of the same difficulties she had already encountered as a lone woman traveller continued to plague her. At Saumur she was again turned away from the inn but found lodging with a pastry-cook. In Nantes she had been told that she would find de Maisonneuve at the house of a merchant called Lecoq, the man who was provisioning the expedition. Unfortunately, this man, the Sieur de la Beaussonière, was known only by the latter name in Nantes so that at first she could not find him. She was obliged to search until finally she encountered him by chance on the street. De Maisonneuve had not yet arrived and was, in fact, not to do so for another two or three weeks, but he had written to Lecoq advising him to expect Marguerite. Even when she had located the man, her difficulties were not over. When he sent her to his house, his wife refused to admit her, and it was only after several returns that the husband was able to prevail on his wife to extend hospitality to so suspect a guest.[116] (The suspicion that Marguerite was to arouse so often at this time suggests that she must have been, at least, a not unattractive woman.) Lecoq was later to show great kindness to her, not only providing her with the water for her voyage to New France,[117] but also supplying her with a mattress and blanket and refusing any payment for her board or passage.[118]

Glandelet also provides several other details about the boat journey to Nantes. He recounts that at one point on the voyage Marguerite's fellow passengers were eight surgeons, a woman with a child, and a young man, all of whom joined with her in the recitation of the Little Office of the Blessed Virgin and the rosary and in devotional reading, and that this group was able to persuade the boatman to travel by night to enable them to attend Sunday mass. Jamet speculates that they may have been a group of pilgrims on their way to one of the well-known shrines, such as that of St Martin of Tours or St Francis of Paula.[119] He also tries to identify the young man who conceived the idea of joining the Montreal expedition and insisted on carrying Marguerite's burdens during her initial difficulties in Nantes. He tentatively suggests François Crusson. *dit* Pilote, aged seventeen in 1653, who had not signed a contract at La Flèche like most of the others, but was already part of the recruitment departing from New France at Saint-Nazaire and who was to die with Dollard at Long Sault seven years later.[120]

While de Maisonneuve continued his enlistment of recruits, mostly in Maine and Anjou, and other arrangements for embarkation to Canada, Marguerite was again – or perhaps still – experiencing doubt and uncertainty. She describes this time in the draft of the letter to Father Tronson already cited. "When I was at Nantes," she writes, "I went to a confessor at the Carmel. He gave me scruples over not becoming a Carmelite when I was being offered the opportunity to do so, as they had written to M. de Maisonneuve when he was at Nantes. This troubled me a great deal. Very depressed, I went to the Church of the Capuchins where the Blessed Sacrament was exposed. At that very moment, all my distress was changed and I returned with great assurance that I must go to Canada."[121] Glandelet says that de Maisonneuve had received an anonymous letter, which he had shown to Marguerite. Her wording does not make clear whether her visit to the Carmelite confessor was the result of this letter, but she does indicate that all her doubts and anxieties seemed to coalesce around the pressure to enter Carmel. In the end, she was set free from her uncertainties, not by any of the often-conflicting advice, solicited and unsolicited, offered from without, but from an inner conviction reached in prayer, perhaps when it was least expected.

Marguerite's reference here to the consolation received in prayer before the Blessed Sacrament recalls another spiritual experience not recorded in her writings but related by Glandelet, who sets it in Troyes. Later biographers have assigned it tentatively to the year 1650.

On the feast of the Assumption of the Blessed Virgin, patronal feast of the [extern] congregation, performing her assigned hour of adoration before the Blessed Sacrament exposed during the king's procession, in contemplating the Sacred Host, she perceived in it a three-year-old child of such great beauty as to be beyond description; from that moment she was, she said, weaned for always from all the beauties of this world, and had no other desire than each day to become more pleasing to God.[122]

Whatever Marguerite told Glandelet about this experience, he has expressed in his own words, for the language is different from that used by her in the very few instances in which she makes any reference to extraordinary spiritual experience. A growing devotion to the child Jesus in seventeenth-century France reflected changing attitudes towards children. It is significant that Marguerite, devoting herself to the education of children, should associate the Eucharist with the *child* Jesus since the "drops of Christ's blood" that she is gathering are the children she educates.

Dramatically, another spiritual experience of confirmation seems to belong to the period at Nantes immediately before the departure for Canada. It is one to which Marguerite Bourgeoys herself attached great importance, for it is recounted, like the event of her conversion, both in the letter to Father Tronson and in the autobiographical writings. In the latter, she recorded: "One morning, when I was fully awake, a tall woman dressed in a robe as of white serge, said to me very clearly: 'Go, I will never forsake you.' I knew that it was the Blessed Virgin. This gave me great courage and I found nothing difficult, even though I feared illusions. This made me believe that if this was of God, I did not have to make any preparations for it [the journey]; consequently, I did not bring a penny for the voyage."[123] Like the conversion of 1640, this experience is connected with an image of

Mary, not this time with a statue, although the reference to the texture of the robe recalls those statues in the churches of Troyes in which every fold and every button is rendered with elaborate attention to detail.[124] And again what is most important to Marguerite is the effect of the experience: in 1640 she had been completely transformed; in 1653 she was filled with certainty and confidence. It is that fact which seems to place the event in her last days in France. It is difficult not to see an oblique reference to it in this statement from the autobiographical memoirs: "When I was at Nantes, I had some confirmation that Our Lord wished me to make the voyage and when I arrived in Montreal, I found the picture which confirmed it all for me."[125] This, with its reference to the picture of the Virgin given to de Maisonneuve by his sister's community, carries implications of a Marian experience. But it is difficult to tell exactly when the early morning vision of Mary took place, and biographers have always located it in Troyes, influenced by its context in the letter to Tronson, which states that meanwhile de Maisonneuve was making preparations for her departure from Troyes with Madame de Chevilly.[126]

It is perhaps easy, now that the centuries have vindicated her choice, to underestimate how painful and difficult the decision to go to Canada was for Marguerite. Some of those attracted to the Montreal expedition were romantic enthusiasts; she was not one of these. As already stated, she was sceptical rather than credulous,[127] and as the words quoted above indicate, she was always wary of illusion. She was a woman who saw and responded to the concrete needs of those around her. In answering the invitation to Montreal, so distant in more than miles from her own experience, she was doing something that was contrary to her own natural temperament. Although she had privileged moments when she experienced extraordinary enlightenment and consolation, she, like most Christians, had to live out her life in the darkness of faith as well as in its light. And it was only in being faithful to those moments of enlightenment that she came to understand them. Faced with the concrete needs of real human beings, she never hesitated, but she was temperamentally unsympathetic to abstract visions and dreams.

Finally, all was ready for departure. On 20 June 1653 the *Saint-Nicolas-de-Nantes*, captained by Pierre le Bresson, put out from Saint-Nazaire[128] on a voyage that, Ransonet writes, "would still be regarded as involving the utmost peril, even in the third decade of the eighteenth century.[129] The destination was a land that he, nearly a century later, was to describe to his fellow citizens as an immense forest bisected by lakes and rivers, a land with so cold a climate that the heedless might suddenly find the flesh of a cheek or a hand frozen, later to rot and fall away, but where the heat was so excessive that grain ripened and was harvested within four months, a land inhabited by a cruel people at whose hands one might meet a painful death.[130]

According to Marguerite, the passengers on the *Saint-Nicolas* included 108 colonists recruited by de Maisonneuve. A hundred of these were to survive the journey, so that 1653 was to be remembered in Montreal and throughout New France as the "year of the hundred men." The ship also carried a few women not destined for Montreal whose names Marguerite had forgotten by the time she wrote her memoirs; another woman travelling with her husband; Marie-Marthe Pinson, who met Jean Milot aboard ship and married him shortly after the group landed; and Marie Dumesnil. Marie, about twelve years old, was on her way to Montreal to find a husband. She was to live with Marguerite until her marriage to André Charly and was eventually to give four daughters to Marguerite's community, of whom one would be the fourth superior of the Congregation.[131]

Once at sea, the ship ran into serious difficulty and began to take on water. At first, an attempt was made to continue the journey by pumping day and night, but 350 leagues out (about 875 miles) this attempt had to be abandoned as futile, and the ship returned to port.[132] Marguerite says that if they had not received assistance from Saint-Nazaire, they would all have perished right then. Whatever eagerness the prospective colonists might have entertained for the journey had now evaporated, and de Maisonneuve was obliged to keep them on an island from which they could not get back to shore while the ship was again made seaworthy. "Otherwise," comments Marguerite, "there would not have been one left."[133] Glandelet reports that she told him she was at first treated with contempt, being regarded as a woman of ill repute and almost certainly de Maisonneuve's concubine, "especially when they knew she was coming to Canada, although the Jesuit priest whom she had consulted in Paris had told her she would find very respectable people there. But the popular belief meant that she was everywhere looked upon with contempt."[134] In her surviving autobiographical writings, however, Marguerite comments, not on the attitude of the men towards her, but on their disposition and state of mind. As the ship foundered before Saint-Nazaire, she was concerned about how ill prepared these men were to die. Later, as they were held on the island, she was conscious of their anxiety and near despair, "There were even some who threw themselves into the sea in order to escape, for they were like madmen, believing that they were being taken to their destruction."[135] This tendency to enter into the thoughts and feelings of others is, again, one of her most characteristic qualities. Typically, by involving herself in the needs of her fellow passengers, she was soon to forget all doubts and hesitations. At long last, the Saint-Nicolas was ready to embark for Canada. On 20 July, the feast of St Margaret and therefore of Marguerite's patron, she finally began her trip to the far-away island whose life was to become her own for her remaining forty-seven years. The ship's destination was a tiny, beleaguered, and fragile settlement whose eleven-year existence had already been fraught with peril and adventure. Marguerite Bourgeoys's decision to go there and the direction that her life now took cannot be understood without a knowledge of the circumstances that had led to the foundation of Ville-Marie on the island of Montreal.

CHAPTER THREE

Montreal: Origins to 1653

The first year they were in Montreal, they made a cross which M. de Maisonneuve carried up the mountain – no light burden up a path as steep as that was. The others carried the pieces of wood for the pedestal. They built an altar there where Father [J. Imbert Du Peron, sj] and those who could leave [their] dwellings made novenas with the intention of obtaining from God the conversion of the Indians, – that they would come submissively[1] to be [instructed] ... All this was done with great fervour.[2]

In leaving Troyes for Montreal, Marguerite was departing from a region where the legends were already old for a place where they had just begun to be created. Montreal, though a city of relatively recent foundation, has this in common with some of the most ancient cities of the world: its origins are the subject of heroic legend. Like Aeneas setting off with the household gods of Troy to establish a new city, the founders of Montreal faced long and dangerous journeys and difficulties and perils without number. However, unlike tales about the founding of cities in the ancient world, many elements in the "golden legend" of Montreal can be documented and so take their place firmly in history, as well as in the realm of epic and romance. To the extent that they belong to the domain of legend, it is that of Christian legend.

The story of the city now known as Montreal begins, not with its founding in 1642, but with the dreams for its establishment in the last years of the previous decade. Those dreams sprang from the great missionary impulse that was part of the religious renewal occurring in seventeenth-century France, specifically from the Jesuit mission to the native people of North America, which began with their arrival in New France in 1611.[3] The missionary impetus of the sixteenth and seventeenth centuries was particularly characteristic of Catholic,

rather than of Protestant, Christianity and was not necessarily connected with European colonization. The English and the Dutch, as
well as the French and the Spanish, were engaged in empire building at this time, but not in the same kind of missionary activity. What
is more, the evangelizing efforts of the Jesuits in China and Japan in
this era were not related to European colonization and empire building.[4]

Although Breton fishermen were sailing to the coast of
Newfoundland as early as 1504, official French interest in the New
World did not begin until 1524. In that year, François I commissioned
Giovanni da Verrazano, the Florentine navigator, to explore the
Atlantic coast in search of a passage to the East somewhere between
Spanish Florida and Newfoundland.[5] This expedition was followed
in 1534 and 1535 by the voyages of Jacques Cartier and the first
known voyage of a European up the St Lawrence as far as the
Lachine Rapids to the island that he called Mont Royal and the
important Iroquois village of Hochelaga, which stood on that island.
Although French attempts at colonization in North America began in
1541, they came to nothing. When Champlain built the Habitation at
Quebec in 1608 and wintered there with twenty-seven other
Frenchmen, it was only the fifth winter spent by Europeans in the St
Lawrence valley, and of Champlain's group only eight survived. In
1611, on an expedition up the St Lawrence, Champlain contemplated
a settlement on the island of Montreal. At the site now known as
Pointe-à-Callère, he built a wall and prepared two gardens and a
square, which he designated Place-Royale, the name it bears to this
day.[6] The name Montreal appears on a map for the first time on one
drawn by Champlain, probably the following year.[7]

In 1612 the Prince de Condé became viceroy of New France, and
the next year the Compagnie de Canada was formed by merchants
from Rouen, Saint-Malo, and La Rochelle. In return for an eleven-
year monopoly on trade in the St Lawrence region, they agreed to
supply a horse to the viceroy each year, to make an allowance to
Champlain, and, most important, to transport six families to begin
the settlement of the country.[8]

From its beginnings under François I, the French enterprise in
America was officially attributed to religious motives. Its purpose,
royal documents were long to maintain, was the evangelization of
the indigenous people of the New World rather than territorial
aggrandizement or the acquisition of riches. Later historians have
regarded with scepticism this claim that French activity in the New
World was religiously motivated and have presented evidence to
refute the altruistic and sometimes grandiose assertions of the

monarch.[9] Yet it might be well to remember that attempts to serve both God and Mammon are a part of religious history. Whatever the mixture of motives that drove king and merchant, there also came to New France those whose unique concern was undoubtedly the conversion of the Amerindians to Catholicism. Indeed, conflict between commercial and missionary motives was to be a dominant motif in the history of New France from the beginning.

This friction was evident even in the first Jesuit mission to New France. It was undertaken by two priests, Pierre Biard and Ennémond Massé, who, after much harassment apparently designed to prevent or at least delay their departure from France, arrived at the tiny and fragile fortified settlement at Port-Royal on 22 May 1611. They were later joined by two other Jesuits, Brother Gilbert Du Thet and Father Jacques Quentin. This mission seems to have been unfortunate in almost every way. Though the Micmacs appear to have welcomed the missionaries (the chief offering to make war on any of his tribe who refused baptism), the governor and the Huguenot traders involved with the colony were considerably less well disposed towards them. Acrimony and conflict were constant. When the Jesuits were participating in an attempt to found another Catholic colony further south, Fathers Biard and Quentin were captured by the English privateer Samuel Argall in an encounter in which Brother Du Thet died, the first Jesuit to do so in America.[10] Constantly in danger from both their English captors and their French enemies in Port-Royal, as well as from the elements, the two priests were finally repatriated in April 1614. Father Massé had been forced to return to France in October 1613.

This first Jesuit mission to North America appeared, then, to have been an almost total disaster; yet in it lay the inspiration for the founding of Ville-Marie some thirty years later. Father Massé, after a year at the Collège de Clermont in Paris, was sent as chaplain to the boarders at the Collège Henri IV in La Flèche. There he was to remain until 1625, nurturing his desire to return to missionary work in the New World and exerting a powerful influence on a remarkable group of people, among them Paul Le Jeune, first editor of the Jesuit *Relations*, and Charles Lalemant, uncle of the martyr and first superior of the Jesuits at Quebec. Also among the students at Collège Henri IV at this time was the man who was to originate the Montreal project, Jérôme le Royer de la Dauversière.

Although it was clerical in inspiration and included important participants from among the clergy, the Montreal enterprise, especially in its beginnings, was a predominantly lay undertaking, both in conception and execution. It was an exemplary collaboration of laypersons and clerics, men and women, single and married, nobles, the middle class, and ordinary working people, such as has been rare in the history of the Roman Catholic Church. *Les Véritables Motifs de Messieurs et Dames de la Société de Nostre-Dame de Monreal pour la Conversion des Sauvages de la nouvelle France*,[11] the document drawn up in 1643 to describe the intentions of the founders of Montreal, insists strongly and at length on the important role of the laity in the propagation of the Christian faith. Though careful to avoid the claim that the laity are empowered with the teaching mission of the church in the same way as the clergy, this document sees Christ's command to go out and make disciples of all nations as addressed to the whole church. Of course, the fact that it states explicitly that no attempt is being made by laymen to usurp the prerogatives of the clergy implies a recognition by its composers that they might be so accused. In answer, the writers stress the role played by the laity in the primitive church: Christianity could not have spread as it did among Jews, Greeks, and Romans without the efforts of lay Christians; the martyrology contains the names of far more lay Christians than clerics.

Women, too, the document points out, were among the earliest followers of Jesus and played their role in the church of the Acts of the Apostles.[12] When the Société de Notre-Dame de Montréal had sought a leader for the expedition to New France, God had sent two, one of each sex, and it is important to note that the document here treats de Maisonneuve and Jeanne Mance as virtual equals. "In 1641 as he [de la Dauversière] was preparing his first personnel and supplies for Montreal, he and his companion had often begged God for people to direct and lead this, His new family they were sending to the uncultivated and abandoned island, and God sent them two leaders at different times and of different sex, station, and place of origin."[13] The importance of the laity and of women in early Montreal was not just a historical accident, a result of the interplay of the personalities involved and the development of events after the foundation, although these too played their role; it was part of the original inspiration.

Many doubts have been raised about the effect on the native people of North America of seventeenth-century missionary activity. Some Christian churches now look back on it with guilt. But the inspiration of the missionary activity in New France was a sincere desire to help the native people "bridge the gulf separating the palaeolithic from the modern age,"[14] however misguided some of those efforts may have been. In the *Véritables Motifs*, the members of the Société de Notre-Dame de Montréal compare the North American native peoples with their own ancestors at the beginning of the

Christian era. They believed that Christians of western and northern Europe owed their faith to the missionaries, clerical and lay, who had left their Mediterranean home to bring Christianity to France, Spain, and Germany. They saw the Christian faith as their most precious possession, but also as a gift involving responsibility: faith was not given only as a personal possession, it must be shared.[15]

Jérôme le Royer de la Dauversière, who stands at the origin of the visionary enterprise that came to be Montreal, was born in 1597 at La Flèche in Anjou. He studied at the Jesuit college that had been founded there in 1604. It was a distinguished school where he would have encountered among his fellow students, not only future Jesuit missionaries to Canada, but also the future philosopher Réné Descartes. In 1618 he inherited from his father the fief of La Dauversière and the office of receiver of the *taille* in La Flèche. Two years later he married Jeanne de Baugé, and the two eventually became the parents of several children.[16] The attempt to found a model missionary settlement in New France was not the first philanthropic undertaking to which his faith inspired him. In an era before the welfare state, he and his elder brother Joseph early began to take responsibility for the organization of charitable undertakings in their town. The fact that no writings which are certainly his own have as yet[17] been discovered makes it difficult to form an independent assessment of his character. Seventeenth-century secondary accounts of him, like those of other men and women reputed for holiness, stress those aspects of his life and character that appeared to their authors as the best evidence of sanctity. They tend, then, to emphasize his asceticism and his extraordinary mystical experiences, just as the early accounts of the life of Marguerite Bourgeoys do. They tell us much about his devotion to the Holy Family,[18] but little of the husband and father. They give abundant proof of his confidence in the vocation of laity as well as clergy in the propagation of the faith, but tell us little about what he made of his vocation in the family, a subject still neglected in Catholic theology and devotional writing. It is impossible to determine now whether this picture reflects his own values or those of his first biographers in a world where theology did not hold the married state in high esteem.

One of the most important statements about de la Dauversière is the letter written by his old friend the Baron de Fancamp to the Jesuit Pierre Chaumonot in Quebec in 1660, after his death in November the previous year. This letter contains a harrowing account of de la Dauversière's physical and moral sufferings, especially his final illness. But perhaps the most moving sentence is this pithy and well-composed tribute: "In spite of all these miseries, he was always on horseback, sometimes on the business of his Sisters, sometimes on the business of Canada, but always on the business of Charity."[19]

In the early 1630s,[20] some time after suffering a life-threatening illness, de la Dauversière had a mystical experience on 2 February, feast of the Presentation of Jesus in the Temple and the Purification of Mary, a feast that brought to a close the Christmas season with its emphasis on the Holy Family. This experience led him to establish the Hospitallers of St Joseph of La Flèche, a religious community of women set up to care for the sick of his native town. That community, which came into existence in 1636, was eventually to send some of its members to the Hôtel-Dieu in Ville-Marie.

In 1635 or 1636[21] a second revelation directed the attention of de la Dauversière towards the native people of New France. The *Véritables Motifs* describes him as having previously had "no particular knowledge of this group," but given his former connection with the Jesuits and the Collège Henri IV, it is obvious that the emphasis should fall on "particular" rather than "knowledge." For some time he hesitated to undertake a project that appeared so much beyond his resources and that he feared would be damaging to his family. By 1639, however, at the advice of the Jesuit François Chauveau, he was ready to go to Paris with his friend the baron de Fancamp to solicit support, "enlightened by an inner vision that clearly showed him the places, things, and persons which he must use," state the *Véritables Motifs*.[22] Daveluy describes Pierre Chevrier de Fancamp as "one of the first, the most generous, and the most faithful of the Montreal associates."[23] The place and date of his birth are both unknown, but he must already have attained his majority (twenty-five) when, in 1634, he made a significant gift of money towards the erection of the Hôtel-Dieu of La Flèche, the first of many such contributions to the charitable works of de la Dauversière. He appears to have been a man of wealth who was also the penitent and friend of Father Chauveau, by whom he was introduced to de la Dauversière and perhaps interested in the Montreal project.[24]

In February 1639 the two made the acquaintance of the man who was to play the third outstanding role in bringing Montreal into being and in sustaining it during its early years. He was Jean-Jacques Olier, at that time a priest in his thirty-first year. Born into the family of a councillor in the Paris Parlement, Olier was, from infancy, destined by his family for ecclesiastical preferment. Though his mother worried that he might be too wild to gratify her ambitions for him, he did well in his studies both at the Jesuit college at Lyon and later at the Sorbonne. By the time he was nineteen but as yet not ordained, he was nevertheless in possession of the revenues from several ecclesi-

astical benefices, including the abbacy of a monastery and the prior-
ship of a convent of Cistercian nuns. He appears at this time to have
lived the same kind of frivolous life as many of his similarly placed
contemporaries, but a visit to Italy was to make a profound and lasting change. In Rome for the ostensible purpose of learning Hebrew,
he contracted an illness that threatened his sight. This misfortune
sent him to pray at the shrine of Loretto, where he experienced not
only physical healing but a spiritual conversion that was to have a
profound effect on the reform of the French clergy. Like Marguerite
Bourgeoys at the time of her conversion a few years later, he at first
considered entering a contemplative order.

Before he could do so, however, he was summoned back to Paris
by news of his father's death and arrived to find that his mother, ever
eager for his advancement in the ecclesiastical career chosen for him,
had obtained for him an appointment of chaplain to the king. There
then began an unresolved and painful conflict with his mother, who
was to remain totally unsympathetic to her son's new-found fervour
and to continue for most of his life her attempts to induce him to
embrace the kind of ecclesiastical career she wanted for him.[25] For
now, instead of the privileged life of a fashionable and ambitious cleric, Olier chose one devoted to the poor. He spent a year with St
Vincent de Paul's Prêtres de la Mission attending to the poor of the
countryside, then in 1633, he was ordained to the priesthood.
Influenced by women such as Marie Rousseau and Mother Agnès de
Jésus and by the Oratorian de Condren, he refused a bishopric in
order to devote his energies more and more to the task of reforming
the French clergy through the establishment of seminaries for their
education. But even in the midst of his early struggles, he also conceived the desire to make some contribution to the evangelization of
the native people of New France. With de la Dauversière and de
Fancamp he was to select the island of Montreal as the site of the
future colony, and with them he was to recruit members of a society
of men and women that would make the venture possible.

Many of the male members of the Société de Notre-Dame de
Montréal were drawn from the ranks of another association to which
the original three already belonged, the controversial Compagnie du
Saint-Sacrement.[26] To this day, accounts of the Compagnie tend to
reflect the values and sometimes the prejudices of their authors
rather than conveying objective information about the group. For
many, the satiric portrait furnished by Molière – for Tartuffe is generally accepted as a caricature of the members of the Compagnie du
Saint-Sacrement – is all that they know of this seventeenth-century
society. The discovery of the manuscript annals of the group in 1885

did a little to correct this situation, but as the society was a secret one, much will never be known.[27] The Compagnie was an important part of the religious revival in France in the first half of the seventeenth century. It had been founded in 1627 by a young married nobleman, the duc de Ventadour, lieutenant-general of the king in Languedoc and viceroy of Canada.[28] The aim of the Compagnie was stated as follows: "To promote the glory of God in doing all the good to be considered true good ... and preventing all the evil to be considered true evil."[29] The description of the spirit of the organization displays what was to be one of the dominant motifs of the Société de Notre-Dame de Montréal: "A universal spirit to work in every possible way to help one's neighbour without causing him any harm, taking for model the magnanimity that religion gave the first Christians."[30] Membership in the group was to be secret because the members were, like Christ in the Blessed Sacrament to whom the society was dedicated, to do good in silence, and it was restricted to men who did not already belong to religious communities.[31] The Compagnie was made up, then, of secular priests and, above all, of laymen from almost every walk of life. If it numbered a prince among its members, as well as dukes, marquises, and counts, it also included merchants, large and small, cutlers, haberdashers, and shoemakers.

Even those most hostile to the Compagnie have never been able to deny the immense good done by the group in relieving the sufferings of the poor, the sick, and the victims of various forms of injustice and mistreatment throughout France. Indeed, it was not so much its members' attempts to promote good as their efforts to suppress evil that were to lead the society into conflict with powerful enemies. Their attack on such vices of the upper classes as duelling and gambling made them enemies at court; their attempt to impose regulations on some forms of trade antagonized elements of the small-merchant class; their attacks on lukewarm priests and endeavours to reform the clergy resulted in hostility among many members of that group.[32] The Compagnie was the unrelenting foe of Jansenism and Protestantism. Its persecution of the Huguenots is perhaps the aspect of its behaviour that is most shocking to an audience today, though intolerance was characteristic of most religious groups at that time, whether Catholic or Protestant. It is also, of course, inevitable that some of the actions of so large a group should have been ill-judged and that some members were hypocrites who acted from motives which would not bear scrutiny. The destruction of the Compagnie du Saint Sacrement by Mazarin and the Parlement in the 1660s sprang, however, more from a jealous desire to safeguard their own power than from any higher motive. In the 1630s, when the Société de

Notre-Dame came into being, the Compagnie was still young, and the impulse to found Ville-Marie sprang from a desire to create something good rather than suppress something evil.

The choice of Montreal as the site for Ville-Marie, as the foundation was to be called, was due principally to the suitability of its location at the confluence of the St Lawrence and Ottawa rivers. In 1640 this island was the property of Jean de Lauson, who had been one of the members of the Compagnie des Cent-Associés at its inception on 29 April 1627. Very active in the organization of the new company, he was soon appointed intendant or director by Cardinal Richelieu and took advantage of his position in the company to obtain large and desirable sections of land in New France for himself and his family; among his acquisitions was the island of Montreal. Lauson, who was later to be governor of New France, favoured the claim of the Jesuits to exclusive missionary rights in Canada over the Recollets and the Capuchins.[33] It was through the Jesuit Charles Lalemant that the society made its overtures to him. According to some accounts, Lauson sold the island for a grossly exorbitant figure, but the Compagnie des Cent-Associés annulled the sale and regranted the island in December 1640.[34] The Société de Notre-Dame was now in a position to look for suitable leaders for the expedition.

Again it appears that Father Charles Lalemant was of service to the Montreal project, for according to Dollier de Casson, it was he who suggested to de la Dauversière the name of Paul de Chomedey de Maisonneuve, a young soldier who had approached him after reading about the priest's experiences at the Jesuit missions in Canada, possibly in the Jesuit *Relations* of 1637. According to Dollier, Father Lalemant arranged for de la Dauversière to go and stay at the inn where de Maisonneuve was putting up in order to take the young man unawares and form an independent impression of him. His perception was favourable, and de la Dauversière's choice was enthusiastically approved by the other members of the society. Thus the expedition now had a leader.

De Maisonneuve was at this time still short of his thirtieth birthday, having been born at Neuville-sur-Vanne in Champagne in February 1612, the eldest son of Louis de Chomedey, seigneur of Chavanne, Germenoy-en-Brie, and other places. There were three other children, two of whom we have already met: Louise, the oldest, member of the Congrégation de Notre-Dame at Troyes; Jacqueline, the youngest, who, as Madame de Chevilly, offered Marguerite Bourgeoys a home for her first attempt to found a community in Troyes; and Odard, a son born in 1614, who died at the age of thirty-three.

Very little is known about de Maisonneuve's life before he became the leader of the Montreal expedition. There is a dearth of documents for the period from 1624 to 1640. However, romantic legend has made him into the very embodiment of what Chaucer called a "parfit gentil knight," as presented in medieval works of idealized chivalry.[35] Nothing is known of the future governor's early education, but Léo-Paul Desrosiers in his 1967 biography signals as evidence of its quality the existence of a grandfather who was a notable writer and scholar, the elegance of the orthography and the clarity and occasional force of expression in surviving documents written by de Maisonneuve, and his ability to draw up early notarial documents in Montreal himself.[36] Dollier's comments were written several years after de Maisonneuve's return to France and, of course, are subject to the caution offered by the author at the opening of his *History*; they are, nevertheless, apart from the *Véritables Motifs*, the closest we come to a contemporary statement about de Maisonneuve's character. Dollier had not arrived in Canada until a year after the departure of de Maisonneuve; accordingly, his comments on the founder and former governor, written about six years later, are based on the statements of those who had known him during the twenty-four years he had devoted to the building of the colony, perhaps particularly the testimony of Jeanne Mance, who had been his partner from the beginning.

As noted earlier, according to Dollier, de Maisonneuve had entered the army at the age of thirteen and had first seen military action in Holland, where France was engaged in fighting the Thirty Years' War. A former soldier turned priest, Dollier would have been able to bring a special insight to both the military and the devout aspects of de Maisonneuve's character. According to him, the young soldier, to keep himself away from the more licentious habits of his comrades-in-arms, took up playing the lute so that with music he might seek solace "to be able to pass his time alone when he had no other companions."[37] De Maisonneuve was to retain his love of the lute all his life; a lute was apparently forgotten and left behind on his departure from Montreal, but the existence of another among the effects disposed of in his will shows that he obtained a replacement in France.[38] It would seem that, at the time of his first encounter with Father Charles Lalemant, de Maisonneuve was at something of a loose end, not having found satisfaction in military life but not having been trained for a civil career. The invitation to lead the Montreal expedition was accepted, and de Maisonneuve was to dedicate all the rest of his active life to the service of the colony. His immediate task was to assist in the recruitment of men who would be effective not only as settlers but also as defenders of a colony to be established in dangerous territory far beyond the assistance of Quebec, itself still a tiny and vulnerable outpost.

The next major figure to enter the story was a woman – Jeanne Mance – who was to be a major support to de Maisonneuve and to the colony in the crucial years of its foundation and early growth. The *Véritables Motifs*, describing her first encounter with de la Dauversière, refers to her as a "great servant of God."[39] Jeanne Mance was to be a close friend of Marguerite Bourgeoys for more than thirty years. Like most close and enduring friendships, this one had its foundation in the fact that, while sharing many qualities and experiences, the two were different in ways that made it possible for them to complement each other. Jeanne was almost fourteen years Marguerite's senior; her baptism had taken place on 12 November 1606. Like Marguerite, she was born in Champagne, though in the then border town of Langres, the daughter of Charles Mance, an attorney in the *bailliage* at Langres, and Catherine Emmonot. Like Marguerite, she came from a large family: baptismal records of twelve children have been located.[40] The death of her mother when she was about twenty would have meant that Jeanne, as the second oldest child, shared the care of younger brothers and sisters, three or four of whom would not yet have been ten years old. In this again, the pattern of events in her family life would have been similar to that of Marguerite.

The two women shared one other important experience, if we are to accept the word of Marie Morin, who had known Jeanne well. Like Marguerite, Jeanne was very close to her father. Sister Morin wrote, "She lived a very devout life in the house of her father, who opposed her in nothing because of the tender love and kindness he felt for his daughter."[41] The information about Marguerite's relations with her father given to Dollier de Casson, most likely by Jeanne Mance, may have been confided as the two women reminisced about their family experiences. As in the case of Marguerite, nothing is known definitely about Jeanne's early education. Daveluy speculates that she might have been a pupil of the Ursulines, who began to teach in Langres in 1613, when Jeanne and her older sister would have been seven and eight respectively.[42]

Again like Marguerite, Jeanne may have performed her first acts of public service among the impoverished and distressed victims of war. As a border town, Langres suffered greatly during the last, or French, phase of the Thirty Years' War from the hostilities, from the presence of marauding armies, whether foreign or French, and from the plague that accompanied them. Local archives reveal the opening of new cemeteries to accommodate the increasing numbers of dead, as in the year 1637 alone, 5,500 people perished in Langres and the

surrounding area.[43] The more fortunate responded to the distress by
setting up hospitals, and under his leadership Bishop Zamet founded an association of devout upper-class women in 1638 oriented
towards the performance of works of charity. Men also joined the
association and took care of its financial administration while the
women devoted themselves to the care of the sick. Daveluy believed
that Jeanne's initiation in the kind of work that she was later to do in
Montreal might have come through membership in this association.[44]
In recent years, emphasis tends to have fallen on her leadership and
managerial abilities and her role of co-leader and co-founder of
Montreal. Her healing skills should not be forgotten, however. One
recent study has recalled her ability to treat sicknesses and injuries
that she had never encountered before her arrival in Canada: her success, for example, in saving scalping victims where previous efforts
had failed.[45]

In many other ways, Jeanne Mance's experience and background
were different from those of Marguerite Bourgeoys. Jeanne came
from a different stratum of society; her family belonged to the ranks
of those we would now call the civil service and, as was characteristic of such families, also included a number of clerics. On a more personal level, Jeanne was apparently very devout from an early age.
There is no suggestion here of a light-hearted and frivolous girlhood
preceding conversion to a more serious and dedicated way of life.
Instead, Marie Morin says that Jeanne Mance *often* told her that she
had consecrated herself to God by a vow of chastity at the age of six
or seven.[46] In the late twentieth century, readers may regard this
statement with incredulity, but until very recently such precocious
fervour in children growing up in a devout family was not uncom-
mon.[47] What has always been rarer has been the continuance of such
devotion into adulthood and the fulfilment of promises, perhaps only
dimly understood, that were made in the first flush of fervour. Jeanne
does not seem ever to have considered entry into a religious community, though there is some evidence that her older sister might, at one
time, have had that intention.[48] Nor, of course, was there any attempt
to found or enter into an experimental group like the little community in Troyes in which the young Marguerite Bourgeoys was to participate. Until quite recently, Catholic religious writers have tended to
see entry into a religious community as so much the norm for the
truly devout that failure to embrace that state had somehow to be
explained. Accordingly, Jeanne's failure to become a nun is sometimes attributed to her weak constitution and habitual ill health. It
seems strange that she, who survived the ordeals of voyages between
France and New France on which so many others perished, endured

the hardships of the foundation of Montreal, and lived to the sufficiently advanced age of sixty-six should not have been a strong and
healthy woman. Yet her weak constitution and poor health are noted
both by Dollier de Casson and by Marie Morin, who says that Jeanne
had been known to keep to her bed for years at a time.[49] However, as
she managed to find the strength for her role in Montreal, something
to which she truly felt called, Jeanne Mance might better be seen as
representing a different kind of ecclesiastical service.

As already seen, Marguerite Bourgeoys was to relate her conversion of 1640 to events important to the foundation of Montreal.
Sixteen-forty was also a decisive year in the life of Jeanne Mance, for
it was then that the idea of going to New France first took hold in her
mind. Her father had died some years previously, certainly by 1635,[50]
and Jeanne had continued to lead a life of discreet devotion in the
family home. Her age and situation were much as those of
Marguerite Bourgeoys would be when she left Troyes for New France
thirteen years later: she was a mature, single woman with some experience in works of charity who had already fulfilled important
responsibilities to her family and was now free to make her own decisions about her future.

Dollier de Casson says that in April 1640 Jeanne was moved by the
enthusiasm of a canon of Langres, who spoke of New France. He
related the news that in the previous year Madame de la Peltrie, "a
lady of quality," had established the Ursulines at Quebec, where she
had accompanied them, and that the Duchesse d'Aiguillon, niece of
Cardinal Richelieu, had established hospital nuns at the same place.
He praised God at this evidence that he wished to be served in New
France by both the sexes.[51] The documents of the Société de Notre-
Dame de Montréal describe many mysterious experiences and recog-
nitions, but to give too much attention to the sensational is to risk
missing the deeper and more important aspects. The growing conviction of a middle-aged woman in indifferent health, settled in a life
of piety in a French provincial town in easy circumstances, that she
was called to brave the discomfort, hardship, and peril of the New
World for the sake of the gospel is a more significant phenomenon
than, for example, the instant recognition of two people who had not
previously met. At first, Jeanne struggled against the idea of going to
New France, but as it persisted, her director finally advised her to go
to Paris to consult Father Charles Lalemant, in charge of the affairs of
the Jesuit missions in Canada, and to seek out as her spiritual director the head of the Jesuit establishment nearest to the place where she
lodged.[52]

The canon who first interested Jeanne in New France has been identified as her cousin, Nicolas Dolebeau, the son of her father's sister.[53] This man, about a year Jeanne's senior, had been educated at the Jesuit college in Chaumont and then continued his studies to become a master of arts and doctor at the Sorbonne. The Duchesse d'Aiguillon had selected him as tutor to her nephew, the young duc de Richelieu, and he was also chaplain of the Sainte-Chapelle at Paris. He was, accordingly, in a position to bring his cousin into contact with the wealthy, the fashionable, and the powerful of the capital. His interest in New France would have been quickened at this time by the departure in 1640 of a younger brother, Jean, a Jesuit, for a mission near the Baie des Chaleurs.[54] It was to this man's sister that Jeanne came in Paris, for Madame de Bellevue, with whom Marguerite Bourgeoys was also to stay on her way to New France, was Jeanne's cousin, Antoinette Dolebeau, residing at this time not far from the church of Saint-Sulpice.[55]

Dollier de Casson says that Jeanne did not reveal the motives for her trip to Paris to her family before her departure, but rather allowed them to suppose that her intention was simply to visit relatives and enjoy the advantages offered by the capital.[56] Marie Morin says that her friends were inclined to suppose that Jeanne was joking about Canada or that she was inventing a pretext "to go to the big city to display herself, as so many others do."[57] Jeanne left Langres the Wednesday after Pentecost, which fell that year at the end of May, and made contact with Father Lalemant at once, only to find that he was leaving for Lyon to transact business important to New France. She was unaware then that this business was the purchase of the island of Montreal for the Société de Notre-Dame. She also sought out another Jesuit, Jean-Baptist Saint-Jure, rector of the Paris novitiate and renowned spiritual director. She does not seem to have made much of an impression on Saint-Jure because, after an initial interview, he was too busy to see her again for several months. As Jeanne joined in the pursuits of her cousins and in their charitable activities, she became acquainted with some of the most influential of the highborn women, who took a lively interest in her desire to become a missionary in Canada. Among these was Madame de Villesavin, who reintroduced her to Father Saint-Jure. As a result, he now became more accessible and began to take an interest in Jeanne's vocation. Dollier de Casson tells us that the wife of the chancellor of France, the Princesse de Condé, and even the queen herself wished to see Jeanne "to question her about so extraordinary a vocation."[58] Years later Marie Morin was to call particular attention to Jeanne's skill and effectiveness as a speaker. "Mademoiselle Mance spoke on these subjects like a seraphim, much better than many learned Doctors would be able to do."[59] Of the ladies she met and impressed at this time, by far the most important for the future was Angélique Faure de Bullion, who was to become patron of the Hôtel-Dieu and one of the principal patrons of Montreal.

Claude de Bullion, Seigneur de Bonnelles, Marquis de Gallardon, and finance minister of France, had died suddenly just before Christmas 1640, leaving his widow in control of an immense fortune. Jeanne met this lady through the good offices of Charles Rapine de Boisvert, provincial superior of the Recollets, who came to the house of his order in Paris early in 1641. As a Recollet he was interested in the Canadian missions, he was previously acquainted with Jeanne Mance, and he was distantly related to Claude de Bullion.[60] After a number of conversations with Jeanne, Madame de Bullion expressed the desire to entrust her with the founding of a hospital in New France and desired her to find out how much the Duchesse d'Aiguillon had spent to establish the one in Quebec.

The earliest accounts suggest that Jeanne was at first taken aback by this offer and only gradually led to accept a responsibility for which she does not seem to have felt herself particularly suited. Dollier de Casson makes no mention of Montreal at this point, and Faillon and Daveluy have followed him, so that their versions of events make it appear that Jeanne had no notion of going to Montreal until a providential meeting with de la Dauversière at La Rochelle when she was already on her way to an undetermined destination in New France. Marie Morin's account is different. It is true that she wrote somewhat after the events described, but she was closer to them than Faillon and writing on a subject important to the history of the Hôtel-Dieu and the Hospitallers of St Joseph in Montreal, in which community she had been the first Canadian to make profession. Since she later fulfilled the offices of bursar and superior, she would have had to be well acquainted with the original bequest from Madame de Bullion. She was also long and well acquainted with Jeanne Mance. In addition, her version of events is more credible.[61] Sister Morin does not deny the role of divine providence in the foundation of Montreal. Indeed, the chapter that describes these events begins with the words: "Divine Providence which had guided and directed the affairs of the Montreal colony to such good effect, knew well that it would need a hospital for the relief of the sick, both French and Indian."[62] The writer then goes on to explain how that providence had worked through human agents to bring the hospital into being. She tells us that the story of the founding of the Hôtel-Dieu in Quebec by the Duchesse d'Aiguillon had caused so great a stir in Paris that it inspired in Madame de Bullion the desire to make the same contribution to the projected colony in Montreal. It is now known that Madame de Bullion was in correspondence with Mother Marie de la Ferre, founder of de la Dauversière's Hospitallers at La Flèche,[63] from which source, if from no other, she could have been well informed about the Montreal project. In the course of several encounters, Madame de Bullion satisfied herself that Jeanne Mance, a woman who had been presented to her as one who wished to become a missionary in New France, was a suitable person to undertake this trust.

So it was that a woman of means chose another woman as the instrument through which her largesse would pass into the missionary project, and Madame de Bullion became, until her death more than twenty years later, one of the major benefactors of Montreal. Jeanne Mance was thus led into playing no small role as financial manager and planner in Montreal in the era of its foundation, an unusual role for a woman at the time. The usual pattern in charitable groups was for the male members to take charge of everything to do with finance while the women were entrusted with the organization and performance of the services. Such would have been Jeanne's previous experience if she had worked in the group organized by Bishop Zamet in Langres.

Though at first hesitant, Jeanne, on the advice of her spiritual directors, especially Father Saint-Jure, at last expressed willingness to undertake the responsibility of founding the hospital in Montreal, and a contract was drawn up. This document no longer exists, but as cited by Sister Morin, it contained, in addition to the provision of funds for the hospital and a lifetime pension for Jeanne Mance, clauses relating to the reversion of her pension to the hospital at the time of her death and provisions for the disposal of funds should the project on the island of Montreal have to be abandoned temporarily or permanently.[64] According to Dollier de Casson, as well as Marie Morin, Madame de Bullion entrusted 1,200 *livres* to Jeanne at this time, promising more when she was settled in New France and could report back about the needs of the hospital.[65] All sources are agreed about Madame de Bullion's insistence on secrecy; even in the contract cited by Sister Morin, the donor remained anonymous.

All sources also agree that Jeanne then journeyed to La Rochelle, one of the two ports from which ships were embarking for Canada.[66] The other was Dieppe, and it was there that her family wanted her to go. Dollier de Casson says that Jeanne left for La Rochelle the day after concluding her business with Madame de Bullion, selecting that port because she wished to practise detachment from her family and because the ships departing from there were to carry priests and she would thus be able to assist at mass on the voyage. It is also likely that she wanted to escape the importunities of her family, intent on dissuading her from so perilous an enterprise. Dollier implies that the agreement with Madame de Bullion still had not specified where in Canada the new hospital was to be located. The happy choice of La Rochelle as Jeanne's port of departure, he claims, providentially brought her into contact with Jérôme de la Dauversière and the Montreal expedition.[67] Marie Morin, however, says that Jeanne wrote to de la Dauversière from Paris knowing him to be, "as it were, the soul of this project and steward of the Gentlemen of the Association."[68] He responded by bidding her to come to La Rochelle to meet him.

Does this version of events contradict the account of the meeting of Jeanne Mance and de la Dauversière in La Rochelle given in "Les *Véritables Motifs*," where each seemed able to recognize and name the other without any previous contact?[69] The purpose of the *Véritables Motifs* was to describe the working of divine providence in the foundation of a missionary colony at Montreal. Perhaps the amazing thing that happened in the first encounter between de la Dauversière and Jeanne Mance was not so much that each knew the name of the other without prior introduction (unless one thinks of "name" in the biblical sense of the inner nature of the bearer), as that a spiritual understanding sprang up immediately between the two. Marie Morin put it this way: "They [Jeanne and de la Dauversière] got there at the same time and, animated with the same spirit, to work and spend themselves for God, opened to each other their hearts, aflame with divine love."[70]

All accounts make clear that de la Dauversière and Jeanne Mance were mutually satisfied by their meeting in La Rochelle. He was able to convince her that allying herself with the Société de Notre-Dame de Montréal would not mean a choice of human over divine help. Father Saint-Jure, applied to in Paris, gave his approval. Jeanne Mance was invited to join the society and became its first woman member. Although she at first expressed some diffidence because her financial resources did not match those of earlier members – she had only a small private income – she was reassured. Her first practical contribution as a member of the society was to persuade de la Dauversière to put his plan for Montreal in writing and to give her copies to send to the wealthy ladies of her acquaintance in Paris.[71] Thus, from the beginning, she showed the resourcefulness in fundraising that was to prevent Montreal from perishing in the first decade of its existence. The *Véritables Motifs*, Dollier de Casson, the *Memoirs* of Jean-Jacques Olier, and the annals of Sister Morin all sing the praises of Jeanne Mance, but perhaps nothing speaks more eloquently of the confidence that she inspired than her emergence in 1641 as not only nurse but also bursar and co-leader of the Montreal expedition.

As planned, the group left France from the two ports of Dieppe and La Rochelle, with de Maisonneuve and Jeanne Mance sailing from La Rochelle on different ships. With de Maisonneuve travelled Father Antoine Fauls, who was to serve the Ursulines at Quebec, and twenty-five men intended for Montreal; with Jeanne Mance, Father Jacques de La Place, who was a Jesuit, and twelve men for Montreal. They embarked on 9 May and would have sailed with the first favourable wind. At first the two ships were able to stay together, but after eight days they were driven apart by the winds. Jeanne's voyage was calm, perhaps too much so, for it took three months to reach Quebec, where the travellers landed on 8 August 1641. There she found that a group from Dieppe had already arrived and were engaged in building a storehouse. But she also discovered, perhaps to her consternation, that there was as yet no sign of de Maisonneuve. As well, within days she had experienced the immense hostility to the Montreal enterprise that existed at Quebec. When de Maisonneuve arrived on 20 August, she was able to warn him about this new and unanticipated problem. His voyage had been more eventful than that of his co-leader. After the separation of the two vessels, he had been compelled by weather conditions and the state of his ship to return three times to harbour. In the process he had lost four of his men, one of them his surgeon, an indispensable member of the expedition. However, at Tadoussac he had encountered the French ships on their way back to the mother country under the command of M. de Courpont, admiral of the Canadian fleet and an old friend of de Maisonneuve. De Courpont had offered the governor his own surgeon, who had agreed – enthusiastically, Dollier says – to become part of the Montreal expedition.[72]

Dollier de Casson attributes the fomenting of bad feeling against Montreal to the agents of the Compagnie des Cent-Associés, resentful of the wide powers bestowed by the king on the Société de Notre-Dame de Montréal, which included the right to name the governor of Montreal, to keep artillery and other weapons there, and to maintain storehouses at Quebec and at Trois-Rivières. He sees their warnings about the dangers from the Iroquois as a pretext for preventing the establishment of Ville-Marie on the island of Montreal, rather than as a genuine concern for the security of the expedition. In his biography of de Maisonneuve, Desrosiers defends the governor of Quebec and its inhabitants by pointing out that the dangers of which they warned were real and far more vivid to individuals already in the country than to those making decisions in France. The new land was very thinly populated – Dollier de Casson put the entire European population at about two hundred – and this population was very spread out.

In establishing the fur trade, Champlain had allied the French with the Algonquins, who occupied the basin of the Ottawa River west of the Rivière Saint-Maurice, and the Hurons, whose territory was south of Georgian Bay. The French thus became enemies of the Iroquois confederacy, or Five Nations, consisting of the Mohawks, Oneidas, Onondagas, Cayugas, and Senecas, who occupied what is now southern Ontario and western New York State as far west as Lake Erie.[73] Because the location of their territory brought them into contact with the French, the Dutch, and later the English, these peoples were to play a role in the imperial conflicts among the European powers. After 1643 the Dutch armed their native allies, while the French continued to deny firearms to non-Christian natives. The 1640s saw the terrible conflict between the Hurons (themselves an Iroquois people) and the Five Nations for the role of middlemen in the fur trade, a conflict that was to end in the destruction of the Huron nation. By 1642 bands of Iroquois warriors, armed by European enemies of France, had come from the south into the St Lawrence valley, attacking and killing bands of Algonquins on their way to pursue the fur trade with the French. In addition, the series of epidemics that was to devastate the peoples more friendly to the French, who served as a barrier against the Iroquois, had begun.[74] In such circumstances, Desrosiers suggests, it was not so much petty-minded as natural to conclude that any new colonists and soldiers should settle near Quebec and contribute to its defence rather than go to a remote island upriver that would inevitably call on the slender resources of Quebec for its defence. It was therefore the delayed arrival of de Maisonneuve, of necessity entailing a winter in Quebec and long second and critical thoughts on the part of its inhabitants, that was the real source of trouble, in Desrosiers's opinion.[75]

The early accounts make clear, however, that Jeanne Mance was aware of the hostility towards the "folle entreprise" long before the arrival of de Maisonneuve. Attempts were made to dissuade her from the expedition and to spread fear and despondency among the newly arrived colonists, who now for the first time heard eyewitness accounts of the terrors that awaited them. It is possible that she was sufficiently alarmed about the situation to go to meet and warn de Maisonneuve at Tadoussac rather than await his arrival at Quebec. The first document to attest to his presence in New France is the baptismal record of a native baby on 20 September 1641, on which the names of de Maisonneuve and Jeanne Mance appear as godparents. The place of the baptism is not given, but the parents were residents of Tadoussac, and the priest who performed the baptism was Paul Le Jeune, who, since he was on his way back to France on the last ship of that year, would most likely have been at Tadoussac.[76]

When de Maisonneuve arrived at Quebec, he was met with the importunities of Governor Charles Huault de Montmagny, who attempted to induce him to establish the new colony on the nearby island of Orléans rather than the distant one of Montreal. The response put into the mouth of de Maisonneuve by Dollier de Casson is one of the most famous dramatic utterances in the history of New France: "Sir, what you tell me would be excellent if I had been sent to look about and select a place. But as it has been decided by the company who sent me that I should go to Montreal, my honour obliges me to go there and found a colony, were every tree on the island to be changed into an Iroquois, and you will, I am sure, approve my decision."[77] However he may have felt, de Montmagny did accept de Maisonneuve's decision, and in early October an expedition was made to reconnoitre the site for the new colony the following spring. Dollier de Casson states explicitly that this journey was undertaken by both de Montmagny and de Maisonneuve. "They set off together at the beginning of October and reached Montreal on the 14th of the same month, on the spot where now stands the building called the Château. Next day, the day of Saint Thérèse, they took possession with due ceremony, in the name of the company of Montreal."[78] Indeed, it would be expected that de Maisonneuve would have seized the first possible opportunity to see the site of the colony he was to head.

Dollier's version of events was accepted by Lanctot and at one time by Trudel.[79] However, the Jesuit *Relations* do not list de Maisonneuve as one of those participating in the October expedition but present him as taking official possession of Montreal on 17 May 1642.[80] This fact has led other scholars (Daveluy, Desrosiers) to conclude that he delegated his responsibility on this trip, perhaps to Father Barthélemy Vimont, who knew the country better than he. They conclude that de Maisonneuve, so recently arrived in the country, may have found himself too absorbed in the organization and employment of his men at Quebec to make such a long journey away from them. In addition, Desrosiers suggests that the object of the trip may have been the delineating of the borders between that section of the island of Montreal which had been ceded to the Société de Notre-Dame and the section to be retained by the Compagnie des Cent-

Associés.[81] What is certain is that de Maisonneuve did visit Sillery at
this time, whether it was on his way back from Montreal as Dollier
states or not, and there encountered someone who was to offer what
must have seemed a truly providential solution to the problem of
where the governor could have his men winter and how he could
employ them until the spring in a way that would keep them away
from the demoralizing influence of the local inhabitants. (It was
events such as this encounter that kept the leaders of the Montreal
expedition convinced that their intentions were truly blessed by God.)

The meeting was with Pierre de Puiseaux, Sieur de Montrenault.
According to Dollier, de Puiseaux, a "good old man, filled with zeal
for the country," was at this time seventy-five years old.[82] After conversation with de Maisonneuve, he asked to be admitted to membership in the Société de Notre-Dame de Montréal, offering to donate to
it almost all his property, including the seigneuries of Sainte-Foi and
Saint-Michel. De Maisonneuve demurred: he would advise the society of the offer, but he did not believe that he could make any undertakings without consultation. His hesitation may have been due to a
realization that it would be better for both sides if an offer made so
impulsively be allowed time for more serious consideration. What he
did accept gladly and perhaps with relief was de Puiseaux's suggestion that some of his men winter at Sainte-Foi, where the plentiful
oak forest would give them material to construct vessels for the trip
to Montreal after the spring thaw. Accordingly, he left a group of men
engaged on this project under the command of his surgeon.

The tensions between the colonists of Quebec and those destined
for Montreal were made very apparent in an incident that took place
around 25 January 1642, an event that displays something of Jeanne
Mance's character and her role in the group at this time, as well as the
style in which de Maisonneuve exercised leadership. The two were at
Saint-Michel with a group of the colonists. The feast of the
Conversion of St Paul was de Maisonneuve's name-day and 1642 the
year of his thirtieth birthday. Jeanne, who was working closely with
the men, handing out to them whatever they needed from the common supplies, including arms, must have been well aware of the
need for some kind of relaxation and distraction for a group experiencing the cold, snow, and isolation of their first winter in New
France. On the night of 24 January, she supplied some of the colonists
with the arms and powder needed to fire a pre-dawn salute in honour of de Maisonneuve. He came promptly to thank them and to
declare a holiday, a day of celebration, which was to culminate in a
special meal, where, for the first time since their arrival, "the good
old wine of France" would be served. However, the Montreal contin-

gent were not long to rejoice, for their salute had been heard in Quebec and interpreted as an act of lese-majesty. The man who had fired the canon was seized, hung with chains, and put in prison by Governor de Montmagny, who claimed that his prerogatives had been contravened.

Indignant as the future Montrealers were, de Maisonneuve decided on a policy of silence and patience in the face of this provocative abuse of power. As a result, de Montmagny rethought his action and released the prisoner, Jean Gorry, a Québécois aged about thirty, who had joined the Montreal expedition after its arrival in New France. (Had his defection from Quebec been a factor in the incident?) All the company turned out to greet Gorry's return to Saint-Michel. De Maisonneuve appeared at their head to declare another holiday, this time in honour of Jean Gorry, and once more the good French wine flowed freely. At the banquet de Maisonneuve announced that he was giving Gorry a raise of ten *écus* and declared him *maître de la chaîne* (master of the manacles). Faillon attributes the following speech to de Maisonneuve: "My friends, although Jean Gorry has been mistreated, do not, for that reason, lose courage. Let us all drink to the health of the master of the manacles. What will we not be in Montreal? There we will be masters. Once we are established there, no one will prevent us from firing our canon."[83]

Unfortunately, these developments, also, were interpreted as a slight by Governor de Montmagny, who closely questioned a number of the Montreal colonists under oath. In the end he concluded that de Maisonneuve was not, in fact, a dangerous rival who sought to supplant him in the government of the colony. These adventures could only have served to increase the mutual loyalty of the Montreal group. The story demonstrates something of the generosity with which de Maisonneuve is reputed to have dealt with his men and something of his ability to resist provocation; it also proves that the devoutness with which the founders of Montreal are credited was not incompatible with humour and *joie de vivre*. On the negative side, it was an omen of future misunderstandings and difficulties between Montreal and Quebec.

And so the long winter passed. De Maisonneuve and especially Jeanne Mance were frequent visitors at the two convents in Quebec, the Hôtel-Dieu and the Ursulines, where Jeanne struck up so strong a friendship with the impressionable Madame de la Peltrie that in the spring she added herself to the Montreal expedition.[84] This woman embodied yet another role that French women were to play in the religious foundations of New France. Marie-Madeleine Chauvigny de la Peltrie was the patron and secular founder of the Ursulines at

Quebec. Born in Alençon in 1603, she had been widowed at the age
of twenty-two after five years of an arranged marriage and the death
of her only child. Despite the efforts of her father to arrange a second
marriage, Marie-Madeleine, always attracted to religious life, was
inspired by reading the Jesuit *Relations* to devote her person and her
fortune to the evangelization of the native people of New France.
After struggles and adventures that included a sham marriage and a
court case to obtain control of her fortune, she personally chartered
and equipped the ship that brought Marie de l'Incarnation and two
other Ursulines to Quebec in 1639 and endowed the Ursuline foundation there. Her departure for Montreal in 1642, which deprived the
Ursulines both of financial resources and furnishings and of her presence, almost led to the destruction of that foundation. However, she
was persuaded to return to the Ursulines eighteen months later,[85] and
although her attempt to become a member of the community when
the novitiate was opened in 1646 was a failure, she continued to live
with the Ursulines as their patron until her death in 1671.[86]

Madame de la Peltrie's romantic impulsiveness contrasts with the
careful consideration that characterized the behaviour of both Jeanne
Mance and Marguerite Bourgeoys before they made their commitment to the Montreal enterprise. The facts relating to her treatment of
the Ursulines in 1642 point up some of the dangers of dependence on
wealthy patrons. They perhaps throw light on de Maisonneuve's cau-
tious response to the generous, but impulsive offer of de Puiseaux.
Several years later Marguerite Bourgeoys was to upset some of her
first sisters when she refused an offer of patronage for her fledgling
community.[87] Her primary motive for this refusal was a trust in providence and a desire to share the material insecurity of the poor. But if
her rejection resulted in the loss of some benefits, it also avoided the
problems that arose when patrons changed their minds.

The forced stay in Quebec that had been the result of their late
arrival would have been useful to Jeanne Mance and de
Maisonneuve. They made frequent visits to the Jesuit residence,
where Jean de Brébeuf was wintering, and became godparents to two
of his Huron converts.[88] There, as elsewhere in the colony, they
would have been able to seek out precious information and advice
about the work they were to undertake at Montreal. Nevertheless, to
these newly arrived Europeans, the Canadian winter must have
seemed interminable, and one can imagine the enthusiasm and joy
with which they must have greeted the spring break-up and the
opportunity finally to set sail for Montreal.

The party set out on 8 May, according to Dollier de Casson's
account, the only early source that advances a precise date.[89] He tells

us that the members of the expedition made their way up the river in two vessels, a pinnace and a barge. They were accompanied by Governor de Montmagny, Father Vimont, superior of the Jesuit mission to Canada, Madame de la Peltrie and her companion, and de Puiseaux. The thoughts of the little group as they sailed up the broad and beautiful St Lawrence, so different from any of the rivers of their homeland, into the heart of this wild, challenging, and dangerous land, have not been recorded. The month of May in the St Lawrence valley is perhaps the loveliest of seasons, an annual miracle as myriad shades of tender green clothe the budding forest. Jeanne Mance always remembered her first journey up the St Lawrence to Montreal, and hers was a memory of the wild flowers, whose brilliant colours lifted her heart after the unrelieved white of the winter snows. Sister Morin writes, "Mademoiselle Mance told me many times at recreation that along the banks of the river ... one could see only meadows enamelled with flowers in every colour of a charming beauty."[90] On 17 or 18 May (depending on whether one accepts the dating of Dollier de Casson or the Jesuit *Relations*) the group finally landed at the site destined for the new colony; de Maisonneuve fell to his knees, blessing God, and all the rest of the company followed suit. The settlers were about forty in number (twelve more were to join them in August). The first party of colonists included only three couples: Jean Gorry and his wife, Isabeau Panie, who had married in Quebec in 1639; Antoine Damien and Marie Joly, perhaps the young woman who had forced herself aboard one of the boats at Dieppe, also married at Quebec the previous October; and Nicolas Godé and his wife, Françoise Gadois. The last named were the only persons accompanied by their children, who were four in number and ranged in age from their early twenties to about five years old, the first European-born family to live in Montreal.[91]

The most pressing task of the newly arrived colonists was to build themselves some kind of shelter. At first this took the form of tents, and it is interesting to see what different similes occurred to two of the earliest commentators on the event. For Dollier de Casson, the former soldier, "At first everyone was under canvas, as in Europe in the army"; for Sister Morin, in a comparison she continues, the likeness is to the Chosen People entering the Promised Land: "The men worked to raise tents or pavillions like true Israelites."[92] But before all this work came the inaugural mass, celebrated by Father Vimont on an altar prepared by Jeanne Mance and Madame de la Peltrie, and a sermon containing these prophetic words, now engraved on the monument to the first settlers at Pointe-à-Callière in Montreal: "What you see is but a grain of mustard seed, but it is sown by hands so pious and so moved by the spirit of faith and piety that Heaven must doubtless have vast designs since it uses such workmen, and I have no doubt that this seed will grow into a great tree, one day to achieve wonders, to be multiplied and spread to all parts."[93]

For the Jesuits, this was a moment of great hope for the mission to the native peoples; as Father Vimont wrote of the island of Montreal, "It gives access and an admirable approach to all the Nations of this vast country; for, on the North and South, on the East and West, there are rivers which fall into the river Saint Lawrence and the river des prairies that surround the Island. So that, if peace prevailed among these peoples, they could land thereon from all sides. *Omnia tempus habent*; all will be done in time."[94] Commenting on the baptism in late July of the four-year-old son of the leader of a group of Algonquins passing by Montreal, a baptism where Jeanne and de Maisonneuve again acted as godparents, he wrote, "This is the first fruit that this Island has borne for Paradise; it will not be the last. *Crescat in mille millia.*"[95]

The colonists passed the first summer making their new home more secure by surrounding it with a palisade of stakes. De Maisonneuve himself performed the ceremonial act of felling the first tree, and the labours of the newly arrived group were supplemented by the discovery of a number of trees cut for firewood by Champlain's men in 1611 and never consumed. Governor de Montmagny stayed until the palisade was completed. Despite all fears – for, hopeful as the Jesuits were, all the early references to the Montreal enterprise make evident their sense of the precariousness of the undertaking – that first summer was peaceful. The Iroquois do not seem to have been aware as yet of the new presence, and there were no alarms or attacks. Dollier's remarks probably once more relay the memories of Jeanne Mance; in contrast with the hardships that were to come, they present the reader with an idyllic world. "This post ... was bordered by a very pretty meadow called to-day the Common ... there were then in the meadow of which we have spoken, so many birds of different warblings and colours that they helped to make our Frenchmen feel at home in this uncivilised country ... God ... gave them time to repose a little in the shade of those trees with which the neighbouring meadow was fringed, where the sight and sound of the little birds, and the wild flowers, helped them to await with patience the arrival of the vessels."[96]

When these ships did arrive, they brought excellent news from France to de Maisonneuve and Jeanne Mance: copies of the report written and circulated at her suggestion the previous year had resulted in a significant increase in the membership of the Société de Notre-

Dame. The group had dedicated the island of Montreal to the Holy Family in Notre-Dame cathedral in Paris the previous February,[97] and 40,000 *livres* had been subscribed for the colony. This money had been spent on supplies that were now aboard the ships of the French convoy. Among the new colonists arriving was one who was to play an important role at Montreal for many years to come. This was Gilbert Barbier, a twenty-year-old carpenter from Nivernais, personally known to and trusted by de la Dauversière. Of him Dollier writes, "Though he was given the name of Minime, the most disparaging among the Latins, he was by no means the least either in fighting or in his trade; we owe the acknowledgement of this truth to his courage and to the services he has rendered on this island, whose buildings have nearly all been made by his hands or by those whom he has taught."[98] This man was to marry in Montreal and with his wife produce a family whose youngest member, Marie, would be the first Montrealer to enter Marguerite Bourgeoys's Congregation and her immediate successor as superior of that community.

One other event from that first summer is recorded in the Jesuit *Relations*. On the feast of the Assumption of Mary, 15 August, a great festival was celebrated at which a tabernacle sent out by the Société de Notre-Dame in France was placed on the altar of a bark chapel constructed by the colonists, as were the names of the colonists themselves. Salutes were fired, and after vespers, there was a procession,[99] to the great admiration of the Amerindians present. The following passage from the Jesuit *Relations* gives a moving view of these individuals, written with perhaps unexpected sympathy:

After the Festival, we visited the great forest which covers this Island; and when we had been led to the mountain from which it takes its name, two of the chief Savages of the band stopped on its summit, and told us that they belonged to the nation of those who had formerly dwelt on this Island. Then, stretching out their hands towards the hills that lie to the East and South of the mountain, "There," said they, "are the places where stood Villages filled with great numbers of Savages. The Hurons, who then were our enemies, drove our Forefathers from this country. Some went toward the country of the Abnaquiois, others toward the country of the Hiroquois, some to the Hurons themselves, and joined them. And that is how this Island became deserted." "My grandfather," said an aged man, "tilled the soil on this spot. Maize grew very well on it, for the Sun is very strong there." And, taking in his hands some earth, he said: "See the richness of the soil, it is excellent."[100]

These aboriginals were eagerly exhorted to return to their own country and inform their people that at Montreal there were those willing to help them build little houses and relearn the agricultural habits lost to them since their dispersal. To the French this seemed an excellent opportunity to initiate the work for which the colony had been established. But the father of the child who had been baptized was the only native ready to make any commitment to this plan. The others expressed interest, but said that they were too much in fear of the Iroquois to settle at Montreal. The success of the Montreal undertaking, concludes the *Relations*, was dependent on the defeat of the Iroquois or the effecting of a stable peace with them.[101]

Even the first winter at Montreal was to pass without some of the problems that had beset previous French colonists during their first Canadian winters. In the first place, and quite remarkably, there was no sickness among the Montreal colonists. Again, we are told, they lived through these first months, not only free from attacks by the Iroquois but in great internal harmony. "The bulk of the French who are here is composed of people very different, indeed, in respect to age and character, – almost as if they were all from different countries," says the author of the Jesuit *Relations* for 1642–43, yet

Since the departure of the vessels, last year, one of the most notable things which prevails in the habitation of Montreal is the thorough unity and the good understanding among all who dwell there. There are about fifty-five persons of various countries, different temperaments, and diverse conditions ... Each one has so well discharged his duty toward God and men, that no cause for complaint has been found in the space of ten whole months. The government has been gentle and efficient, obedience easy, and worship universally loved by all.[102]

This satisfactory state of affairs the Jesuits attributed to the common missionary purpose that animated the group, to the quality of leadership exercised by de Maisonneuve, and to the example set by de Maisonneuve himself and the other "persons of distinction."

If the idealized portrait of the first Montrealers today arouses scepticism about the objectivity of early commentators, it would be well to note that Dollier de Casson also tells the story of the colony's first scandal. In the summmer of 1644 there arrived in Montreal a certain Sieur de La Barre, who does indeed sound as if he escaped from one of Molière's plays. "At La Rochelle he wore at his belt a large rosary with a big crucifix which he had almost continually before his eyes ... This person, looking like Virtue herself, stayed in Montreal all the following year, but he was finally discovered through the frequent walks that he took in the woods with an Indian woman, whom he made pregnant, thereby making clear the falsity of his fine pretences."[103] La Barre was compelled to return to France, where he later got into more serious trouble. Perhaps the acknowledgment of one man's hypocrisy makes the sincerity of the others more credible.

In the first winter, however, danger did arise and from an unexpected source: the little fort was built at the point where the Rivière Saint-Pierre met the St Lawrence, and in December the waters rose higher and higher. This meant that the colonists were forced to consider abandoning the shelter they had prepared for the winter just at the moment when the most severe weather was imminent. Everyone in the colony prayed, and de Maisonneuve affixed to a cross on the edge of the flood waters of the petite rivière a prayer begging God to cause the waters to recede if he willed the foundation of Ville-Marie to continue in that place. The governor also promised that if the flood subsided, he would personally carry a cross up Mount Royal. To the relief of the settlers, the waters began to recede at Christmas. Trees were cut, a cross fashioned, a road cleared, and on 6 January, the feast of the Epiphany, de Maisonneuve lifted the cross, "although very heavy," on his shoulders, and the whole group in formal liturgical procession climbed about a league up the slopes of the mountain. There de Maisonneuve planted the cross, and the prayers described by Marguerite Bourgeoys in the passage quoted at the beginning of this chapter were offered.[104] To this day, the cross atop Mount Royal recalls this event.[105]

The relative tranquility of that first year in Montreal was deceptive; the next decade was to be fraught with difficulties for the new colony, whose continued existence from year to year does appear in retrospect to have been something of a miracle. There were achievements, however. Louis d'Ailleboust de Coulonge arrived in Montreal with his wife and sister-in-law in the autumn of 1643. Another native of Champagne, this military engineer redesigned and rebuilt the fort. The following spring he planted the first crop of wheat (the crops grown in Montreal the previous year had been peas and Indian corn) and demonstrated the possibility of growing this necessary commodity even in so harsh a climate.[106] The cost to the colonists of New France of goods imported from the homeland made such discoveries essential to their survival.[107] D'Ailleboust was to assume de Maisonneuve's authority in Montreal during the temporary absence of the latter in France in 1644–46 and to replace de Montmagny as governor of New France in 1647.[108]

Another colonist, who arrived in 1646, was to have a profound influence not just on the history of Montreal but also, through his illustrious sons, on that of all North America. He was Charles Le Moyne. The son of a Dieppe innkeeper, Le Moyne had come to New

France as an indentured employee of the Jesuits in the Huron country in 1641 at the age of fifteen. His abilities both as interpreter and as soldier were to make him an invaluable asset to Montreal in the 1640s. At the same time, the colony faced immense difficulties: the European population grew very slowly; there were financial problems, especially when support from the Société de Notre-Dame in France foundered; worst of all, the discovery by the Iroquois of the settlement at Montreal in the summer of 1643 marked the beginning of a guerilla war that was to escalate as the decade drew to a close.

In his study of the origins of Montreal society, Marcel Trudel refers to the years from its foundation to 1653 as a period of stagnation. Considerably fewer than one hundred new colonists arrived in the first decade, if one discounts the *camp volant* sent to contribute to the defence of Montreal in 1649. Nor was the European population swelled by births: only six married couples were added to the original three, and to the whole number only one child was born.[109] Not all the original group stayed. The autumn of 1643 saw the departure of both Madame de la Peltrie and de Puiseaux, she to return to her work with the hard-pressed Ursulines in Quebec and he for France. Their loss was not simply one of personnel but also of material resources: de Puiseaux had suffered an incapacitating stroke and was forced to revoke the gifts he had made to the Société de Notre-Dame in order to provide for himself on his return to the homeland; Madame de la Peltrie, of course, gave her support once more to the Ursulines in Quebec.

Nor was the loss of patronage the only financial problem faced by Montreal. In the autumn of 1644, de Maisonneuve was summoned to France to deal with matters arising from the death of his father. He concluded both his personal business and that of the colony expeditiously and returned to Canada the following spring. While in Quebec he attended a meeting of the Communauté des Habitants, which had replaced the Compagnie des Cent-Associés and there frustrated the attempts of the members of the Council to vote themselves an increase in pay.[110] But he was not able to finish his trip and reach Montreal, for a letter sent after him by de la Dauversière informed him that his brother-in-law had been murdered and that his mother was contemplating a disastrous remarriage. He had to return to France at once to deal both with these family crises and with additional business of the colony. On this trip he was himself offered the governorship of New France, but maintained his commitment to Montreal and suggested d'Ailleboust instead. The unexpected trip did give him an opportunity to remain in close contact with the

Société de Notre-Dame de Montréal, thus providing him with some assurance of its continued support.[111]

However, bad news arrived with the spring ships of 1649. Jeanne Mance's hospital had been completed in October 1644, and Madame de Bullion had remained the anonymous, but steadfastly generous supporter of the colony. But in December 1648 Father Rapine de Boisvert, the Recollet who had been Jeanne's intermediary with her patroness, had died. The previous year had also seen the death of the Baron de Renty and the falling away of a number of members of the Société de Notre-Dame. Worst of all, de la Dauversière was critically ill and his own financial affairs in considerable disorder. This time Jeanne Mance herself went to France, where she worked for the colony so successfully that on her return to Montreal at the end of October, she was able to report that "her dear foundress [Madame de Bullion] was as well disposed as ever ... that the company on her urging had now organised itself under a contract in proper legal form and that M. Olier had been made director of the company ... that in this new union everyone had shown such a revival of good-will towards the enterprise that there was every reason to hope the best therefrom ... in Montreal God has made choice of a work which to all appearance He wishes to encourage."[112] She also reported that an attempt had been made to persuade the Associates to divert their aid from Montreal and apply it instead to relieve the miseries of the Hurons. The latter piece of news draws attention to what was by far the greatest obstacle to the establishment and survival of Montreal and ultimately of all of New France: the continuous warfare with the Iroquois.

According to Dollier de Casson, the Iroquois first discovered the settlement at Montreal by accident in the spring of 1643 as they pursued a party of Algonquins who had taken refuge there. The first confrontation took place in June that year when a party of about forty Iroquois made a surprise attack on six carpenters and woodcutters, killing three outright and carrying off the other three as captives. Two of these were later burned, while the other managed to escape to bring the story back to Montreal.[113] This encounter was typical of many that were to occur over the next few years as it became more and more dangerous for the French to travel even the smallest distance from the fort. One incident, which took place on 30 March 1644, was somewhat different in character and has been permanently commemorated in Montreal's Place d'Armes, supposed to be the spot where it occurred. According to Dollier, the men of Montreal became restless at always being the victims of Iroquois attack while not being allowed any attempt at retaliation. De Maisonneuve, habitually a prudent leader unwilling to risk life unnecessarily, would not permit them to make a sortie against the Iroquois, who greatly outnumbered them and were much more skilled in the only type of warfare that could be practised in the forest. However, he seems finally to have decided that doubts about the courage and judgment of its leader constituted an even greater danger to the safety of the colony than an encounter with the Iroquois. So when the watch dogs, especially the bitch Pilotte, gave warning of the presence of intruders in the vicinity, de Maisonneuve responded in an unexpected manner to the urging of his men. "'Sir, the enemy are in the wood ... are we never to go after them?' To this he retorted curtly, in a way unusual with him: "'Yes, you will see them; make ready to set out very soon; I trust that you will be as brave as you say you are. I will lead you.' "[114]

Dollier de Casson, the former soldier, describes the subsequent events in some detail. The struggle was unequal from the beginning: the thirty Frenchmen who confronted a party of two hundred Iroquois were not adequately equipped with snowshoes, so that they were "hardly as mobile as infantry are compared with cavalry." After losses on both sides, de Maisonneuve ordered a gradual and orderly retreat towards a track over which wood was being hauled for the building of the hospital. Once they had attained this road, however, the men fled into the fort at top speed. De Maisonneuve, who had remained last to assure himself that the wounded had reached safety, found himself at some distance from the fort alone with the enemy. His capture seemed inevitable. But the Iroquois who were closest to him hung back in order to allow this prize – for they recognized him as the commander of the French – to their own leader. The Iroquois leader was almost successful in capturing the governor because the first pistol that de Maisonneuve drew misfired. Only the fact that his adversary ducked gave him the chance to draw his second pistol. Even when this shot found its mark, de Maisonneuve escaped only because the attackers closest to him decided to bear away the body of their leader rather than continue their pursuit. Nor was the danger over, for one of those left inside the fort decided to fire the canon. "Fortunately," says Dollier, "the priming was so bad that the gun did not go off. Had it done so, it was laid so truly along the little road by which they approached, that it would have killed them all."[115] At some cost, this incident seems to have established the military authority of de Maisonneuve in the colony once and for all. There were apparently no more incidents of this type and no more murmuring.

But the deaths did not cease, and the women, so few in number, were scarcely safer than the men. In May 1651, in an incident that might easily have cost Jeanne Mance her life, Jean Boudart was killed in an attempt to save his wife, who despite all his efforts was carried off to torture and death.[116] Another incident involving one of the women of Montreal had a happier ending and shows something of the courage and stamina of these women. In the summer of 1652 Martine Messier (Mme Primot) was attacked near the fort by three Iroquois, who threw themselves upon her with their hatchets to kill her. They had, however, met more than their match:

The woman defended herself like a lioness, but as she had no weapons but hands and feet, at the third or fourth blow they felled her as if dead. Immediately one of the Iroquois flung himself upon her to scalp her and escape with this shameful trophy. But as our amazon felt herself so seized, she at once recovered her senses, raised herself and, more fierce than ever, caught hold of this monster so forcibly by a place which modesty forbids us to mention that he could not free himself. He beat her with his hatchet over the head, but she maintained her hold steadily until once again she fell unconscious to the earth, and so allowed this Iroquois to flee as fast as he could, that being all he thought of for the moment.

When the French rushed from the fort to assist Madame Primot, one of them, who picked her up and embraced her, was rewarded with a heavy blow: "'Parmanda,' answered she in her patois, 'I thought he wanted to kiss me.'"[117] Known for the rest of her life by the nickname Parmanda, this woman, through her niece and adopted daughter Catherine Thierry, who married Charles Le Moyne, became an ancestor of the Sieur d'Iberville and his famous brothers.

But such escapes were rare. Although there was some relief in Montreal in 1648–49 as the Iroquois turned their full power against the Huron, this was only the moment of stillness before the full fury of the storm broke. After the deaths of Jean de Brébeuf and Gabriel Lalemant and the destruction of the Huron mission at Sainte-Marie on Georgian Bay in the autumn of 1649, the situation of Montreal and all of New France became desperate. As the remnants of the Huron nation fled towards the French settlements, the colonists thought that they too would soon be slaughtered. Dollier quotes them as saying, "If our handful of Europeans is no stronger than the 30,000 Hurons who have just been defeated by the Iroquois, we may reconcile ourselves to be burnt in the most horrible fashion over a slow fire, as all these people have been."[118] At the same time, Marie de l'Incarnation was writing that the destruction of the Hurons might "make the French fear a similar fate unless help comes promptly ... If France fails us, we must in brief either leave the country or perish."[119]

Throughout the preceding years the offering of refuge to other tribes fleeing the Iroquois had severely strained the resources of the French settlements, barely able to feed their own inhabitants. As the refugees became a flood, it was not only soldiers and military supplies that were desperately lacking. By the summer of 1651, Jeanne Mance had been obliged to withdraw from the hospital and move back into the fort, and those colonists who had built houses outside the fort were forced to abandon them. Dollier sums up the situation in these words: "One saw nothing but enemies every day, no one dared open his door at night, and in the daytime no one dared to go more than four steps from the house without being armed with musket, sword and pistol. Finally, as we grew weaker daily whilst the enemy grew bolder, on account of their great number, everyone saw quite plainly that unless powerful aid appeared very shortly from France, all would be lost."[120]

For the second time in two years, Jeanne Mance acted to save Montreal and, some would say, New France itself. As he watched his settlers fall one by one and no apparent help was forthcoming, de Maisonneuve was increasingly convinced that the only way he could fulfil his obligations to the survivors was by removing them from danger and abandoning the Montreal project. With the future of the colony at stake, Jeanne Mance offered to put at his disposal 22,000 livres given for the establishment of the hospital by Madame de Bullion, her secret benefactor, so that he could go to France to recruit men able to defend Montreal. De Maisonneuve accepted this offer, an act that, although it seemed the only way of giving continued existence to the colony at this time, was later to help bring an end to his career in New France. Jeanne also revealed to him the identity of her benefactor and advised de Maisonneuve to approach Madame de Bullion without betraying any knowledge of that woman's previous connection with Montreal. In 1651 de Maisonneuve turned over responsibility for the defence of the colony to Jean-Baptiste d'Ailleboust des Muceaux, the nephew of d'Ailleboust de Coulonge, and left for France in a last-ditch attempt to save it. The governor succeeded in his approach to Madame de Bullion, and in 1653 returned with a sufficient force of recruits to make the event a second founding of the city. One of these was Marguerite Bourgeoys, come at last to play her part in the history of Montreal and of Canada.

CHAPTER FOUR

The Fort and the Stable,
1653–1658

There were about eight years when no one could bring up children; and this gave us great hope because God was taking the first fruits ... Four years after my arrival, M. de Maisonneuve decided to give me a stone stable to make into a house to lodge the person who would teach there ... I moved into [the house] on the feast of St. Catherine of Sienna.[1]

De Maisonneuve's acceptance of Marguerite Bourgeoys as school-mistress at Ville-Marie had been ratified at a plenary session of the Société de Notre-Dame de Montréal in 1653 before her departure from France.[2] The establishment of a school as well as a hospital at Montreal had been among the original intentions of the society.[3] But it was to be many years before she could fulfil the role of schoolmistress in the tiny colony, for reasons that the previous chapter has made obvious. How then was she to occupy her first five years in Canada? She began as she was to continue throughout her long life among the people of New France: she looked around her and saw the needs of those among whom she was living; she then found ways of responding effectively to those needs. She began this kind of involvement at once, on the very voyage across the Atlantic.

At the beginning, as throughout her forty-seven years in Canada, Marguerite Bourgeoys exemplified what has sometimes been described as the most distinctive quality of seventeenth-century French spirituality. She shared important characteristics with St Vincent de Paul, who can himself be seen as typifying that spirituality. The two illustrate a statement made by David Maland in his remarks about religious fervour in this period. In France, he says, unlike Spain and Italy, "A combination of mystical enthusiasm with much practical common sense and organising ability led not to passive contemplation but to active service."[4] One of St Vincent de Paul's biographers has written: "In him the man of action can be explained only insofar as he was determined and conditioned by the spiritual man. We understand nothing of his work if we do not recognize in the least of his achievements the intentions of the great mystic."[5] Like Marguerite, whose reticence has already been noticed, "He guarded jealously what went on in the depths of his soul; and he believed moreover that this was of interest to no one."[6] Neither of them was an ideologue, a theorist, or a "visionary" in the pejorative sense of that word. Both shared an immense sensitivity to the needs of others, a willingness to respond to those needs, and a genius for finding the means to do so. The work of each of them took shape, not in fulfilment of some predetermined set of ideas, but out of their lived responses to the people and situations they encountered. If St Vincent's teaching "sprang from the circumstances and encounters of his life, from difficulties to be surmounted,"[7] so did that of Marguerite. The Mary who inspired her was not just the Virgin of the Visitation or of the Cenacle; it was the Mary of Cana who in the Gospel of John was the first to be aware of the embarrassment of a young couple and eager to afford them help, a Mary who, in Marguerite's view, made herself, from her very childhood, skilful in all kinds of work so that she might be of service to others.[8] Marguerite had that special kind of inner security that not only set her free from many of the class attitudes of her time, but also enabled her to perform with total unselfconsciousness services that many people, both then and now, would regard as demeaning. Yet she did so without compromising her dignity as a person and as a woman.

As a result of de Maisonneuve's two-year sojourn in France, 153 prospective colonists had signed contracts with the Société de Notre-Dame de Montréal. An attempt was made to recruit hardy young men capable of defending the colony, who also possessed those skills necessary for building a self-sufficient society. Among their number were men trained in such occupations as surgeon, mason, carpenter, locksmith, miller, baker, brewer, tailor, hatter, and shoemaker, as well as land clearers and future farmers. These men contracted to remain in the colony for five years, and the Montreal Associates undertook to transport them there, to return them to France when their contract expired if they so desired, and to pay them salaries commensurate with their occupations (even at that time the surgeons received the highest remuneration). Most of these men received advances on their salaries so that they could outfit themselves before leaving France.[9] In keeping with the missionary purpose of the settlement, the prospective colonists were also supposed to be good Catholics, but the difficulty of enlisting candidates made it necesary to include some Huguenots.

This recruitment was financed in part by the 22,000 *livres* to which Jeanne Mance had given de Maisonneuve access, as well as by a further 20,000 *livres* donated by Madame de Bullion. According to Dollier, de Maisonneuve, following the advice given him by Jeanne Mance, had obtained access to Madame de Bullion through his sister Jacqueline, who was attempting to reach a friendly out-of-court settlement of some legal dispute with her. If their conversation actually followed the course described by Dollier de Casson, the two played an elaborate and subtle game. De Maisonneuve acquainted the benefactor not only with the plight of Montreal but also with Jeanne Mance's decision to put the gift of her unknown founder in his hands. The patron questioned him with interest and sympathy, but without revealing any prior knowledge of the foundation at Montreal. In Dollier's view, had Madame de Bullion opposed the use to which her previous gift was being devoted, now would have been the time for her to make those objections known. Her further gift to Montreal at this time testifies to at least a tacit approval of the actions of Jeanne Mance and de Maisonneuve.[10]

Of the 153 recruits who had signed contracts, 50 did not take them up. Therefore 103 men embarked on the *Saint-Nicolas-de-Nantes* at the same time as Marguerite Bourgeoys. In addition, there were more than fifteen women aboard, of whom she names three: Perrine Mousnier (already the wife of Jules Daubigeon, one of the contracted settlers), Marie-Marthe Pinson (later to marry Jean Milot at Ville-Marie), and Marie Dumesnil. The last named was a young orphan entrusted by de la Dauversière to Marguerite's care. Her exact age at this time is not known. Because women were so few and the pressure for them to marry consequently so great, later historians tended to calculate their age by assuming that they were twelve at the time of their first marriage, this being the minimum age required by canon law. Marie may not have been quite as young as the ten years she has sometimes been assigned, but she may not have been much more than twelve at the time of her arrival in Montreal. She was to remain with Marguerite until her marriage about a year later, a marriage that was to produce, among other issue, four of the earliest members of Marguerite's Congregation. Marguerite says that there were about 120 passengers aboard the ship.[11]

As already seen, the voyage was not uneventful. After the mishaps that had dogged the first attempt to sail, it may have seemed to Marguerite a good omen that this second departure took place on the feast of St Margaret. Whatever doubts she may have had in the past, there is no indication of any diminution in her confidence in her call to Montreal during the long delay. Aboard ship, she soon found much to occupy her. The morale of the passengers must by this time have been uncertain, to say the least, and the worst was not yet over, for soon serious illness struck the Montreal contingent. Marguerite devoted herself to caring for the sick: "She nursed them with extraordinary care," wrote Dollier de Casson.[12] Soon she had also to console the dying. In the absence of a priest, she offered them what spiritual help she could in the face of imminent death and afterwards saw to whatever could be managed in the way of funeral rites. In a society with a strong belief in an afterlife and divine judgment, assisting others to die well was an exceedingly important activity. Eight of the Montreal recruitment died before the ship finally reached Quebec. There the ill-fated vessel hit a sandbar, from which it could not be dislodged even at high tide. In the end, it had to be burned. This had been a journey that would surely destroy in most people any taste for ocean travel. The newcomers were greeted with jubilation by the inhabitants awaiting them in New France, but this reception could scarcely have surpassed their own joy at feeling the steady earth beneath their feet. For a time at least, the terror of the Iroquois which lay before them must have seemed small in comparison with the terror of the sea from which they had just escaped, and they must have joined wholeheartedly in the solemn Te Deum sung to welcome their arrival. It was 22 September, three months and two days since the original departure from Saint-Nazaire.[13]

One amusing incident from this voyage was recorded by Marie Morin, presumably based on information provided by Marguerite Bourgeoys herself. It is trivial, but like many such episodes, throws more light on character than do accounts of some grander occasions. It seems that de Maisonneuve had been given some laces and fine linen by his sister Jacqueline while he was in France. (Jacqueline may not have cared much for her brother's mode of dress.) The linens were presumably for use on ceremonial occasions when he would be called upon to assume the dress of a seventeenth-century gentleman. Marguerite had collected this finery in a package, perhaps for laundering, but accidentally dropped it into the ocean when the ship was a few days out from France. Her best efforts to fish the parcel out were unsuccessful, and she approached the owner to report the loss in some trepidation, because, says Sister Morin, she did not yet know him well. His reaction was to laugh heartily and to assure her that both of them were now better off without having to worry about these ornaments of vanity.[14]

Two of the characteristics attributed to de Maisonneuve by Sister

Morin are apparent in this episode. One is his indifference to the display so dear to others of his country and class: his habitual dress was the grey homespun of the ordinary colonists.[15] The other was his capacity to respond to setbacks with laughter, an aspect of his character already demonstrated in the affair of the salute on his first name-day in Canada. Sister Morin writes, "He was without equal in his constancy in the face of adversity; what would have cast down or enraged someone else only entertained him and made him laugh." Then she adds a comment from her own observation of him in his last years in Montreal, after she herself had entered the Hôtel-Dieu.

It is a valuable corrective to those accounts of the founders of Montreal that, in an attempt to depict their virtue, succeed rather in portraying them as dour and joyless people deficient in ordinary humanity. Sister Morin says that when de Maisonneuve faced problems which especially worried and troubled him he went to see Marguerite Bourgeoys or Judith de Brésoles (first superior of the Hospitallers of St Joseph at the Hôtel-Dieu in Montreal) in order "to laugh his fill. They [the women] laughed with him too and gave him great joy in his trials, something he enjoyed very much." She continues, "Monsieur Souart [first parish priest of Ville-Marie] was also among his friends on these occasions; I have seen them laugh for hours at a time on like subjects, etc."[16] The account of the lace incident shows the beginning of the understanding and friendship that was to exist between Paul de Chomedey de Maisonneuve and Marguerite Bourgeoys.[17]

During de Maisonneuve's two-year absence, the raids by the Iroquois had continued, and they had won a considerable victory at Trois-Rivières in 1652. Although a peace was concluded with one of the Iroquois tribes just before the arrival of the reinforcements from France,[18] none of the French had any confidence in its long continuance. Jeanne Mance had come to Quebec the previous summer in expectation of de Maisonneuve's arrival, but had been obliged to content herself with a letter in which he reported on the force being recruited for the colony and promised a return the following year. Early in the summer of 1653 she had again come to await him in Quebec, a journey that would have been impossible had she delayed, for shortly after her arrival, a large group of Iroquois laid siege to Trois-Rivières and blockaded the river. A letter arrived with news of de Maisonneuve's coming, but as the year drew on without any sign of his ship, a great fear settled over the colonists of New France, unaware of the difficulties faced by the Saint-Nicolas. The Blessed Sacrament was exposed and public prayers offered in Quebec. Earlier in the year the pinnace sent up to Montreal from the capital had been ordered not to land unless Frenchmen could be perceived around the fort. Because there was fog when the pinnace approached Montreal, the inhabitants were not sure that they saw a boat and so did not emerge to signal and greet it. It had, accordingly, returned to Quebec without landing, to report the apparent fall of Montreal.[19] As further evidence of the terror gripping New France in 1653, the governor had promulgated an order prohibiting anyone from leaving the colony without his signed permission and forbidding ships' captains from accepting aboard their vessels anyone who did not possess such authorization.[20] It was the relief experienced throughout New France when, almost against all hope, this desperately needed aid arrived from the homeland that caused 1653 to be forever known as the "year of the hundred men."

On disembarking, de Maisonneuve had first to pay ceremonial calls on Governor Jean de Lauson,[21] who had replaced d'Ailleboust in 1651, on the Jesuits, and on the other religious communities. He then repaired at once to Jeanne Mance to describe in confidence his adventures in France and no doubt to receive a report on what had transpired at Montreal in his absence. It was time too for him to introduce Marguerite Bourgeoys, the fellow Champenoise who was to join them at Montreal, in the enthusiastic terms attributed to him by Dollier and already quoted earlier. The tribute makes clear that he believed her natural qualities of intelligence, good sense, and amiability and not just her fervour would make her a signal asset to the little community in Montreal.[22]

Marguerite now had her first opportunity to see the new country to which she had come. She was at once aware of isolation and poverty. "In Quebec," she recalled, "there were not more than five or six houses and in the lower town the storehouses of the [Jesuit] Fathers and of Montreal. The Hospital Sisters were dressed in grey; everything was so poor that it was pitiful."[23] De Maisonneuve and Jeanne Mance were to return to Montreal at once with the new contingent, but he had difficulty in getting the boats to transport his men. Lauson wished to keep them in Quebec and was only compelled to arrange the necessary transportation when de Maisonneuve produced a letter obtained from the king by the Société de Notre-Dame de Montréal earlier in the year, apparently in anticipation of difficulties with the governor.[24] As it was, de Maisonneuve sent Jeanne Mance ahead, while he brought up the rear to make sure that all his contingent got away from Quebec. Because some of the men were still too ill to make the trip and had to remain at the Montreal storehouse in Quebec, it was decided that Marguerite would stay behind to take charge of them. She was invited to lodge at the convent of the Ursulines but declined with thanks. "That was not where I wanted to stay," she wrote.[25] Instead, she chose to share the living conditions of the ordinary settlers, to see to their needs, and to nurse those who still required her care. Years later she was to advise the members of her community, "When the sisters are travelling and it is necessary to sleep away from home, they ought to choose the homes of the poor where they ought to give very good example and always give some informal instruction."[26] As she had done on her journey across France, Marguerite elected to share the living conditions of the ordinary people, of the poor. She rejected for herself, as she was later to reject for her Congregation, any preferential treatment, any comfort or mark of honour that separated her from the people she had come to serve. This characteristic, so rare in any period, was perhaps what gave some of her earliest biographers such a misunderstanding about the social and economic situation of her own family.

There was another reason that Marguerite stayed with the settlers, something she herself says gave her "great joy":[27] these men had been transformed in the course of the voyage she had shared with them. Before, they had been a rough enough crowd ready with their lewd or bawdy suggestions about her aims in coming to Canada and her relationship with de Maisonneuve. One of her great concerns when the ship was foundering off Saint-Nazaire was that these men did not appear ready to die. To try to convey the change wrought in them by the journey, she says that they were now "as gentle as true monks"[28] and, in a more homely and domestic simile, "they were changed like linen that had been sent to the laundry."[29] Desrosiers observes that the men had made a retreat preached by the example of a woman of thirty-three and that from then on there existed unbreakable ties between Marguerite Bourgeoys and the people of Ville-Marie.[30] In later life she expressed confidence in the capacity of people of goodwill to achieve harmony and understanding and in the power of good to inspire good in return.[31] Experiences such as the voyage of 1653 would have confirmed her in this confidence.

By November the new settlers were sufficiently recovered that, at long last, Marguerite was able to leave for Montreal, a trip that would have been very different from that Maytime voyage of the founders, made through the flowery meadows in the spring of 1642. Instead of a month before Midsummer Day, it was a few weeks short of the winter solstice. Now the days were brief and dark and the trees bare, and no birdsongs brightened the journey, for if May is the loveliest of months in the St Lawrence valley, November is the bleakest. Pierre Boucher, her contemporary in New France, wrote that in Canada there are only two seasons, summer and winter, and that winter comes rushing in immediately after All Saints' Day,[32] perhaps the very day that Marguerite began her journey. She first set foot in Montreal in mid-November on a date that she describes as fifteen days after All Saints'.[33]

For the next several years she was to live in the governor's house inside the fort, to which, of course, the whole population was confined at the time of her arrival. A plan found among the papers of Jean Bourdon, seventeenth-century Quebec engineer, surveyor, cartographer, businessman, and syndic, may depict the Montreal fort in about 1647.[34] In this diagram, the gate gives onto the river. Within are depicted guardhouses on both sides and then a single road leading to the governor's house, which stands at the far end beyond a military exercise ground, while on each side of this road and facing it are several buildings. At the left, near a bastion, is a blacksmith's shop and then along the road, two houses providing living quarters for the men with, behind them and nearer the river, a little building marked "privé" on the plan. Beyond these on the road stands the large building marked "magasin": this would have been not only a storehouse but a weapons depot. Between it and the governor's house is a small building that would have served as kitchen, balanced on the right side of the road by a similar building, designated the oven. Opposite the magazine stands the chapel, flanked on each side with little buildings for the use of the priests. Opposite the lodging houses on the left are two more sets of living quarters for the men. The governor's house, with its steep Norman roof and large chimneys at either end, dominates the other buildings in the plan. Windows are indicated at three levels. Even if the drawing is not a depiction of the Montreal fort, the plan for the colony was probably quite similar.

When Sister Morin describes the understanding and friendship that existed between Marguerite Bourgeoys and de Maisonneuve, she points out that Marguerite had lived in his house for the first five years that she was in Montreal. She goes on to say that during that time, Marguerite saw to the care of his linen and the maintenance of his private quarters. To form a correct picture of the situation, one must remember that the governor's house was not a private residence but the centre of administration in the colony. Apart from the priests' quarters and the barracks for the men, there was, in fact, nowhere else to live, so that it would have been the residence of several others besides the governor and Marguerite. The other women from the recruitment of 1653 must have lived there until their marriages, as must other new arrivals and visitors, as well as the children for whom she soon began to care. Marie Morin expected her readers to understand the function of the governor's house.

She is concerned, however, that the services performed by Marguerite might lead to a misunderstanding of her position, for she adds that Marguerite looked after all de Maisonneuve's interests and later states, "He did not look on her as a servant but as someone given him by Our Lord to help him toward salvation, and for whom he had a deep respect."[35] She has made it clear elsewhere that de Maisonneuve was served by a single valet, to whom she says he gave as little trouble as possible: the man was served by the master as much as the master by the servant. Back in France in later years, de Maisonneuve went out himself to get them food, and a visitor to the former governor in Paris reported that the host himself went out to an inn to get them a bottle of wine.[36]

But it is important to note here that Marguerite herself did not regard any kind of service as demeaning, whether to the governor, the poorest of the colonists, or the native people, even though her writings imply that her attitudes were not always shared by all of her first companions in the Congregation. Many years later she was to present to her sisters the life of Mary as an inspiration for their own. Her account of the events in the early life of the Virgin derives from the apocryphal gospels mentioned in an earlier chapter, works that made the life of Mary approximate to that of a cloistered nun and removed her from the everyday concerns and activities of ordinary women. Not for the young Mary in the Temple the degrading domestic toil that was the lot of most women; instead, her life was devoted to needlework and prayer. But this was not Marguerite's vision. She saw Mary as attending a school for girls in the Temple. There she impressed others, in the first place, by her good example. Her teaching (and Marguerite believed that even at this point Mary was a teacher) and her action bore fruit because she was willing to take "upon herself the functions of a servant, rendering her companions all the services she could and teaching them various kinds of honourable work."[37] The fact that Marguerite makes this point more than once in her surviving writings suggests that it was one some of her sisters found difficult to accept.

Sister Morin's account of the relationship between Marguerite and de Maisonneuve may have another implication, according to Leo-Paul Desrosiers, who was not afraid to use his sympathetic imagination in the biographies he wrote of both.[38] In the context of her remarks about the friendship that existed between the two, Sister Morin recounts that when de Maisonneuve consulted Father Jérôme Lalemant about certain spiritual difficulties he was experiencing, the Jesuit counselled him to marry. He chose, however, to seek the opinion of Marguerite Bourgeoys about this matter, and her advice, with which he complied, was rather to make a vow of chastity. Marguerite would have been in her middle thirties at this time, de Maisonneuve in his early forties. Desrosiers puts his suggestion very carefully, aware that he treads on dangerous ground. In his opinion, the significance of de Maisonneuve's question lies in the fact that he posed it to Marguerite at all. Was this, he wonders, a subtle way of sounding out Marguerite's sentiments towards him, an oblique proposal of marriage? Desrosiers points to what must strike anyone who attempts to write a biography of Marguerite Bourgeoys, her great reticence and reserve: "She will not reveal her inner secrets until the end of her life and under the pressure of necessity." In such circumstances, Desrosiers believed, the governor would not yet have known about her previous mystical experiences and the depth of her commitment to her private vows. He might well have believed her free.

Of Marguerite's sentiments in this matter, we know nothing, but, Desrosiers wrote, "What appears indisputable is the profound Christian friendship that existed between her and the governor ... It can be read in the various documents, contracts, proceedings – standpoints that cannot deceive." Of course, he continues, she was already irrevocably committed to God and to Mary and never considered abandoning her mission, but she was human and not impervious to other attractions. At the time that Desrosiers was writing, the Le Ber portrait of Marguerite Bourgeoys had just been restored, and he saw support for his theory in the sensitivity, the suffering, the conflict, that for him made her face so surprisingly moving. He concluded: "Without ever giving words to their feelings, this man and this woman will remain totally faithful to their vocations, but testifying by their reciprocal acts of thoughtfulness to the sentiments they felt towards each other and the deep sympathy that expressed a mutual understanding."[39] This theory may seem too romantic or sentimental, but it suggests a possibility that is difficult to avoid as one follows the flow of ideas in Sister Morin's manuscript, the document that gives the fullest account of the friendship between the two, and when one examines other documents that conclude with de Maisonneuve's will made a few hours before his death.

Marie Morin writes that at the time of the arrival of the recruitment of 1653, there were only fourteen women and fifteen children in Ville-Marie.[40] Although there were not yet enough children for the establishment of a school, Marguerite was given charge almost at once of the first child who had survived in the colony. The first records of the colony show that she was the fourth child of French settlers to be baptized in Ville-Marie, but Jeanne Loysel, baptized on 21 July 1649, was, according to Marguerite, the first child to survive.[41] She went to live with Marguerite at the age of four and a half and would remain there until her marriage to Jean Beauchamp in November 1666.[42] But the events of 1654 gave promise that soon there would be children in the colony.

There had been only thirteen marriages among the Montreal group since the foundation, but there were fifteen in 1654,[43] beginning with a triple wedding on 7 January immediately after the Christmas celebrations. On that day, three of the women who had come on the *Saint-Nicolas* married three colonists already established in Montreal. One of the single women who arrived on that voyage married at Quebec, and all the rest at Montreal within the year, including Marie Dumesnil. The women in their twenties married first, and those in their teens in the later part of the year. Four of the bridegrooms were from the same recruitment, the rest being already in the colony. (Most of the men from the recruitment of 1653 did not marry until later in the decade after they had had time to establish themselves.)

Marguerite's charge, Marie Dumesnil, married André Charly, called Saint-Ange, on 31 October. The arrival of this young man in Montreal at the end of 1652 is described by Dollier de Casson. Governor Lauson had promised de Maisonneuve ten soldiers and obtained the advance of their pay from him before the latter's departure for France that autumn. These soldiers were eventually dispatched in a shallop "so late and so unprovided that they were like to die with cold." When they arrived on 10 December, "They were looked on here rather as living ghosts ... like skeletons ... People doubted that they were indeed men, and were only sure of the fact when they saw them at close quarters." At the close of his remarks about the state of health of the new arrivals, Dollier identifies "two of them [who] were indeed still children though they have in truth since become very good settlers, one of them being called Saint-Ange and the other La Chapelle."[44]

The history of the Congrégation de Notre-Dame records an anecdote about the immediate aftermath of the wedding of Marie Dumesnil and André Charly. Next morning the bride returned to Marguerite in tears, sobbing so hard that she could hardly be understood: "'They deceived me,' she said, 'or maybe I didn't understand. I didn't know what it was going to be like or I would never have consented. I can't stay with that man; he doesn't love me a bit, and he'll never see me again.'" Records differ as to the ages of this groom as well as of the bride, but it is apparent that both were very young. Marguerite had to console her protégée and bring about a reconciliation between the two, a task that required prayer as well as persuasion.[45] Despite this unpropitious start, the marriage seems to have worked out well. The couple prospered and became the parents of a large family. Four daughters joined the ranks of the Congregation and no doubt carried the story into its annals.

Two of the other marriages that took place that year are of interest. One is described by some commentators as the most important one ever to take place in New France. It was the union of the twenty-eight-year-old Charles Le Moyne with thirteen-year-old Catherine Primot (adopted daughter of "Parmanda"), which was to produce such illustrious offspring. The other was the marriage of Anne Archambault to Jean Gervaise. Anne had been married in the summer of 1647 to one Michel Chauvin at Quebec. When it was discovered that he already had a wife in France, the pregnant Anne was left without a husband. An indication of the support offered her in the colony is the fact that when her daughter was baptized, d'Ailleboust Des Muceaux and Jeanne Mance served as godparents. Anne found a second husband in the recruitment of 1653: Jean Gervaise, a widower in his early forties at the time of his arrival in Montreal, was to become one of the first church wardens when Ville-Marie became a parish; he also served as fiscal procurator and substitute judge. One month after the marriage of these two, de Maisonneuve contracted to pay Anne the same wages as her husband was receiving from the Montreal Associates as long as the family remained in the service of the society and provided for the welfare and education of Charlotte Chauvin, Anne's child by her first, invalid marriage. When the couple, in turn, became parents of a daughter, de Maisonneuve and Marguerite Bourgeoys acted as godparents and the child was named Marguerite.[46] In his history, Dollier praised Anne and Jean Gervaise and their children as "a blessed family, in good repute throughout the country, with an endowment of virtue exceeding that of this world's goods."[47]

As might be expected, the result of so many marriages was a sharp increase in the birth rate in 1655 and 1656. The stories of Marguerite's life that have survived, from the one about Marie Dumesnil's wedding night to a later one about a mother who had been responsible for the accidental death of her daughter,[48] portray a woman whom others found easy to approach, someone to whom they could turn in trouble without fear of judgment. In so tiny a community as Montreal was in the 1650s, Marguerite must have been intimately acquainted with the struggles and difficulties of the young families coming into being around her. Was it the experiences she shared at this time that would make her so determined, a decade later, even against the opposition of her companions, to take a special house and live with the young *filles du roi* who arrived as propective settlers' wives in 1663?[49]

The mid-1650s were years when the colony was changing every day; in the metaphor of Leo-Paul Desrosiers, Montreal ceased to be a monastery and became a village.[50] In comparison with the period immediately before and the terror that was to come at the end of the decade, these were years of relative peace. Two Iroquois tribes that had been a great menace to the French, the Onondagas and the Mohawks, both wanted to incorporate into their midst the Huron survivors who had settled under French protection on the Ile d'Orléans. Both wished to swell their numbers to gain a greater advantage against the Senecas further west, and they vied with one another for French backing. There were incidents in which the peace was broken, but the colonists were freed from the daily harassment that had caused withdrawal into the fort in 1649. Jeanne Mance was able to move back into the hospital in the spring of 1654, and presumably the colonists who had built outside the fort returned to their dwellings.

The recruits of both 1642 and 1653 had pledged themselves to remain in the colony for a limited period: in the first case, three, and in the second, five years. Their numbers were made up almost exclusively of unattached men. But it was the hope of the Société de Notre-Dame de Montréal from the beginning that as many as possible of these men would settle permanently at Ville-Marie and establish families. Most of them, however much or little they may have understood or shared the missionary dream of the leaders, came to seek a better life for themselves and their future families. While some may have dreamed that the fur trade would bring them wealth with which to return in triumph to the homeland, others had more modest hopes of land, a house, a farm, and better opportunities than those available in the country they had left behind. De Maisonneuve had made the first land grants to the colonists in 1648–51. To encourage permanent colonization, at the end of 1653, he inaugurated a plan that in various versions was to be employed in the colonization of Canada into the twentieth century under the French, British, and Canadian regimes. In December of that year, he offered to colonists ready to establish themselves permanently material help in building houses. Further, he proposed to forgive the debt owed to the Société de Notre-Dame de Montréal by those colonists bound for five years who had received an advance on their salary.

In January 1654 the colonists began to take advantage of his offer: forty of them were to draw up contracts with him that year and a dozen the next. Among their number were many of the new bridegrooms. In each case, the help de Maisonneuve, pledged in the name of the Société de Notre-Dame, was based on the value of the services offered by the beneficiary and on his need. The amount was arrived at in consultation between the governor and the colonist. These grants compare favourably with the royal grants offered later to encourage settlement in New France. The new concessions were in three areas, Place d'Armes, the region called Saint-Joseph in Pointe-Saint-Charles, and Côteau-Saint-Louis to the west of the fort. The new developments were linked to the fort by paths, and to ensure the safety of the colonists, a redoubt was erected for the protection of those settling at Saint-Louis. In addition to the construction of homes and fortifications for their defence, the colonists were also employed from the summer of 1654 in the building of a church attached to the Hôtel-Dieu, the chapel in the fort having become so inadequate to the needs of an expanding Ville-Marie that two masses had to be held, one at four in the morning for the men and a second at eight for the women. When the colonists were unable to complete the financing of this church, the remainder of the cost was paid by the Société de Notre-Dame.[51] In his biography of de Maisonneuve, Desrosiers paints an attractive imaginary picture of the Montreal coming into being in these years, with so many young couples establishing homes and families, filled with the hopes and plans that characterize this period of life.[52]

Life was not idyllic, however; there were interruptions of the peace. During one of these in 1654–55 a party of Mohawks attacked a group of the French at Isle-aux-Oies, killing everyone except the four young daughters of the Moyen and Macart families, who were carried off as prisoners.[53] When de Maisonneuve was successful in negotiating a peace and an exchange of prisoners, these children were recovered and brought to Montreal, where they went to live with Jeanne Mance. In August 1657, at the age of sixteen, the eldest of them, Élisabeth Moyen des Granges, married Lambert Closse, the town major, whose exploits figure large in the defence of early Montreal.

Another incident was one of the few that has found its way into the writings of Marguerite Bourgeoys, involving, as it did, people she already knew well. On 25 October, Nicolas Godé, Jean Saint-Père, his son-in-law, and a servant were killed as they roofed their houses. Nicolas Godé was the father of the first family in Montreal, the only one to have come with the founding group in 1642. Saint-Père was the colonist chosen to head the campaign to build the church in 1654 and Montreal's first notary. Legends about these deaths are recounted by both Dollier de Casson and Marguerite Bourgeoys. Saint-Père had such a magnificent head of hair that the Iroquois cut off his head to take back to their own country. But according to later report, the head reproached them, speaking in the Iroquois tongue, a language not known to Saint-Père in life. Even after the native warriors had removed the scalp and thrown the head away, the voice continued to address them. An interesting difference in the story as told by Dollier and by Marguerite Bourgeoys lies in the message that each attributes to the voice. For Dollier, it was one of coming French triumph over the native population: "You murder us, you commit a thousand cruelties against us, you want to destroy the French, but you will not succeed; the day will come when they will be your masters, and you will obey them; it is vain for you to struggle."[54] For Marguerite, the message was, rather, a declaration of faith: "You think that you do us harm, but you send us to paradise."[55] Both are careful to advance the account as one that has been attested to by credible witnesses rather than as the assertion of something to which they can themselves testify. Marguerite's story contains a detail not mentioned by Dollier, to which she was a witness. When some of the Iroquois who had taken part in this attack were caught and brought to the fort, "The two widows came [to the fort] to beg that they would not be harmed and brought them some food."[56] For Marguerite, who valued charity above all things, this heroic act of forgiveness on the part of a mother and daughter who had lost both husband and father was a more remarkable sign of divine grace than stories of miraculously talking heads.[57] The way to peace between the French and Amerindian peoples lay through mutual forgiveness, understanding, and reconciliation, not violent conquest.

There was also poverty in early Montreal. One of the stories in the *Histoire de la Congrégation de Notre-Dame*, perhaps deriving again from Marie Dumesnil's daughters, demonstrates how great were the hardships faced by some of the less well equipped colonists as well as revealing generosity on Marguerite's part. As the weather grew colder during her first winter in Montreal, she was approached by one of the men, perhaps one of her former patients on shipboard or in the shed at Quebec, who begged for something to help keep him warm during the night. Marguerite gave him the bed presented to her in Nantes by M. LeCoq. When his fellows saw his good fortune, they approached her one after another until she had given away her mattress and each of her two blankets. She and Marie Dumesnil, who shared her quarters, were left with only the pillow and their aprons on which to sleep, a situation that might have been rather hard on Marie.[58]

According to Dollier, de Maisonneuve too could respond with generosity and sympathy to the needs of the colonists. There were very few ways for them to obtain money with which to buy the goods they needed, especially the expensive products that were imported from France. One way was by engaging in the fur trade, either by doing their own trapping – one of the young surgeons recruited in 1653 was captured by Amerindians while out trying to catch some beaver – or by engaging in trade with them. Each year the Hurons and Algonquins arrived at Pointe-à-Callière, their canoes laden with beaver skins, for the annual fair of furs. All the colonists were eager to trade whatever they could for the furs, which they would be able to sell. It was one of the high points of the year. One year de Maisonneuve noted the distress of one of the men who had distinguished himself in the defence of the colony, and on questioning him, he found that it was because the man possessed nothing to trade. As the colonist was a tailor by training, the governor took him to his own quarters and bade him cut down the curtains from his bed and make cloaks of them. The man was only too happy to comply; he set to work at once and so was enabled to take his part in the annual fur trade.[59]

Besides building up an intimate knowledge of the joys, struggles, and griefs of the Montreal community, Marguerite was also charged with or undertook certain specific tasks for the colony during these first years in Montreal. She herself makes mention of the re-erection of the cross on Mount Royal. Soon after her arrival, in fulfilment of a promise he had made to her, de Maisonneuve detailed thirty men to accompany her on a pilgrimage to the site at which the cross had been erected in January 1643. They found that it had been overthrown by the Iroquois. Plans were made for a new cross, and Marguerite was placed in charge of the project by the governor. She went with a party of men that included Gilbert Barbier ("Minime"), the carpenter, and the group spent three days cutting trees, erecting a new cross, and enclosing it with a palisade of stakes. While there, Marguerite found the remains of the banner given to de Maisonneuve by the Congrégation de Notre-Dame of Troyes, with its message still legible: "Holy Mother of God, pure Virgin with a royal heart, keep us a place in your Montreal."[60] This discovery was extremely important to Marguerite. As her writings make clear in more than one context, she saw in it a confirmation of her vocation to Montreal. It was one of the great moments of insight in her life, like that of the Rosary procession of 1640 and the vision of Mary telling her to leave France without fear. Sister Scott wrote in the notes that she was preparing for a biography of Marguerite Bourgeoys that the site of the cross on the mountain was "a prophetic and holy place" for her. Allusion has already been made to the essential connection that existed in Marguerite's mind between her own conversion of 1640 and the foundation of Montreal so that the mention of one almost always evokes a reference to the other.[61] That connection seems to have come into existence at this moment. She apparently realized when she discovered the banner during this re-erection of the cross that the place being saved by the Blessed Virgin in Montreal was for her and that the previous thirteen years had been a preparation for her work in Montreal. Sister Scott believed that, in Marguerite's view, it was no accident that this was the first place where the native people came to be instructed, the boys by the Sulpician Fathers and the girls by the Congrégation de Notre-Dame.

But in 1654[62] that development was still far in the future. Danger of Iroquois attack soon made pilgrimages to the cross on the mountain impossible, and Marguerite turned her attention to the erection of another place of pilgrimage for Montrealers, a chapel closer to Ville-Marie that would be dedicated to Our Lady. Today, even devout Christians find it much easier to understand and admire the Marguerite Bourgeoys who befriended the people of Montreal, established schools for the education of the girls of New France, and set up institutions to help poor women learn to earn their living than the founder of Notre-Dame-de-Bon-Secours chapel. But the foundation of the chapel was very important to her and to her contemporaries.[63]

The exact date at which it occurred to Marguerite to undertake the building of a Marian chapel at some distance from the fort is uncertain. Marie Morin says that it was 1655,[64] and Jamet accepts this date in the belief that Marguerite must have discussed her plans with de Maisonneuve before his departure for France in that year, when renewed attacks by the Iroquois made pilgrimage to the cross on the mountain too perilous.[65] The longest reference to the origins of Notre-Dame-de-Bon-Secours chapel in her writings begins with the fragment of a sentence that appears to refer to some of the ornaments and perhaps vestments from France still waiting for the building of a parish church. Sister Scott pictured Marguerite, sacristan of the chapel in the fort, looking regretfully at these beautiful gifts from the homeland, which could not as yet be put to use. The larger chapel that now served the inhabitants of Montreal at the Hôtel-Dieu was dedicated to St Joseph. There was as yet no place of worship devoted to Our Lady, the inspiration not only for Marguerite but also for the Société de Notre-Dame de Montréal. She was never given to idle dreaming. When she believed an idea worthwhile, she at once took steps to make it a reality. Those that she took to make a beginning on the chapel of Notre-Dame-de-Bon-Secours exhibit concretely her

powers of organization and characteristic mode of proceeding, as
well as her gift for persuading others to participate in projects where
she herself set the example as the hardest worker.

De Maisonneuve was involved from the beginning. He and
Marguerite must have gone together to examine possible locations
before they chose the site where a chapel still stands today, beside the
St Lawrence slightly downriver from the spot where the original fort
stood. But the participation of the governor was much more effective:
not only did he make the land grant and detail men to fell trees for
the framework of the chapel, but he himself helped to drag these
trees from the woods to the appointed site.[66] Marguerite was well
aware that their time and labour were the only commodities the men
of the fort had to exchange for the means of subsistence. She was
apparently also aware of what tasks these bachelors found themselves unable to perform. Rather than expecting them to contribute
their efforts to the building of the chapel without return, she made a
contract with them: for each day that they spent gathering stones for
the construction, she offered her services to do such sewing and
mending as they needed. To recompense the masons, she collected
alms from those better able to afford them.[67]

Of course, she also sought and obtained the ecclesiastical approbation necessary to proceed with the project. Claude Pijart, the Jesuit
charged with the Montreal mission, was pleased not only to approve
the plan but also to choose the dedication for the chapel, a title of
Mary that must have seemed very appropriate for the still-vulnerable
little colony: Notre-Dame-de-Bon-Secours, or Our Lady, Help of
Christians. The title would also have pleased Marguerite, who saw in
Mary both an example to be emulated and her own sure and stead-
fast help. Other communities might rely on wealthy patrons and secular founders. For her, the only patron, founder, and protector of her
Congregation would be Our Lady. Simon Le Moyne, another Jesuit
missionary, who was passing through Montreal at the time, laid the
first stone, and Lambert Closse, the town major, who replaced the
governor during his absence in France, had a copper plate engraved
with the necessary inscription. The cooperative project was apparently proceeding to the satisfaction of all concerned when the work
was interrupted in the autumn of 1657 for reasons to be discussed
later. The chapel would remain uncompleted for almost another two
decades, though even at its completion, it would still be the first
stone church on the island of Montreal.

In the spring of 1658, however, an even greater and older dream
was to be realized by Marguerite: she was finally able to open her
school. Glandelet, her first biographer, states that she did not wait for

a building to begin teaching the children of Montreal. Besides instructing Jeanne Loysel, who joined her soon after her arrival in Montreal, and the slightly younger Jean Desroches, who was entrusted to her shortly afterwards, even during those first five years, Glandelet writes, Marguerite taught the girls to read without charge and instructed them wherever she could, sometimes in one place, sometimes in another.[68] Robert Rumilly pictures her going from house to house, catechism in hand, teaching the children and women, consoling them in their difficulties, perhaps bringing from the house of the governor such news as there was of negotiations with the Iroquois and the possibility of recovering hostages.[69] Her manner of working may have been not very unlike the one she had experienced in Troyes as a member of the lay congregation, except for the numbers of people with whom she dealt and the degree of destitution she encountered. In all the events of her life, she displayed an extraordinary capacity for adaptation and immense patience. But she had come to Ville-Marie to be a teacher, and it must have filled her with joy to be able to give to her work the stability and accessibility that a school would provide.

The building she was given stood on the edge of the common set aside since the 1640s for the pasturing of cattle belonging to the settlers. It had been vacant since Antoine Roos, the cowherd, had been killed by roving Iroquois in 1652.[70] The original documents relating to the first school in Montreal have been lost, but the archives of the Hôtel-Dieu in Montreal contain a series of four acts drawn up on parchment by the notary Benigne Basset in 1666.[71] The first was made from an original in de Maisonneuve's writing; it is followed by three more copies made by Basset of records that make it possible to reconstruct the early history of the school and of the Congregation.

The act drawn up by de Maisonneuve is formulated with what Sister Scott described as "customary thoroughness and detail." By virtue of his function as governor of Montreal and in the name of the society for the conversion of the heathen of New France, he confers on Marguerite Bourgeoys a stone stable. The building is thirty-six French feet in length and eighteen in depth, and stands on a tract of land measuring forty-eight *perches*. It is to serve as a schoolroom for the girl children of the settlement and a residence for their women teachers. The concession is made to serve for the instruction of the girls of Ville-Marie during the life of Marguerite Bourgeoys and after her death in perpetuity, her heirs having no right to direct it to any other purpose. Should the building or land cease to be used for purposes other than teaching and the housing of teachers, the hospital administered by Jeanne Mance, which is nearby, is to have first claim on the property and may take it over in its entirety by paying only for the buildings erected on it, the price of which is to be set by a competent appraiser. Even given the proclivity of those who draft legal documents to provide for all eventualities, the reference to women teachers seems to imply that from the beginning some kind of community was anticipated, a conclusion confirmed by Marguerite's reference to the stable and the site as having been "given us for a community."[72] It also calls into question the idea that there was still an intention of installing the Congrégation de Notre-Dame of Troyes in Montreal.

An additional statement, copied by Basset, records that on that same afternoon in midwinter an assembly of the notables of the colony met with Marguerite at the hospital to signify their acceptance and approval. This is a separate act in which she accepts the concession. Her age is given as thirty-eight, her place of origin as Troyes in Champagne, and her residence as Ville-Marie. The signatories, besides Marguerite herself and the notary, are the two Sulpicians recently arrived from France, Gabriel Souart and Dominique Galinier; Major Closse; the first wardens of the newly organized parish, Gilbert Barbier, Jean Gervaise, and Louis Prud'homme; Marin Jannot, and Charles Le Moyne. The two other acts appended are land grants of 1666.[73]

It is impossible that Marguerite with her great devotion to Mary did not think of Bethlehem as she contemplated her stable, impossible that she, who had seen the Christ child in the Host confirming her vocation to educate the children of New France, did not associate the preparation she would now make with those made on the first Christmas. As she went about the refurbishment of the sturdy building that was to cradle the beginnings of her life work and her Congregation, she must have had no difficulty following the counsel that she later gave her sisters to imagine the Blessed Virgin doing the same work when she was on earth. Even in the primitive world of Ville-Marie, there was much to be done before a disused stable could serve as school and living quarters. First of all, and with the help of the children themselves, she had to remove traces of the former inhabitants, the cattle that had occupied what would be the downstairs schoolroom, and the doves that had made their home in the upstairs dormitory.[74] Children, unlike animals, could not survive without heat in the harsh climate, and so Marguerite had a chimney installed. Because the building was outside the fort, certain precautions had to be taken to ensure, as far as possible, the safety of the children and their teachers: a ditch was dug, and a ladder up to the loft could be withdrawn at night. In addition, in a colony where material goods were not plentiful, it was necessary to collect the basic furnishings and equipment necessary for the future pupils, their teacher, and her helper. On 30 April 1658, the feast of St Catherine of Sienna,[75] all was at last ready; almost five years after her departure from France, Marguerite was able to welcome the children into her first schoolroom. Public education had begun on the island of Montreal.[76]

It is surprising, therefore, to discover that within a few months, Marguerite Bourgeoys was to leave her newly opened school and set off for France on the first of her return voyages to the homeland. This journey was made advisable by events within the colony with which she was not personally involved. Leaving Ville-Marie at such a time may at first have seemed impossible to her, yet the journey could have presented itself as a providential opportunity.

In 1655 de Maisonneuve had taken advantage of a temporary peace with the Iroquois to make another trip to France. Although it was not the reason made public, his purpose was to obtain a secular clergy who would set up a parish in Montreal, a fact well known to his intimates, among whom Jeanne Mance at least had been consulted. Dollier records: "So far his chief endeavour had been to increase the size of the colony by the men whose coming he contrived. But now he was anxious to set up here clergy for their salvation, and so on this account he risked his life in crossing the ocean again, though he gave another reason for his journey."[77] At the request of the Société de Notre-Dame de Montréal, Jesuit missionaries had ministered to the colony from its beginnings, but now they had served notice that they might soon be unable to find personnel to continue. Most commentators on these events have accepted this statement at face value.[78] Without question, the Jesuits had come to Canada to work among the native peoples rather than to look after the French settlers, they had a vast territory to cover, and they had lost many of their men to death at the hands of the Iroquois or through sickness and accident. Lanctot, however, attributes the Jesuit threat to withdraw and de Maisonneuve's subsequent decision to seek other clergy for Montreal to an increasing hostility to Montreal on the part of the order. Certainly, the pressures brought to bear on the Sociéte de Notre-Dame in France at the end of the 1640s, which had resulted in the defection of some of its members and the transfer of their financial support to the work of the Jesuits among the Hurons, had come from friends of the Jesuits. Lanctot says that after 1653, mention of the colony at Ville Marie disappears from the Jesuit *Relations* and that it was probably in the following year that they began to suggest to de Maisonneuve that they might abandon the mission there. In addition,

Father Paul Ragueneau, superior of the Jesuit mission in Canada from 1650 to 1653 and confessor to Governor Lauson, is perceived by Lanctot as operating with Lauson against the interests of Montreal. These two dominated the Council at Quebec, and Lanctot believed that de Maisonneuve felt doubly compelled to seek the aid of other clergy "in the face of an administrative antagonism and an ecclesiastical disaffection that seemed to go hand in hand."[79]

Father Ragueneau's biography strikingly illustrates the strengths and weaknesses that characterize a number of influential ecclesiastical figures in seventeenth-century New France. No one would question his devotion to the Hurons and his dedication to his work among them. As superior of the Huron mission, he was responsible for the Relations of 1646–50, including the description of the martyrdoms of Jean de Brébeuf and Gabriel Lalemant, and of the migration of the Huron survivors to the region near Quebec. He had the bodies of Brébeuf and Lalemant recovered and buried, and then had the bones removed to Quebec when it was necessary to abandon Huronia. What is more, he undertook to assemble the documents and sworn statements of witnesses related to these and other martyrdoms in the "Manuscrit de 1652," an official and canonical document that would be used later in the canonization process of the North American martyrs, showing a forethought not common in his time. A statement he wrote in 1648 also shows him as a man far ahead of his time. He advised missionaries to the native peoples:

One must be very careful before condemning a thousand things among their customs, which greatly offend minds brought up and nourished in another world. It is easy to call irreligion what is merely stupidity, and to take for diabolical working something that is nothing more than human; and then, one thinks he is obliged to forbid as impious certain things that are done in all innocence, or, at most, are silly but not criminal customs. These could be abolished more gently, and ... more efficaciously, by inducing the Savages themselves to find out their absurdity, to laugh at them, and to abandon them – not through motives of conscience, as if they were crimes, but through their own judgment and knowledge, as follies. It is difficult to see everything in one day, and time is the most faithful instructor that one can consult.[80]

Patronizing as this advice may sound today, it shows, for its time, a remarkable degree of tolerance and understanding. Father Ragueneau was so respected in New France in 1650 that he was suggested as a likely bishop when a diocese would be erected in New France.

However, that situation was to change when, as Jesuit superior, he became a member of the Council at Quebec. "Once he became rector of Quebec and superior of the Canadian missions, he displeased the missionaries as superior by mixing too much in the civil and religious affairs in the colony, and as a member of the Council he by the same token offended a large number of the settlers," wrote Rochemonteix.[81] This gifted man, though he was highly regarded by Governor Lauson and later by Governor Pierre Dubois Davaugour, dissipated much of the goodwill that he and his fellow Jesuits had built up earlier. Some of his Jesuit confrères must at times have disagreed with him as strongly as anyone else in the colony. The tragic aspect of the battles that were soon to become so common among major clerics in New France is that they most frequently sprang, not from the conflict of good and evil, but from conflicting visions of good among men of strong convictions and character. The situation was exacerbated by the fact that so many of the men who came to the struggling church in New France were men of strong conviction and character, the time-servers, those with merely worldly ambitions, and the lukewarm having stayed behind in the more comfortable and prosperous church of Old World.

De Maisonneuve hoped to complete his arrangements in France expeditiously, but it was again to be two years before he returned to the colony. Besides his official business for Montreal, he found himself with family affairs to see to, for he arrived in France to shocking personal news: his sister Jacqueline de Chevilly, who had sheltered Marguerite Bourgeoys's first attempts to found a community in Troyes, had been murdered like her husband before her. On 20 August she had been shot dead on her way to vespers at Neuville-sur-Vanne, the site of the family manor and estates. The murderer was her cousin's husband. Was de Maisonneuve struck by the irony of arriving to such news from the "violence" of New France? Desrosiers has commented with surprise on the fact that no word of this event finds its way into Dollier de Casson's history or into any of the documents connected with the Sulpicians or the Société de Notre-Dame de Montréal.[82] As the sole surviving male in his family, the governor must have been involved in the legal proceedings related to the murder, in the settlement of his sister's affairs, and in the arrangements to be made for his two nieces. These duties would have involved several trips to Troyes and perhaps added to the length of his stay in France. There were also problems relating to his own estate of de Maisonneuve at this time. But his official and more important business was in Paris, where he formally requested Jean-Jacques Olier to send Sulpicians to Montreal.

This community had come into being as part of Olier's effort to bring about a reform in the French clergy. Influenced by St Vincent de Paul and by de Condren, second superior of the Oratory in France, to whom he is supposed to have confided his plans before the death of the latter in 1641, Olier began to gather a group of secular priests around him, first at Vaugirard on the outskirts of Paris and then at the parish of Saint-Sulpice, where he became curé in October 1642. The Séminaire de Saint-Sulpice, which was to play such a great role in the education and inspiration of the French clergy, was begun in September 1649. It was natural that de Maisonneuve would appeal to Olier, who had himself once wanted to be a missionary in New France and who had played so leading a role in the activities of the Société de Notre-Dame de Montréal. Olier was at this time a very sick man, but in one of his last acts as superior of Saint-Sulpice, he appointed four men to the Canadian mission. The superior of the four was to be Gabriel Thubières de Levy de Queylus. As a member of the Compagnie de Saint-Sulpice and the Société de Notre-Dame de Montréal since 1645, founder of four previous Sulpician community groups, and a man of considerable personal wealth, which he was willing to spend on Montreal, he seemed the ideal and obvious choice. His companions were two priests, Dominique Galinier and Gabriel Souart, and a deacon, Antoine d'Allet. When Olier died on 2 April 1657, the four received the news as they waited to embark at Nantes. They sailed on 17 May, with ecclesiastical powers conferred on them by the archbishop of Rouen, who claimed jurisdiction over New France. The archbishop had also bestowed on de Queylus further powers that were to cause considerable conflict in Canada as well as in France. The Sulpician carried letters patent making him vicar general and official representative of the archbishop of Rouen for the whole of New France.

The idea of endowing a bishopric in New France had occurred to the Société de Notre-Dame de Montréal in the mid-1640s, and some members saw de Queylus as the ideal man to occupy a newly created see. When he left France, he did so in the expectation of becoming the first bishop of Quebec. Unfortunately for the fulfilment of his hopes and for the peace of the church in New France, his candidacy did not meet the approval of the group who since 1632 had guided the church in Canada, the Jesuits. Influential historians of the nineteenth and much of the twentieth century were to see the ensuing conflict as a confrontation between Gallicans and papalists in the French church, but in two articles on the struggle over jurisdiction in the Canadian church of the seventeenth century, Jean Blain has argued that this is an oversimplification, if not a deformation, of the facts. He situates the dispute in the conflict between two visions of

French Canada, the mystical and evangelizing view and the economic. Blain argues that earlier historians, such as Faillon, Gosselin, and Rochemonteix, were misled by the prevailing ultramontanism of their own time and gave insufficient attention to the conditions and attitudes of the period in which these events took place.[83]

The Recollets and the Jesuits who had come to Canada had received their powers directly from the pope because they came as missionaries to the Amerindians. Problems arose with the immigration of French settlers: did the powers derived from Rome for the mission to the native people apply to the French settlers also?[84] The Jesuits had sought advice on the question of the rights held by the archbishop of Rouen, from whose diocese many of the missionaries came and where most of them embarked. In 1649 they obtained from him letters appointing the Jesuit superior at Quebec vicar general, but they did not make this appointment public until 1653, taking care first to forestall protests from Rome or the court in Paris.[85] As the appointment of de Queylus extended to the whole of New France but did not revoke the jurisdiction already granted to the Jesuit superior, it made clashes inevitable.

But these did not come at once. After a rough journey, the Sulpicians, in a party that included Louis d'Ailleboust as well as de Maisonneuve, reached Quebec on 29 July. They were greeted at the Ile d'Orléans with every mark of respect and courtesy by the Jesuit superior, Father Jean de Quen. "After these congratulations and compliments," Dollier de Casson says, "the abbé was invited by one of the Reverend Jesuit Fathers to make use of his authority for Quebec, which he did not at first wish to do, though at length he yielded to their entreaties. There was nothing gentler or more agreeable in a savage country like this than to see such charming actions. But this fine weather soon began to be overcast; the thunder pealed out, and our four newly arrived missionaries did not run away because of its threats."[86] The Sulpicians arrived in Montreal in the first week of August, but in September de Queylus returned to Quebec leaving to Gabriel Souart the task of setting up the first parish in Montreal. The Sulpicians made a temporary home at the Hôtel-Dieu. In November the parishioners elected the first wardens, Gilbert Barbier, Jean Gervaise, and Louis Prud'homme, the three who were soon to witness the deeding of the stable to Marguerite Bourgeoys.

It was during de Queylus's sojourn at Quebec that she wrote to inform him of the project already underway to build the chapel of Notre-Dame-de-Bon-Secours. He forbade her to continue. "Through an excess of scruples," Desrosiers says, "Marguerite then wanted to obtain a second permission from M. de Queylus"[87] (having already obtained the authorization of the Jesuits, in charge when the chapel had been begun). However, immediate events demonstrate that she either showed better insight into the character of the new vicar general or had a higher regard for peace than some of her ecclesiastical contemporaries, perhaps both these things. Had others acted with the same circumspection, a nasty chapter in the history of the church in New France might have been avoided. There can be no doubt that Marguerite Bourgeoys, a woman who both in her words and in her life confirmed the primacy of charity, would have believed it better to postpone the Marian chapel, even for a decade, than provoke an incident like those that were soon to cast the church into turmoil. The events of her life had already taught her how to wait, and she trusted that if God willed it the chapel would one day come to be.

De Queylus had made his precipitate departure from Montreal for Quebec because he believed his authority had been flouted. On arrival there, he had confirmed the Jesuit Joseph-Antoine Poncet as parish priest. But when, at the instruction of the Sulpicians and without consulting his superior, Poncet proclaimed from the pulpit the Bull of Indulgence granted by Alexander VII on his elevation to the papacy, Father de Quen replaced him with Claude Pijart, displaced by the arrival of the Sulpicians in Montreal. Poncet, on his way to the country of the Iroquois, stopped at Montreal and told de Queylus what had happened. De Queylus repaired to Quebec in high dudgeon, removed Father Pijart, and installed himself as parish priest. He proceeded to preach inflamatory sermons such as one on 21 October 1657 in which he compared the Jesuits to the Pharisees. When a Jesuit wrote a letter saying that de Queylus was more troublesome in his war against the Jesuits than the Iroquois, a statement that was probably all too true, someone made sure it fell into the Sulpician's hands. In November de Queylus even attempted to have the Jesuits evicted from their house in Quebec, claiming that it was a presbytery being used illegally by them as a residence. Abetted by the parish wardens, he brought his case to court, but lost in the judgment handed down by Louis d'Ailleboust, who was once more acting as governor.[88]

The Jesuits appear to have been the first to attempt a reconciliation. This was at first rejected, but somehow, by summer, a rapprochement had been achieved. When Pierre de Voyer d'Argenson, the new governor, arrived in the summer of 1658, he was pleasantly surprised to find the church at peace. But already the affair had provoked a reaction from beyond the shores of Canada, for the last ships of the previous autumn had carried news of the dispute back to the homeland. With the intention of establishing peace in the church of New France, the archbishop of Rouen on 30 March 1658 signed an act making de Queylus his vicar general for the island of Montreal and Father de Quen vicar general for the rest of New France. When the ships arrived from France that summer, they brought the news of this decision and the necessary documentation. For a time, de Queylus procrastinated, but finally, in August, he withdrew with some bitterness to Montreal. For a time, at least, the scene of the battle switched from New France back to the home country.

Although at the time of his appointment, the Jesuits appear to have accepted the candidacy of de Queylus, they favoured as prospective bishop, François de Montmorency Laval, a man who had been educated by the Jesuits and was sympathetic towards them. In January 1657, even before the departure of de Queylus for New France, Laval's candidacy had been presented to the pope in the name of Louis XIV. The progress of the affair was very slow, but on 3 June 1658 the bull was signed appointing Laval as vicar apostolic in New France with the title of bishop of Petraea. As vicar apostolic, he was not subject to the jurisdiction of the archbishop of Rouen, whose authority Rome refused to recognize in any case. However, because Quebec itself was not yet a bishopric and therefore Laval was not yet its bishop, the jurisdictional disputes continued as the court vacillated. When this action on the part of Rome became known, there was an indignant outcry at what was perceived by many as an unlawful infringement on the prerogatives of the French church.

Tiny, fragile Ville-Marie seems a long way from these disputes exercising the French church, but events were to bring both Marguerite Bourgeoys and Jeanne Mance to Paris shortly after the consecration of the new bishop there in December. On 27 January 1657 Jeanne had broken and dislocated her right arm. The medical care that she received at Montreal and later at Quebec was ineffective, so that in the summer of 1658 she was still suffering excruciating pain and was largely incapacitated.[89] In addition, de Maisonneuve, as well as arranging for the coming of the Sulpicians to Montreal on his last trip to France, had also advanced plans for the Hospitallers of St Joseph of Anjou to serve in the Hôtel-Dieu in Montreal. This was the community, founded by de la Dauversière, whose eventual coming to Montreal had been among the original intentions of the Société de Notre-Dame de Montréal. Jeanne had, then, a double reason for a voyage to France: to seek better medical attention and to bring back the nuns who were to work in her hospital. In her present state, however, she needed a companion to help her on the journey. That person was to be Marguerite Bourgeoys.

Marguerite's writings tell us about one other event of the summer

of 1658, an event that was of more immediate importance to her than
ecclesiastical squabbles about jurisdiction. In August that year, she
adopted an Iroquois baby. Some aspects of this story now appear
shocking, especially when one reads that the father later came looking for his child and could not find her. The child, a girl about nine
months old, was apparently not being adequately cared for by her
mother. Marguerite says that the mother "elle négligeait assez"[90]
(somewhat neglected her), but knowing her propensity for under-
statement and her reluctance to condemn, the phrase may imply a
high degree of negligence. Marguerite was to demonstrate on her
return voyage from France how quickly and effectively she responded to a baby in distress, and so her hesitation about taking this child
is perhaps surprising. Yet hesitation there undoubtedly is. Pressure
was brought to bear on her by Marguerite Picart,[91] the young woman
who was living with her. Both Father Simon Le Moyne, a Jesuit who
had already spent time among the Iroquois, and Charles Le Moyne,
so knowledgeable not only about the language of the native peoples
but also about their psychology, agreed with Marguerite on the inad-
visability of keeping the infant. But Souart, the parish priest, offered
the mother a porcelain necklace worth thirty *livres*, and she agreed to
give the child up to be a daughter of the governor.[92]

Because hesitation in the face of distress, especially the distress of
a child, is so at variance with everything known about Marguerite
Bourgeoys's normal reactions, there must have been some strong reason for her reluctance. Was it because her departure for France was
imminent? Was she reluctant to make such a commitment in view of
the new work she was about to undertake? Would it be anachronistic
to conclude that she was troubled about a possible injustice to the
native people or to the parents of the child, or was she worried about
the consequences for the child? Conflicts between the individual
right of a child to proper care and the collective rights of parents and
cultural communities are not easy to resolve, even today. When, in
later years, Marguerite's sisters taught Amerindian girls at the mountain mission and even included native women among their number,
she, like some of the other experienced missionaries of her time,
expressed her opposition to attempts to impose European customs
on the children.[93] In this case, however, opinion in favour of adopting
the child prevailed, and the little girl was baptized on 5 August, the
feast of Our Lady of the Snows, and given the name that must have
seemed so fitting to both the day and the child, Marie-des-Neiges. De
Maisonneuve himself was godfather, and the young Madame Closse,
who had lived among the Iroquois as a captive and was expecting her
own first child at the beginning of October, was godmother.

Marguerite had to place the child with someone to be cared for during her absence.[94] She left her with one of the women who had been a fellow passenger on the *Saint-Nicolas* in 1653, Marie Regnault, married to Mathurin Langevin, called Lacroix, who was also a recruit from that year. Marguerite must have known the couple well, and as they appear to have been childless,[95] the woman was perhaps eager to act as a substitute mother. On her return from France, Marguerite took the child back to live at the stable-school with her and apparently loved her very much. Writing about the episode years later, she as usual tells us nothing of her own feelings. She points out the historic significance of the event – "Father LeMoyne affirmed that this was the first Iroquois to be baptized" – and states quite simply, "She died at the age of six in our house."[96] It is left to Dollier de Casson to tell us of Marguerite's affection for the child: all her pain and trouble were repaid by "the pleasure the child gave her," and out of love for this little girl Marguerite kept her name alive in other adopted children after the death of the first Marie-des-Neiges on 11 August 1663.[97] Perhaps she, however, does leave a clue to her feelings about the child, because when she describes the events so many years later, she still remembers the baby's laughter. "We wanted to give her to a nurse but the child would never take the woman's breast and laughed when it was offered to her."[98] Because of the death of that first Marie-des-Neiges, Marguerite would afterward be able to speak to bereaved parents out of her own experience.

Before the departure of Marguerite Bourgeoys and Jeanne Mance on the first lap of their journey to France, one other incident occurred that is described fully by Dollier de Casson, in whose remarks sympathy for Jeanne prevails over his desire to be charitable to de Queylus. As was proper, Jeanne informed de Queylus fully about her projected voyage as well as the reasons for it. During his stay in Quebec, he had made the acquaintance of the Hospitallers who served the Hôtel-Dieu there, had been favourably impressed by them, and now conceived the plan of introducing them to Montreal. Later historians of Montreal and biographers of Jeanne Mance have tried to make excuses for him, suggesting, for example, that not having been a member of the Société de Notre-Dame de Montréal from the beginning, he was not sufficiently aware of the original intention of installing at Montreal the nuns from de la Dauversière's La Flèche foundation.[99] But the stealth with which de Queylus set about implementing his plan suggests that he knew perfectly well that it would meet strong opposition. His intention seems to have been to face Jeanne Mance and de Maisonneuve with an accomplished fact. Without a word to either of them, he sent Gabriel Souart to Quebec to bring back Mother Bouillé, one of the Hospitallers, with a companion.

Father Souart, who, in this instance, does not seem to have been aware of the way that he was being used, had studied medicine before entering the priesthood and was persuaded to prescribe a change of air as treatment for an ailment from which the hospital sister had been suffering. The first that Jeanne Mance knew of the project was when de Queylus arrived at her door after the nuns had landed in Montreal with the announcement, "Here are two good hospital nuns, come because one of them needed a change of air; they are going to come and call and ask for shelter."[100] Jeanne was, not unnaturally, "amazed" and not at all slow in perceiving the implications of this arrival. "You are coming, and I am going," she observed to the two nuns, though she nevertheless took them in and tried to make them comfortable, physically at least. As soon as she could, she went to talk to de Maisonneuve about this new development. The propensity of de Queylus for trouble-making is apparent at the beginning of the ensuing scene, for at first de Maisonnuve, not suspecting the audacity of his ploy, received his long-time associate with some reserve, believing that she had made arrangements for the hospital without consulting him. Once he grasped that the surprise was mutual, the governor was able to join Jeanne Mance in making counter-plans to hoist de Queylus with his own petard. Since Mother Bouillé had come to Montreal to rest, there could be no question of making her or her companion responsible for the hospital. Instead, Jeanne entrusted its administration during her absence to another secular woman, Madame de la Bardillière, a widow.[101] And Marguerite Bourgeoys did her part, not only to help de Maisonneuve and Jeanne Mance, but also to provide a place in the life of Montreal for those other victims of de Queylus's plotting, the two nuns from Quebec. To them she entrusted the instruction of the children in her stable-school during her absence. Perhaps, in the end, their presence too seemed like a providential arrangement.

De Queylus and Marguerite Bourgeoys present a striking contrast in styles of behaviour. There can be little doubt that de Queylus was a devout and generous priest. He was a rich man and could have lived in all the comfort that his century and country might provide. Instead, he chose the danger and discomfort of Canada – Dollier compares the Sulpicians assembling their belongings for the journey to New France with Isaac binding up the faggots for the trip to the mountain of sacrifice with his father.[102] Perhaps not unnaturally, de Queylus came with his own plans for Montreal, plans conceived before he even saw the place and with no great awareness of or respect for the experience of those already there. When Marguerite came to Montreal, she arrived without preconceptions, and for five years she served the colony in whatever capacity she could. By the time that she opened her school, she had an intimate knowledge of the children who were to be taught, of their families, and of the environment in which they would have to live their lives. When she made her plans for Montreal, they sprang from a long-shared experience of life in the colony.

Now Marguerite believed that it was time for a new step. When she had left Troyes, Father Gendret had told her that the community God had not brought to pass in France, he might will to be in Canada, and she had remembered his words. If the growing number of children at Ville-Marie were to be offered education without charge, a group of women would be necessary, rather than a single individual, for they must not only teach the children but maintain themselves in some way. From the beginning, it was the essence of Marguerite's vision that the community she was to form would depend, not on patronage or dowries, but, like the colonists of Montreal among whom they lived and whom they served, on the labour of their own hands. In addition, a community of women could give to the task of educating the children a stability that no one individual could guarantee. Jeanne Mance and Marguerite Bourgeoys embarked from Quebec on 14 October 1658 on a voyage whose consequences for Montreal would be singularly far-reaching.

CHAPTER FIVE

Towards a Community, 1658–1659

Five years later, I returned to Troyes to bring back some young women to help me teach the few girls and boys able to learn. We would live in community as we had planned it and in conformity with what we had planned in France.

I promised ... that we would have bread and soup and that we would work for our living.[1]

The ship carrying Jeanne Mance and Marguerite Bourgeoys took two months to reach France. All that is known of the voyage is contained in a single reference in Marguerite's surviving writings. Because the two women had left their departure to the end of the season, all others returning to the homeland had left ahead of them (which meant that various versions of events in New France were in circulation before their arrival). There was no priest on the ship; in fact, with the exception of the two women and five or six men, it carried only Huguenots, who sang their hymns publicly morning and evening and also at other times. Jeanne Mance was in constant pain, and the two women spent almost the entire journey in the gunroom. When they reached what would now be French territorial waters, Jeanne asked the Huguenots to desist from their hymns, warning them that she would, on arrival, be called upon to give an account of what had happened on the voyage, they complied with her request at once.[2] It is impossible to guess Marguerite's attitude from her typically non-judgmental description of this incident. Sister Scott wrote that, having grown up on the edge of the Huguenot quarter of Troyes known as "little Geneva," she may have found their devotions less disturbing than Jeanne Mance did.[3] Faillon sees in this incident evidence of Jeanne's ability to command respect, even from heretics.[4] Because there is no record to tell us, we can only imagine the feelings the women experienced when finally the distinctive towers of La Rochelle were sighted: the relief after the monotony, discomfort, and danger of the voyage; the lifting of the heart felt by most expatriates at the sight of the native land, however great an attachment has been formed for the country of adoption.

While the women were still at sea, an event had taken place that was to have a profound influence not only on the future of the church in New France but also on fulfilment of the purposes that brought the two women to France at this time: the establishment of communities of nursing nuns and teaching women at Montreal. On 8 December 1658 François de Montmorency Laval had been secretly consecrated bishop in the lady chapel of the abbey of Saint-Germain-des-Prés in Paris. This event was both the symptom and the outcome of conflict within the church of New France, to which reference was made in the previous chapter. Though it was intended to settle that struggle, its immediate effect was rather to bring it out into the open.

As we have already seen, the existing problems sprang from the appointment of de Queylus as a second vicar general in New France and his acceptance by the assembly of the clergy of France as episcopal candidate in 1657, problems that his subsequent behaviour did nothing to diminish. The Jesuits made known their opposition to his appointment, and the court realized the unwisdom of appointing a bishop who did not meet their approval. This was so not only because the Jesuits had served the church of New France with single-minded and heroic devotion, but also because no other group in France had promoted and provided for the colonies with such success. Through the influence of their powerful supporters and the publicity they provided in the widely read *Relations*, which appeared in France year by year, the Jesuits had done more for colonization in New France than any of the companies established for that purpose. The queen mother (Louis XIV was still in his minority) invited the Jesuits to submit the name of one of their own members for the post of bishop. They declined to do so, but instead suggested one of their former students, François de Montmorency Laval.

Laval came from one of the oldest and most distinguished families of France. His Montmorency ancestor is supposed to have been the first of the Frankish nobles after King Clovis to receive baptism at the hands of St Remigius in 496, and Bishop Laval was to incorporate the family motto "Dieu ayde au premier baron chrestien" (May God assist the first Christian baron) into his own coat of arms. The family had continued in succeeding centuries to render significant service to the kingdom, though the branch to which the bishop belonged was no longer particularly wealthy. Even if it was not his noble antecedents that prompted the Jesuits in their choice of Laval, such a background could only be useful to the man who would be called upon to protect the church of New France against colonial administrators as well as French churchmen. Certainly, the Jesuits could never be accused of presenting a candidate who would be their puppet: Laval would never be anything else but his own man.

In 1658 he was thirty-five years old. He had been educated by the Jesuits, first at the same college in La Flèche that had produced de la Dauversière and so many of the Jesuit missionaries to Canada and then at the college in Clermont. As a younger son, Laval was intended from birth for the ecclesiastical life, but before his ordination the death of his two older brothers in battle made him head of the family. Though he took time away from his studies to put the family affairs in order, he resisted pressure from his mother and his uncle, the bishop of Évreux, to abandon his plans for an ecclesiastical career in order to marry and fulfil his secular duties as head of so distinguished a house. He was ordained subdeacon in 1646, and priest the following year. But Laval did not seek the kind of ecclesiastical preferment that his rank and abilities would have made it so easy for him to attain. In the year after his ordination he devoted himself to the care of the sick and the teaching of abandoned children in Paris, as well as to the administration of his family affairs. He also continued to participate in a group with whom he had been associated at La Flèche and who offered one another support in the effort to lead a devout life.[5]

In 1648 Laval was appointed archdeacon of the diocese of Évreux where he obtained administrative experience that was to prepare him for the office of bishop. Since 1642 he had cherished the idea of becoming a missionary, and in 1652 his was one of the names suggested by the Jesuits to the pope who was looking for candidates for the posts of vicar apostolic in Tonkin and Indochina. One of his warmest supporters was St Vincent de Paul.[6] Laval was in fact selected for Tonkin, but for political reasons the appointment was never made. The Congregation for the Propagation of the Faith was unwilling to endorse a position that would maintain and perhaps even enhance the power of the Jesuits in the Far East, and the Portuguese, in whose territories these two appointments were to be made, were not willing to countenance a French cleric. At this point, Laval resigned his archdeaconry, made over his patrimony to a younger brother, and in seclusion devoted himself to prayer and works of charity, displaying not only great piety but also considerable administrative ability. In the efforts to put him at the head of the church in New France, he took no part at all.

In January 1657 Louis XIV wrote to the pope presenting Laval as his candidate for the bishopric in Quebec. Many difficulties had still to be overcome, however. The archbishop of Rouen objected not only on personal grounds but on behalf of the Gallican church, of which he was a strong advocate. He was joined in his resistance by other Gallican clergy in France. In the end, the Jesuits and their supporters were forced to compromise: Laval became vicar apostolic and bishop of Petraea (an ancient, extinct diocese), and Quebec did not yet become a diocese in its own right. The Gallican clergy at first refused to recognize the newly created office of vicar apostolic and were able to prevent the first attempt to consecrate Laval in October 1657. The result was the secret December consecration by the papal nuncio. Even though it was effected in a chapel outside his jurisdiction, this event, which took place within his diocese but without his authorization or knowledge, gravely offended the archbishop of Paris. Such was the state of the struggle when Jeanne Mance and Marguerite Bourgeoys arrived in France.

The ship carrying the passengers from Quebec reached port sometime in the Christmas period, and the two women left at once for La Flèche, an agonizing journey for Jeanne Mance. The jolting of the coach on badly maintained winter roads caused her so much pain that she had finally to be transported on a litter, cared for always by Marguerite, now her nurse as well as her companion. Two stops were made along the way, one at Saumur to pray at a celebrated shrine of Our Lady and a second in Baugé at a hospital operated by the Hospitallers from La Flèche. Marie Morin says that the two arrived at the convent of the Hôtel-Dieu at La Flèche in time to assist at midnight mass with the community on Christmas Eve[7] and spent the holidays with them, but Marguerite herself says that they reached La Flèche on the feast of the Epiphany, a discrepancy due perhaps to confusion over two different establishments of the Hospitallers.[8]

Pain of quite another kind was waiting for Jeanne Mance at La Flèche. As already noted, the women were the last of the 1658 travellers from Canada to reach France. Long before their arrival, de la Dauversière had been informed of the presence of the two nuns from Quebec at the hospital in Montreal. That he too concluded that these Hospitallers could not have come to Ville-Marie without the knowledge and consent of Jeanne Mance is a further indication of the enormity of the actions of Abbé de Queylus. According to Dollier de Casson, Jeanne was at first distressed by what she perceived as coolness on de la Dauversière's part. He appeared to believe not only that she was deserting the Montreal project, something that might perhaps be expected, given the state of her health, but that she had already, without his knowledge and consent, entrusted to another group of women the hospital intended from the beginning to be staffed by the community that he had founded at La Flèche.[9] It seems surprising that after so many years of working with her, both de Maisonneuve and de la Dauversière should apparently have been so quick to believe that Jeanne Mance had failed them. It must be remembered that in his references to the coldness of both de Maisonneuve and de la Dauversière, Dollier is recording the perceptions of Jeanne Mance. At the time these incidents occurred, she was a sick woman in constant pain. She was also very upset by de Queylus's behaviour. Her assessment of the reactions of both de Maisonneuve and de la Dauversière may have been coloured by her own physical and emotional state. De la Dauversière was himself close to death at this time, so that his perception may also have been dulled and his spirits at a low ebb.

De Queylus had entrusted Marguerite Bourgeoys with a letter for de la Dauversière in which he claimed that everyone in Montreal wanted the Hospitallers from Quebec to take over the hospital in Montreal, even Marguerite. This statement implied, of course, that her opinion about Montreal had become important. De Queylus may have based his claim on the fact that Marguerite had temporarily turned over her school to the two hospital nuns. When the contents of the letter were made known to her, she was able to clarify what she had actually said to de Queylus,[10] and the two women could reassure de la Dauversière in such a way that he continued his plans to send the Hospitallers of La Flèche to Montreal. To accomplish this, however, Jeanne must go to see Madame de Bullion and appeal once more to the generosity of this great benefactor. Marguerite accompanied Jeanne to Paris and did not leave her until she was safely established in the home of her cousin, Madame de Bellevue, where her sister was waiting to receive her.[11] Now at last Marguerite was free to fulfil her own purpose in returning to France: the enlistment of women willing to live in community with her and teach the children of Montreal.

The first place towards which she looked for such women was her own native city of Troyes, and she journeyed there in late January. Because no description of her first return home survives, we can again only imagine the feelings with which she revisited the city she had not seen for six years and the devotion with which she must have prayed once more before the Beau-Portail of the abbey of Notre-

Dame-aux-Nonnains, whose beauty had first attracted her to such unexpected paths, and before Our Lady of the Visitation in her old parish church of Saint-Jean-aux-Marché, the journeying Virgin. Above all, she must have rejoiced to renew old relationships. There were her brothers and sisters to see, and nieces and nephews, some born since her departure, to be admired. In later years, three of the little girls, daughters of her sister Marie, were eventually to accompany her to Canada, and two of them would enter her Congregation; at this time they were about six, four, and two years old. Surely it must have given the family great happiness to see once again this sister, who all her life inspired so much love, return to them, even briefly, from the perils of Canada. Of course, there would also have been sorrow. Marie Bourgeoys Semilliard, the sister closest to Marguerite in age, was certainly dead by the time Marguerite again left Troyes, for on 29 March 1659 she signed a contract with Orson Semilliard, who is named as the father and guardian of the minor children of himself and his deceased wife.[12] The record of Marie's death has not yet been discovered, but she may have died at the birth of her youngest child two years earlier. It is possible that Marguerite's youngest sister, Madeleine, was living with her brother-in-law and caring for the motherless children, for she signed this document with Marguerite. There would, then, have been grief as well as happiness for the family to share, but the imaginary picture of Marguerite's first return to her old home in Jamet's biography is surely too bleak.[13] His supposition that her youngest brother and sister had died during her absence in Canada is certainly wrong: in March 1659 Marguerite signed an act before the family notary, Bourgeois of Troyes, transferring her share of the family inheritance to Madeleine and her brother Pierre.[14]

At the same time, and perhaps marking a more definitive separation, Marguerite took up residence during these days in Troyes, not with members of her own family, but with the sisters of the Congrégation de Notre-Dame of Troyes.[15] Louise de Chomedey would probably have had many questions about the welfare of her brother, and the whole community must have heard with fascination about Ville-Marie, the faraway settlement to which Marguerite had gone in their stead, and about her discovery on Mount Royal of the banner that affirmed their place, and hers, in this great missionary enterprise. Surprising, perhaps, is the lack of any reference to Father Gendret in Marguerite's description of her attempts at this time to find companions to fulfil the vision that she had shared with him of a community dedicated to emulating the "journeying life" of Mary. The year of his death has not yet been discovered; the last date on which it is certain he was still alive was 31 December 1657.[16]

Not long after Marguerite's arrival in Troyes, she had unexpected and welcome news from Jeanne Mance: her colleague had been cured of the paralysing condition that had for so long incapacitated her and filled her life with pain. There are three accounts of Jeanne's cure: her own attestation, written immediately after the event, and the descriptions in Dollier de Casson's History and Marie Morin's *Annales*. They are identical in all their most moving details and especially in their spirit. They are perhaps, of all that has been written, the documents that bring us closest to Jeanne Mance herself.

When she arrived in Paris, the members of both her own family and the Société de Notre-Dame de Montréal were shocked to see the state of her arm. An immediate effort was made to provide her with the best medical attention available in France, and she was examined by a large number of doctors, among them the personal physician of Louis xiv. Their common verdict was that it was too late to do anything for the injured arm, which had already atrophied, and that she should beware of any physician who offered to achieve a cure; such a claim could only be made by a charlatan intent on cheating her. This was the state of affairs when on 2 February, the feast of the Purification, Jeanne went to visit Saint-Sulpice. The feast of the Presentation of Jesus in the Temple and the Purification of Mary, which concluded the festivities of the Christmas season, was not just a major feast in the liturgical calendar; it had special significance in the history of the Société de Notre-Dame de Montréal as the anniversary of the mystical experiences of de la Dauversière that had led eventually to the founding of Montreal. On the same feast in 1636, Jean-Jacques Olier had first been drawn towards the Canadian mission as he listened to the words of the aged Simeon, "Lumen ad revelationem gentium" (A light for the revelation of the gentiles) being sung, and on this day in 1642 the island of Montreal had been consecrated to the Holy Family.

This was Jeanne's first return to France since the death of Olier, and on a visit to M. de Bretonvilliers, Olier's successor as superior at Saint-Sulpice, she asked to be allowed to pay her respects to the mortal remains of the founder. As was frequently the practice at the deaths of those whose sanctity had been highly esteemed, Olier's heart had been removed: his body lay in the private chapel of the Sulpicians while his heart was enshrined in the superior's room.[17] De Bretonvilliers had arranged for Jeanne's visit to the seminary to take place while the liturgy of the feast was being celebrated in the church: as women were not normally allowed into the private chapel, he wished her visit to be as discreet as possible in order not to antagonize others who had not been accorded the same privilege. He himself would say mass for her in the chapel, to which he would bring the reliquary containing Olier's heart.

Jeanne Mance's own testimony written immediately after the event is the best authority as to what happened that day. In its eloquent simplicity, it shows us something of her powers of communication, so admired by Marie Morin. She says that in approaching Saint-Sulpice that day, she no longer had any hope that her arm would be cured, even by a miracle, and had accepted her incapacity as the will of God for her. She approached the tomb of Olier not to beg favours but "with the intention of honouring him, esteeming him as a very great servant of God."[18] As she drew near the chapel, she experienced an overwhelming sense that Olier was close to her, and the thought came to her that perhaps, through the intercession of her old friend and associate, God would grant her some relief from pain and enough strength to perform some of the simple tasks of everyday life. She prayed, "O my God, I do not ask for a miracle, for I am not worthy; but a little relief from pain and to be able to use my arm a little."[19]

As she entered the chapel, she was overcome by a sense of joy so extraordinary and so intense that it surpassed any other experience in her life. This sense of being "surprised by joy" emerges with great power in the attestation that Jeanne wrote immediately after the event and also in the descriptions she gave much later to Dollier de Casson and Marie Morin. Her joy assumes far greater importance than the cure, which seems simply to flow from a miracle already accomplished.

As I entered the chapel, I was overcome by a great rush of joy so extraordinary that in all my life I have never felt anything else like it. This joy so filled my heart that I can find no words to describe it. My eyes were like two fountains of tears that could not be dried up; something which came about so gently that I seemed to melt without any effort or work on my part to excite such a state, one to which I am not naturally disposed. I cannot explain my experience except in saying that it was an effect of the great joy I felt at the happiness into which the blessed servant of God [Olier] had now entered. I spoke to him as if he were there before my eyes, and with much greater confidence, certain that he now understood me much better than when he was in this world; that he saw my needs and the sincerity of my heart which had hidden nothing from him.[20]

Dollier says that when de Bretonvilliers approached Jeanne to hear the confession then customary before Communion, she could only say to him, "Monsieur, I am possessed by so great a joy that I can say nothing to you."[21] Sister Morin, most unusually for her, turns to the language of human love so often used in the attempt to convey mystical experience: "She approached the altar to pray and was drawn into a state of prayer in which she tasted God, His intimate and unique sweetness, and received many caresses from his Majesty."[22] Jeanne's remark that she was not normally given to emotional transports in prayer makes her testimony sound all the more authentic. Like Marguerite Bourgeoys, she was disposed neither to sentimental piety nor to transports of enthusiasm, so that the meagre accounts both women give of the great spiritual experiences of their lives assume a special power from the very contrast with their habitual sobriety.

Jeanne's sense of enjoying a taste of the blessedness already experienced by Olier continued throughout the mass and her reception of Communion. Afterwards, when de Bretonvilliers left with her the reliquary containing Olier's heart, she took it in her left hand and applied it to her injured arm, which was much bandaged and in a sling. Immediately, she reports, she was able to feel the weight, but was free from any experience of pain while a sensation of warmth filled the arm.[23] Revealing nothing to the porter who conducted her out of the building, she hurried home. Her sister was out, but on her return was shown the effects of the miracle by a Jeanne still scarcely able to speak. Neither woman was able to eat dinner, and at two o'clock they both hurried back to Saint-Sulpice to acquaint de Bretonvilliers with what had happened. There Jeanne wrote with her right hand a first, brief attestation to her cure, the writing clear but still displaying the effect of the strong emotion that was to possess her for another week. On 13 February she was to record the detailed attestation quoted above in a calmer hand differing not at all from her manner of writing before her accident.[24] One of the first tasks to which this newly restored writing skill was applied was to convey the good news to Marguerite Bourgeoys in Troyes. Marguerite says, "I received a letter in which she [Jeanne] told me she was cured, a letter written by her own hand." Then she adds with the caution that so strongly marks her approach to events reputedly miraculous: "I showed it [the letter] to a doctor and to another person and told them about the way her arm had been broken. Each of them told me that it could not happen except by a miracle."[25]

In her search for the first members of the community to be established in Montreal, Marguerite had turned to the Congrégation de Notre-Dame of Troyes and to the extern or secular congregation of which she herself had for so long been a part. Two of its members volunteered to go to Montreal: Marguerite's former associate, Catherine Crolo, who had so wanted to accompany her in 1653, and Edmée

Chastel, whom Marguerite might also have known before her own departure for Canada. Both these women were slightly older than Marguerite herself. A third woman from Troyes was added to their number, Marie Raisin, at that time between twenty and twenty-five years old and therefore, according to the law of the time, still a minor. Later, in Paris, a fourth woman, Anne Hioux, was to join the party.

To what were these women committing themselves? Specifically, they were undertaking to journey to the distant and dangerous missionary colony of Ville-Marie, where in return for simple food and shelter they would teach the children by day, and by night do such other work as would enable the group to support itself. Thus they would be able to offer free education to the children of the colonists and to any native children who came to be taught. The commitment was initially a temporary one, like those of the colonists who had previously contracted to go to Ville-Marie under the auspices of the Société de Notre-Dame de Montréal. At the same time, it was clear that they were not going there simply as a group of secular teachers who would inhabit the same house. Of her intentions in seeking women to return with her from this voyage, Marguerite later wrote, "We would live in community as we had planned it and in conformity with what we had planned in France."[26] The form that the community was to take could not yet be clearly defined, but it would find its inspiration in the missionary life of Mary the mother of the Lord, who never knew the inside of a cloister, as Father Gendret had suggested so many years earlier. Marguerite still had the Rule drawn up by Gendret for the attempt to establish a community in Troyes. Now this community was to take form in a definite place, the infant church of Ville-Marie, and to perform a particular service in that church, the education of children in the stable-school.

In an attempt to highlight the heroism of the women who joined Marguerite at this time, some of her biographers have stressed the deprivations, perils, and hardships that she would have described as lying in store for them.[27] No doubt she would have warned them about the difficulties: not to have done so would scarcely have been a wise way of finding suitable companions for such a difficult and dangerous enterprise. It would also be an error to underrate the attraction among the devout in seventeenth-century France to heroic self-sacrifice and martyrdom. But the records of their lives indicate that these women were neither unrealistic romantics nor masochists. They did not come *because* of the difficulties, though they would necessarily have been women who responded to a challenge. Surely, what must have inspired them was Marguerite's growing appreciation of the role of Mary and the women disciples in the early church and her ability to communicate to them the opportunity to play a similar role in Ville-Marie. They were called to be like Mary, even if only "as living water, crystal clear, springing up from the fountains of the Saviour and refreshing all who come to it is compared with muddy, dirty water,"[28] or as "a snowflake which falls in the shape of a star and melts at the least warmth [is like] a star in the firmament,"[29] as Marguerite was to say in another context, evoking images that would have been especially vivid under the vast wintery skies of Canada.

The contents of the Rule devised with Father Gendret for the little community in Troyes are now unknown, but she stated clearly and unequivocally, "The rule of charity is the one the Blessed Virgin prescribed to all those who had the honour of following her, even the first Christians, for the love of God and of neighbour includes all the law."[30] She was one day to write this description of an ideal sister of her Congregation: "She esteems all devotions but attaches herself to the principal devotion which is to love God with one's whole heart and one's neighbour as oneself and to find ways of serving Him in the occasions which are offered."[31] Marguerite's existing writings are also unequivocal on another aspect of her vision for the community she founded: it was of fundamental importance to her that her Congregation be egalitarian, that its members should not reproduce the distinctions and hierarchies of the world around them. The role played in the Congregation by the first women to join her is a striking illustration of this point. Writing about her desire to find in Troyes three women willing to become her associates in Ville-Marie, Marguerite says, "One of them I hoped would be strong in order to assist us."[32] This was to be Catherine Crolo, the old companion from the secular congregation who was to be with Marguerite almost to the end, at her side in the infirmary in their old age and predeceasing the founder by less than a year.

According to the history of the Congregation, Catherine was born in 1619 at Lauzon in Lorraine of parents who moved to Troyes soon afterward.[33] Towards the end of Catherine's life, Marie Morin wrote of her: "In operating the school, Sister Crolo's share of the work was the management of the farm, where she consumed her strength and her years, thereby rendering great service to her sisters, in doing the laundry during the day after soaking it all night and in making the bread. She was an indefatigable worker, looking on herself as the servant of all and the donkey of the house. She is still alive today, aged eighty, and with a great reputation for holiness."[34] Implicit in Sister Morin's statement is Marguerite's sense that all her sisters played a role in the educational apostolate of the Congregation whether they were instructing in the classroom or performing the tasks that made free education possible for the children of New France. In Marguerite's view, physical labour was as honourable as any other kind: it had been performed by Mary the mother of the Lord in her household and wherever else she could be useful, as well as by Jesus in Joseph's carpenter shop. Although there was to be only one superior in the Congregation until long after Marguerite's time, it was Catherine who was to take charge of the farm in Pointe-Saint-Charles when it was set up by the community. Marguerite must frequently have felt grateful for the presence of this strong, capable, and willing woman at her side.

According to Marguerite, Catherine's contract of employment was drawn up by Edgar Chastel, notary apostolic, at the same time as he drew up that of his own daughter, Edmée, the second of the women of Troyes to bind herself temporarily to the proposed community.[35] The solemnization of Edmée's baptism (she had been baptized at birth by the midwife) is recorded in the register of the parish of Saint-Nizier in Troyes for 25 October 1619, making her some months older than Marguerite. Marguerite was deeply touched by her encounter with Edmée's father, which is recounted in two similar passages in her surviving writings. "M. Châtel asked me how we would live in this country. I showed him the contract [for the stable-school], which was not very much. 'All right,' he said to me, 'that takes care of lodging. But for the rest, what will you do?' I told him that we would work and that I promised them bread and soup. This brought tears to his eyes."[36] Showing once more her appreciation for the feelings of parents, Marguerite adds that "he loved this daughter very much." Chastel consulted the bishop, but when the latter counselled him to give his blessing to his daughter's intentions, he drew up the two contracts noted above, and they were signed in his study. He also made what arrangements he could to guarantee his daughter's comfort and safety. Besides arranging a chest for her clothes and a box for her linen, he wrote to all the places through which the party was to pass asking that she be given whatever she needed to return to Troyes if she so desired. He also had her sew into her corset 150 *livres* in gold pieces, forbidding her to reveal this fact to anyone, including Marguerite. This measure was to make certain that she had the means to enable either the whole party or Edmée alone to return to Troyes if she wished.

Edmée herself renounced her property in favour of her godchildren before she left home. The document making this official was signed on 8 March 1659 and states that her motivation in making the journey to New France was her desire to spend her life "in a congregation of women which is established in the said region on the island of Montreal to care for young French girls and even Indians as far as this is possible."[37] It would be two years before she revealed her secret insurance to Marguerite.[38] Whatever else may have been uncertain about the community to take form in Montreal, this document makes two things abundantly clear: this new group was to be a missionary community established at the very edge of the French world, and it was to be dedicated to the education of girls, the children of both the French colonists and the native people. Marguerite's descriptions of her discussions with her first companions and their parents in France also makes it evident that these women committed themselves to simplicity of life and to the stable-school of Montreal.

The third and youngest of the women from Troyes to join the new group was Marie Raisin, baptized on 29 April 1636 and, like Marguerite Bourgeoys, at Saint-Jean-au-Marché. She would have been almost seventeen at the time of Marguerite's first departure for Montreal, and as her father's house was, like Marguerite's, close to the "Belle Croix," the two were most likely known to each other. Marie's father, Edme Raisin, was a master tailor, a traditional occupation in the family.[39] He had apparently prospered, and his son, Nicolas, born in 1634, was a lawyer in the Paris Parlement. Nicolas and Marie were their father's only children, and he was at first most unwilling to part with his daughter, especially when her destination was the danger and hardship of Canada. Marie was still a minor and therefore required her father's consent to join the project, but in any case, Marguerite was always reluctant to accept a subject whose parents were not reconciled to their daughter's decision. Her writings suggest that she had already met Edme Raisin in Troyes, where he had apparently inquired about her work in Canada with no suspicion that it would touch his own family so closely. Marguerite says that he "had never dreamed that his daughter, who was young, would think of this voyage."[40] When Marie reached her decision, her father was in Paris, where he now spent much of his time, and there she went to try to obtain his consent. At first, afraid of weakening, he would not even see her. However, "She begged him, she wept, she did everything she could. Finally, she obtained his permission."[41]

For this beloved child the father was eager to make generous financial provision. Marguerite says that Raisin "had a contract drawn up for her like the two others in Troyes. He gave 1,000 livres for the trip and for her clothes, of which I took only 300 livres. I left him the rest which I did not need. But every year, he sent us 35 livres on the 700 livres and after his death, his son continued it. And at the death of his son, a lawyer to Parliament, besides these bequests, we had an income of 300 livres on 6,000 livres."[42] Marguerite had now enlisted in her native Troyes the number of women she had hoped to take back to Montreal with her, but the recruitment was not yet complete. In Paris they were to add another to their number.

Where the women stayed in Paris is unknown, perhaps with relatives of Jeanne Mance and almost certainly in the same area of the city. Jeanne would have had much to tell Marguerite about the meetings of the Société de Notre-Dame de Montréal she had been attending and about the difficulty in getting the new bishop to accept the establishment of the Hospitallers from La Flèche in Montreal, for Bishop Laval was inclined to support the Jesuits and de Queylus in his intention of bringing the Quebec Hospitallers to Montreal. Though these proceedings did not directly involve Marguerite, she must have met some members of the society, for it was through one of them that yet another member was added to her nascent community. Anne Hioux was the twenty-one-year-old niece of Pierre Blondel, procurator for the Hospitallers at La Flèche. She was an orphan under the guardianship of her uncle, in whose household she had apparently heard a great deal about the foundation at Montreal. Marguerite says that Anne "was the first to be formally received into the community."[43] Her obituary in the history of the Congregation explains the remark in this way: "Although Mlle Hyoux had come with the three first companions of our Foundress, she is not ordinarily mentioned with them for this reason: 'Sisters Crolo, Raisin, Châtel, after having their contracts of engagement notarized, had been received by Mgr de Laval, without any ceremony, in the church of Saint-Germain-des-Prés; while Sister Anne Hioux, given to our Foundress immediately before her departure from Paris, was not received by the Bishop until his pastoral visit to Ville-Marie in 1676. This is what makes our Mother say that she was the first to be received *formally*.' "[44]

Marguerite also mentions two other additions to her party, though it is not certain at what point they joined her. One was a young girl much the age that Marie Dumesnil had been on the first voyage and, like her, an orphan entrusted to Marguerite's care by de la Dauversière until the girl could find a suitable husband in Ville-Marie.[45] Marguerite Maclin was to live with the Congregation until her marriage to Jean Chicot in October 1662. Marguerite Bourgeoys was one of the witnesses to the signing of the marriage contract.[46] A widow with two children less than five years later, she remarried, became the mother of ten more children, and lived to the age of ninety-five.[47] The final member of the group was not destined for so long a sojourn in Ville-Marie. Marguerite says of him: "A young man, a student, also offered himself to serve this house, to give himself to the service of God for his whole life. He followed us on the voyage and took his quarters near ours. But while he was on board, he was attacked by dysentery from which he died in our house two years after his arrival in Montreal."[48] By the time that Marguerite left Paris, she had also been joined by other women. She observes, "We were in Paris sixteen women bound for Montreal."[49]

The group journeyed to La Rochelle, where Jeanne Mance was to join them later. The trip was not without difficulty: on both the journey from Troyes to Paris and now this one from Paris to the coast, the carters they first hired were not authorized to carry passengers such long distances, and they were forced to begin each journey twice.[50] Meanwhile, Jeanne Mance was encountering obstructions of a very different nature in achieving the purpose of her visit to the home country: the departure of members of the Hospitallers of St Joseph of La Flèche to staff the hospital in Montreal. Only the continued support and determination of the members of the Société de Notre-Dame de Montréal made it possible to overcome the opposition of the Jesuits, de Queylus, and Bishop Laval. The new bishop is supposed to have attributed his opposition to a desire not to displease de Queylus, though his behaviour once he arrived in New France gives little evidence of an inclination to defer to the wishes of the Sulpician. He might, however, have hoped that de Queylus would subsidize the foundation. Assurances on the part of the Société de Notre-Dame de Montréal that de Queylus would comply with their wishes and with those of his superior, de Bretonvilliers, had no effect on Laval, who, in any case, would have been far more likely to listen to the Jesuits. Nor was he inclined to give any weight to the contract signed during the visit of de Maisonneuve in 1655. Money was finally the deciding factor: the foundation of the Hospitallers of La Flèche in Montreal had a patron in Madame de Bullion; the other group did not.

As she had been charged by de Queylus before her departure, Jeanne Mance approached the Duchesse d'Aiguillon, patron of the Hôtel-Dieu at Quebec, with the request that she continue her generosity by establishing that group at Montreal. One wonders about the judgment of de Queylus in entrusting such an enterprise to someone committed to the establishment of the sisters from La Flèche, even though, as administrator of the hospital since its beginnings, Jeanne was obviously the most suitable person to make such an approach, quite apart from her reputedly considerable charm and powers of persuasion. Her biographers insist that, distasteful as the task was to her, she would nevertheless have given it her best efforts.

However that may be, she cannot have been displeased with the outcome: her efforts to solicit funds from the duchess were unsuccessful, and she was met by a categorical refusal.[51]

Meanwhile, Madame de Bullion did not fail the enterprise to which she had already given such faithful support. She now provided Jeanne with 22,000 *livres*, of which 20,000 was immediately paid over to de la Dauversière as procurator of the Hospitallers of La Flèche.[52] On 29 March 1658 the contract between the Société de Notre-Dame de Montréal and the Hospitallers of La Flèche was signed before the notary Marreau. It provided that three hospital sisters and one lay one should go to Montreal, laid down financial conditions, and made Jeanne Mance administrator of the hospital for life. After her death, this function was to be filled by two administrators appointed for three-year terms.[53] Jeanne now invited the sisters designated for the Montreal mission to meet her in La Rochelle for embarkation.

The problems were still not at an end. Once more, difficulties came from the hierarchy of the church, for Henri Arnaud, bishop of Angers, refused to permit the sisters to leave his diocese for Canada. De la Dauversière, seriously ill, was further distressed by communications from the Société de Notre-Dame de Montréal in Paris demanding to know the reasons for the delay. However, he made a partial recovery, and in May Bishop Arnaud's objections were withdrawn. The three sisters carefully chosen for the mission were finally free to travel to the coast. All were mature and experienced women; the youngest of them, the superior, Judith Moreau de Brésoles was a month older than Marguerite Bourgeoys, while Catherine Macé was forty-three and Marie Maillet forty-nine at this time. Each of these women had attained maturity before her entry into religion.

Judith de Brésoles had wanted to be a nursing nun from a very young age, but could not obtain the approval of her parents, although they were ready to assent to her entry into a more established community such as the Sisters of the Visitation. In order to follow what she believed to be her vocation, she was finally forced to leave her home secretly when she attained her majority at the age of twenty-five, and the Hospitallers accepted her, by exception, without a dowry. She was a skilled pharmacist. Marie Morin wrote that Sister de Brésoles's reputation for making remedies from wild herbs was such that she was sought out even by the wealthy and fastidious in the colony with greater confidence than were the doctors and that the sick believed that while under her care they could not die.[54] She says elsewhere that the Amerindians gave Sister de Brésoles a special name in their own language that meant "the sun that gives light," because she gave back life to her patients through her care and her medicines as the sun gives life to the growing things of the earth.[55] Sister Macé, the second of the hospital sisters to come to Montreal, had been twenty-seven when she entered the Hospitallers, and Sister Maillet had, at thirty-five, been living independently and comfortably on her own income for several years before her entry into the convent. These sisters were accompanied by a servant and also by two young women interested in entering their community, since it was believed that it would be many years before there would be any Canadian recruits.[56]

Still, the difficulties did not cease for this group. A rumour was circulated in La Fléche that the departing nuns were being abducted and shipped to New France against their will, and a mob collected around the convent. The Montrealers who had been sent to accompany them to La Rochelle had to ride through the crowd with drawn swords and scatter it "by the fear they inspired, not a difficult thing in country towns that are not on the frontier," observed that experienced soldier, Dollier de Casson.[57] In an attempt to explain this incident, commentators have suggested that the townspeople did not want to lose any of the nursing nuns who served their community. They have also speculated that perhaps some of the young people previously recruited as colonists for Montreal, though willing enough to go themselves, might have done so in opposition to the wishes of their parents. It has even been suggested that, as a tax collector, de la Dauversière could have become a scapegoat for anger against the government or that the confusion in his own financial affairs could have provoked the disturbance. There was also the fact that this community, not yet canonically approved, was seen by families of the nuns as offering too little security to their daughters.[58] But the hostility to the Société de Notre-Dame de Montréal in some high places cannot be completely forgotten. It would be interesting to know where the damaging rumour originated.

Another anecdote related by Dollier illustrates how widespread and insidious was the hostility towards the Montreal group. Jeanne Mance apparently travelled to La Flèche on horseback. A few leagues from the city, she was thrown from her horse when, startled by some dogs, the beast leaped a ditch. Jeanne landed heavily on her right arm, but amazingly, she suffered only some slight scratches. Someone in Paris wrote to a Jesuit in La Rochelle who was an expert on breaks and dislocations suggesting he go to inspect the arm. The tone of the letter made it clear that the writer believed her earlier claim that she had been cured to be fraudulent and this new accident was simply an excuse to cover up the fact that there had been, in reality, no miracle. It was in the expectation of unmasking her deception that the Jesuit approached her, although he was obliged instead to acknowledge the validity of her claim.[59]

By the time that Jeanne Mance and Marguerite Bourgeoys were reunited in La Rochelle, Marguerite was surrounded, not just by her own immediate party, but also by the group of young women – estimates of their number vary – recruited for the colony. Dollier writes that she "acted as a mother to them during the journey, and afterwards until they were settled, which moves us to remark on their good fortune in having fallen into such good hands as hers."[60] He also relates that at this time Marguerite refused the patronage of a wealthy member of the Société de Notre-Dame de Montréal. He recognizes that there are those who disapprove of her refusal, and perhaps, indeed, some more worldly and prudent part of himself can see their point. At the same time, his admiration is clear, as he acknowledges all that God can accomplish through those who trust him completely.[61] Marguerite's trust and detachment were to be tested at once.

The harassment of the recruits for Montreal was not yet over; although all the important voyages of recruitment for Montreal were attended by drama and difficulty, that of 1659 was by far the worst. It was, of course, a voyage that was extremely important to the survival of the settlement not only in providing a much-needed influx of new colonists but also by bringing the women who were to give permanence to those essential social services, health and education. The sisters for the Hôtel-Dieu were informed by representatives of Bishop Laval that, because he wished them to delay their departure for another year,[62] they would not be permitted to land in Canada, but would be sent back to France at once. Worse was to occur. The ship on which the voyage was to be made was the *Saint-André*, and until this point, arrangements with the captain seem to have been satisfactory. Marguerite says that she and her party were to have been taken aboard for 50 *livres* each, a sum that was also to cover their food and the transportation of their belongings. Now the captain demanded 175 *livres* each, to be paid in advance. He refused to accept de Maisonneuve as security and wanted Marie Raisin to return to Paris to have her father pay the necessary sum.[63] This new demand has sometimes been attributed to pure cupidity; perceiving the urgency of the expedition to depart, the owner of the ship simply decided to claim as much as he could extract from its members. Of the captain himself, Marguerite Bourgeoys, always so restrained in her comments about people and events, says he was "a very upright captain."[64] It is difficult not to wonder whether some other influence had been brought to bear as part of a larger campaign against this attempt to reinforce the colony in Montreal, though later events were also to reveal a callous disregard for human life on the part of the ship's owner.

Somehow Marguerite Bourgeoys and Jeanne Mance both managed to make new financial arrangements with the captain. Marguerite presented two promissory notes, one on the Société de Notre-Dame de Montréal payable at once and a second on Edme Raisin, due when the vessels returned from Canada if the first had not already been paid. She also observes that, as happened so frequently in her life, God provided for her without the need for recourse to wealthy patrons. "When I arrived in Montreal, a boy loaned me some beaver and all was paid."[65] Jeanne Mance borrowed the necessary funds from a merchant on the strength of a contract she had drawn up with seven families from Varens who were part of the new recruitment for Montreal.[66] This document was signed on 25 June 1659. On 29 June embarkation took place, and finally, on 2 July, the ship sailed. The first members of the Congrégation de Notre-Dame of Montreal left their native land for Canada on the feast of Our Lady of the Visitation, which was to become the patronal feast of the community. Except for Marguerite, these women, like most settlers who came to New France, were never to see that native land again.

The day the ship sailed was when the group began their life together as a community. Her research convinced Sister Scott that, in Marguerite's opinion, the Congrégation de Notre-Dame de Montreal came into being 2 July 1659 aboard the Saint-André. It was born, not in seclusion, but as it was intended to continue, with its members living, eating, and sleeping literally side by side with those it was founded to serve. Sister Scott believed that Marguerite's statement of this fact had long been misinterpreted by her biographers as referring to the organization among the young women of Ville-Marie of a confraternity like the lay congregation to which she had belonged in Troyes. In a correction she had prepared for the relevant footnote in the French and English editions of Marguerite's writings, she wrote:

The original reads "et commençames la Congrégation séculière le jour de la Visitation." "Séculière" is the word used in document after document to distinguish the Congrégation sisters from the Hôtel-Dieu, or "religieuses". Most often they (we) are called 'filles séculières de la Congrégation," or sometimes just "filles séculières." The explanatory note is incorrect and is not supported by the manuscript text, which is reproduced correctly in the main text, but changes radically in the footnote. Thus: on p.54: "On fit voile le jour de la Visitation, et on arriva [au Canada] le jour de la Nativité [de la Vierge]." Marguerite was bringing back to Ville Marie four recruits. The first time all five women came together as a group was on shipboard, at the time of the embarkation from La Rochelle.[67]

There is no doubt that Marguerite did establish a religious confraternity for the girls and women who were beyond school age.[68] The difficulty is to distinguish references to this group from references to members of the Congrégation de Notre-Dame of Montreal. The sisters themselves were officially "filles séculières" (secular women) not, canonically, "religieuses" (nuns), and both Marguerite Bourgeoys and Marie Barbier signed themselves "Congréganiste" in their correspondence with Father Tronson as late as the 1690s.[69]

The recruitment of 1659 was to be the last major one undertaken by the Société de Notre-Dame for the colonization of Montreal. Documents in the archives of the Hôtel-Dieu in Montreal list 109 persons whose passage was paid or guaranteed by those who directed the recruitment, including individuals such as Marguerite and Jeanne, who were returning rather than arriving for the first time.[70] Marguerite was therefore a fellow passenger with the aspiring colonists at each major influx of new citizens for Montreal after the voyage of foundation in 1641. On this, even more than on her previous voyage, she would come to know them in the most harrowing of circumstances.

At its best, the ocean journey from France to Quebec was scarcely a pleasure trip. Like immigrants from other parts of Europe who were to make the voyage to Canada in the nineteenth and early twentieth centuries, these colonists of the seventeenth occupied the cheapest kind of accommodation aboard ship. The common food provided was prepared by one of the sailors and was not attractive, over-plentiful, or even clean.[71] While those who could afford it brought aboard their own food (including livestock) and cooked it themselves, their personal store of provisions could run out, and they might be forced to share the common rations if the voyage was prolonged. Besides the hardship created by living conditions, especially those that resulted from the confinement of such assorted groups in close proximity for a long time, there was also danger from hostile nations if the home country was at war. England and Holland, the most frequent enemies of France in the seventeenth century, were both naval powers. Above all, the weather was a constant source of peril. Aboard the *Saint-André* in 1659, however, lurked an invisible and even more deadly enemy: the plague. For the previous two years the vessel had been used as an army hospital ship, and it had not been disinfected before being released for this voyage to Canada.[72]

Soon after the ship left port, there was an outbreak of the plague aboard. Almost everyone was ill to some degree. Jeanne Mance, who was extremely sick, was incapacitated for the rest of the voyage. The two Sulpician priests, Guillaume Vignal and Jacques Le Maistre, though infected themselves, were called upon to minister to the dying and to assist at their burials at sea. Marguerite Bourgeoys wrote of Le Maistre that "he took [the bodies of those who had died of the plague] with their blankets in which he wrapped them before lowering them into the sea."[73] Dollier records that after eight or ten people had died, the Hospitallers on their way to the Hôtel-Dieu in Montreal were allowed to care for the most seriously stricken in a kind of hospital, after which, he says, "no one else died, though there were plenty of sick."[74] According to Marie Morin, this work was undertaken by Sister de Brésoles and Sister Maillet since Sister Macé was too ill herself to care for the sick until close to the end of the journey, when Le Maistre gave her charge of some of the more distinguished passengers.[75]

Although not untouched by sickness herself,[76] Marguerite was able to move about freely in the care of the ordinary passengers during this terrible voyage. While the two priests occupied a private cabin, Jeanne Mance shared another with the Hospitallers and the two aspirants to their community, and all this group ate together at a private table, Marguerite and her companions shared their quarters and living conditions with the group of women coming to Montreal.[77] These first members of the Congregation were expected from the beginning to seek no special privileges but to partake in the lot of the ordinary people. "Sister Marguerite Bourgeoys," Dollier writes, "worked with great zeal during the voyage, and ... God endowed her with strength therefor, so that whilst the labours of the voyage were heavy, its solaces were not few, especially in the pious end which these poor plague-stricken people made."[78]

The context of Dollier's statement suggests that he had in mind primarily the spiritual consolation that she offered the sick and dying, but a pathetic story related by Marguerite herself shows that the help she offered was also of an immediate, practical nature. Though occupying only a few lines in her memoirs, this story tells a great deal about the difficulties, hardships, and sorrows facing immigrants to New France in the seventeenth century and also about her own character. Among the families from Marans aboard ship were Mathurin Thibaudeau, his wife, Catherine Aurard, and their four children, Catherine, Jacques, Jeanne, and finally Marguerite, who was only a few months old.[79] The parents and three older children were stricken with the plague. "The Thibaudeau family were all near death," Marguerite says, "except the little girl who was still nursing at the breast. No one was willing to take care of her. I asked for her against the advice of our entire group who were all ill. But I had heard them speak of throwing her into the sea and that was too pitiful for me."[8] This passage demonstrates Marguerite's most characteristic qualities: her awareness of the needs of others, whether of a desperate family or her own companions, her willingness to help even without being asked, her consultation of her companions and weighing of their wishes, and yet her ability to make unpopular decisions when she believed they were right. Nowhere in this account are there any recriminations: Marguerite condemns the behaviour of no one involved in the incident, not the crew, not the parents, not the women who were with her. But she was beginning to find out that in gathering together companions to help her in her work, she was sacrificing some of her own freedom. Already, the day was foreshadowed when some members of her Congregation would find it difficult to meet the challenge proposed to them in their founder's way of life or, at least, would be unable to accept her point of view on questions affecting the community. The quarters occupied by Marguerite and her companions were shared with a large group of women coming to Montreal, but her words suggest that opposition to admitting the crying baby was universal and therefore seems to have included her new companions.

The story of the Thibaudeau baby did not have a happy ending. By the time the ship reached Quebec, the three older children had all been buried at sea.[81] Marguerite returned the youngest to her parents, who were somewhat recovered, "to keep until our departure for Montreal in order to give our young women some relief from the child's crying."[82] Unfortunately, the parents left the baby too close to a large fire built to keep the group warm, and her back was badly burnt. Marguerite took the baby into her care once more for the trip to Montreal. "She was suffering a great deal and I had no ointment to dress her burns. This troubled me a great deal during the trip," wrote Marguerite. In Montreal she gave the baby to a wet-nurse, but in vain. After so brave a struggle, the baby died, and her death was attributed to her having been put back at the breast on arrival in Montreal. The only references that Marguerite makes to her own feelings in all these events are her responses to the plight of the baby: her pity when there was no one to care for the child and her sorrow that she had no means of alleviating the pain of the burns.[83]

All the passengers must have had their fill of sickness and fear by the time the *Saint-André* docked in Quebec on the evening of 7 September 1659. As they sailed through the channel between the Île d'Orléans and the north shore, they must have looked with relief at the first small church dedicated to St Anne, special patron of sailors, on the slopes of Beaupré.[84] They had been at sea for more than two months when they finally disembarked at Quebec. They reached Quebec on the eve of another major feast of the Blessed Virgin Mary, on this occasion that of her nativity on 8 September. Their arrival was ultimately to contribute to the strength and stability of Montreal and thus to making permanent the French presence in the New World. In the immediate future, however, they had to face the period characterized by Léo-Paul Desrosiers in his life of de Maisonneuve as "les années terribles" (the dreadful years). In a little over two years both the Sulpicians who arrived with this group, as well as many other Montrealers, would have been killed by the Iroquois.

But at least for a moment, there must have been relief and hope for those who had survived the terrible journey. The new colonists, like those of 1653, stayed in the Montreal warehouse. This time Marguerite did not remain at Quebec with those unable, as yet, to make the trip upriver to Montreal. Instead, she accompanied the first group ready to leave. They arrived in Montreal on 29 September, the feast of St Michael the Archangel, a year to the day since her departure with Jeanne Mance for France. This time she did not arrive as a stranger, but as an established member of the Montreal community. She came to a house in which she and her companions could begin at last to give concrete form to the dream of a community of women who, like Mary the mother of Jesus, would work towards the building up of an infant church. Their contribution would be through the education of its children in their stable-school, and they would live, not separated from, but among the ordinary people of Montreal, sharing their hardships and trials as well as their hopes and dreams. Because she had returned to Ville-Marie within a year of her departure, Marguerite was able to retain a task in which her devotion to the Eucharist always gave her delight: "The sacristy and everything associated with it that a woman can do were given back to me."[85]

CHAPTER SIX

Planting the Seed,
1659–1665

I compare this Community to a square in a large garden. For all Christendom is a great garden created by God and all the communities are as so many plots in this large garden ... The sisters of the Congregation are as so many plants which occupy one of these squares in the garden ... the Community.

When God in His divine goodness gave New France to the Blessed Virgin as her domain because of the prayers of the first settlers to her, she wished to have the little girls formed as good Christians so that they might later become good mothers of families. For this she chose poor women without learning, without distinguished bearing, without talent and without money.[1]

The six years between the arrival of the *Saint-André* in the autumn of 1659 and de Maisonneuve's last departure from Canada in the autumn of 1665 were ones of irony and contradiction in the history of Montreal and in the life of Marguerite Bourgeoys. They were years of extreme danger and hardship, yet in her later life she was to bring them to mind again and again as representing better and happier days in her Congregation, when life had been shared with the ordinary people of Montreal with an intimacy and a generosity lost in a more secure and prosperous era. They were a time of new beginnings as, finally, families came into existence and began to grow. Jeanne Mance saw the fulfilment of her desire to establish the Hospitallers from La Flèche at the Hôtel-Dieu, and Marguerite Bourgeoys the realization of her dream of a community of women whose life would emulate that of the Virgin Mary in the early Christian church. But they were also years of endings; the disappearance of the Société de Notre-Dame de Montréal and of Montreal's large degree of autonomy would profoundly alter the reasons for the colony's existence. The arrival of Jean Talon and the Carignan-Salières regiment, which coincided with de Maisonneuve's departure, would assure the survival of Montreal, but not the community of which its founders had dreamed. If the years between 1643 and 1665 were seed-time in Montreal, those seeds were to grow and bear fruit in a world very different from the one envisaged by their planters.

Dollier de Casson characterized 1658–59 as a year when little worthy of record happened in Montreal, but Marguerite, on returning from France, would have observed that some physical changes had taken place during her absence. The Sulpicians had built defensive posts, each of which could house a number of men, at Sainte-Marie and Saint-Gabriel, the two outer limits of the colony. Their construction had provided not only a more secure defence but also work and therefore income for many of the poorer men of Montreal. Dollier says that de la Dauversière had employed a pious stratagem in persuading the Sulpicians that they need bring no workmen with them from France because he knew something of the poverty faced by all the settlers at that time and wished to create employment and income for them. In later years, as economic conditions improved, the men would prefer to work for themselves.[2] Another change was disappointing to Marguerite. After visiting the site of the projected chapel of Notre-Dame-de-Bon-Secours, she wrote, "On my return from France, I found the materials which had been collected for the chapel all scattered."[3]

This time it was Marguerite who brought de Maisonneuve the news from France, while Jeanne Mance, too ill to travel, remained with the rest of the recruitment at Quebec. There, difficulties were to continue for the unfortunate passengers of the *Saint-André* as they unintentionally carried a scourge to the tiny capital. Father de Quen, superior of the Jesuits, who had carefully recorded the arrival of the ship on 7 September, hurried at once to greet Jeanne Mance and the Hospitallers who accompanied her and to bring them fresh food. As a result of this visit, he himself contracted the plague, of which he died on 8 October. Nor was he alone; the contagion was to spread to many others in Quebec, and the new bishop was to distinguish himself in the care he offered to those stricken with the disease.[4]

Her weakness prevented Jeanne from doing anything to help the Hospitallers during those early days at Quebec. Fortunately, they demonstrated from the beginning that they could look after themselves. They sought out Bishop Laval at once and, despite his earlier threats, were received with great kindness. He urged them to visit the Quebec Hospitallers and then to accept an invitation from the Ursulines to stay in their convent; however, he would not give them permission to go to Montreal. Instead, they were subject to immense pressure both from the bishop and from the Jesuits either to sever connections with their own community and join the Hospitallers of Quebec or to return to France. Much of the bishop's lack of enthusiasm for their establishment in Montreal was the result of his determination to centralize the church in Canada. Lanctot suggests that he was also suspicious of the Rule of the Hospitallers of La Flèche because it had been written by a layman, de la Dauversière, and a married layman at that. A more likely concern of the bishop was that this community still made only simple vows and had not yet adopted a specific religious habit.[5] Moreover, as indicated in the previous chapter, the uncertainty surrounding this very new community might have given the bishop pause without any particular prejudice on his part.

But the newly arrived Hospitallers were no more to be discouraged than de Maisonneuve had been in 1641. The heroic terms in which Marie Morin describes their response is reminiscent of his famous refusal to be deterred from his mission by the warnings he received at Quebec. "They did not listen to these speeches for a moment. The superior, who was a true Judith in her courage and fidelity, replied for her companions, whom she knew to be dauntless in their intentions, that they would do neither of these things [join the Quebec Hospitallers or return to France]."[6] Eventually it was Bishop Laval who yielded. On 2 October he accorded the three sisters permission to take up their work in Montreal, but warned them that they could never hope to be established as a canonical community or receive Canadian-born women as novices.[7] The sisters no doubt decided to leave the future in the hands of God; time would show that their forced delay in the Ursuline convent had won them the admiration of eleven-year-old Marie Morin, a boarding-school pupil who at this time conceived the desire to become a member of their community. Jeanne Mance advised them to leave for Montreal at once, perhaps fearing that the bishop might change his mind, and they promptly did so under the conduct of Father de Vignal. Contrary winds so delayed them that the trip up the St Lawrence took two weeks. As they approached Montreal near the end of the month, they saw in the distance another boat coming towards them. It bore the two Quebec Hospitallers away from Montreal and back to their convent in Quebec.

Nor were these two sisters the only departures from Montreal that year, for important letters had also arrived aboard the *Saint-André*. De Queylus had gone to Quebec in early August, greeted the new bishop, submitted to his authority, and promised to accept no further appointment from the archbishop of Rouen. But when he received two letters, one from the archbishop and another from Louis XIV confirming his powers as vicar general, he sought to have those powers recognized. Unfortunately for him, the king had later changed his mind, and a letter to Governor d'Argenson cancelled the earlier authorization. Bishop Laval had de Queylus served with a later letter. When the *Saint-André* sailed on 22 October, it was the Sulpician and not the Hospitallers of St Joseph who returned to France.

With the arrival of the Hospitallers in Montreal, one of de la Dauversière's dreams for the colony had been realized; the three members of the Holy Family at Nazareth were represented by three different religious groups: Jesus by the Sulpicians, Mary by Marguerite Bourgeoys and her companions, and Joseph by the Hospitallers. Montreal in the autumn of 1659 was described by Governor d'Argenson after his first visit.[8] Its population numbered about 160 men, of whom 50 were heads of families. The settlement consisted of about forty houses so situated as to be able to defend one another in the event of an Iroquois attack. Besides the protection offered by the fort, the settlement was also defended by a redoubt, and a mill had recently been constructed on the Saint-Louis side. Given an influx of 100 new colonists and the consequent necessity of providing housing for them, it is easy to see why Jeanne Mance, on her arrival some three weeks later, found that the quarters for the hospital sisters had not yet been completed.

Now Marguerite could begin in earnest the work for which she had come to New France six years before: the education in her school of the children of Ville-Marie, whose numbers were at last beginning to grow. There is no definite information as to how many children attended the stable-school in the first half of the 1660s, but certain deductions can be made from the census of June 1663.[9] Trudel estimates that there were about thirty pupils in the school conducted by the Congregation in that year.[10] He bases this estimate on the information compiled for that census: there were fifty-three children between the ages of six and twelve in 1663, thirty of them girls. But the number of children in the school may have been considerably higher. Marguerite states that Jeanne Loysel, the first child to survive in Ville-Marie, was entrusted to her at the age of four and a half.[11] There is no explanation as to why she took charge of such a young child. As Jeanne was born in July 1649, she must have come to Marguerite soon after the latter's arrival at the end of 1653. Other mothers later might have been relieved to send their children to school at a young age. When the eldest of the Barbier children was drowned in February 1657 at the age of five and a half, there were four younger children at home, a fifth, one of twin girls, having died at the age of two days. Women in such a situation might have been only too glad to entrust their children to the safety of the school as early as possible.

The passage in Marguerite's writings that refers to Jeanne Loysel as the first child to survive in Montreal and Jean Desroches as the second has traditionally been interpreted in the Congregation as implying that he too became a pupil.[12] Whatever the original intentions of the Sulpicians, the quarrel between de Queylus and Laval and the deaths of two Sulpicians at the hands of the Iroquois prevented them from opening a school for boys until 1668. It is possible that the boys were given religious instruction by Father Souart, who might have prepared them for First Communion at the age of twelve. However, it is generally accepted that both boys and girls attended Montreal's first school until after the middle of the 1660s.[13] At least for a time, the exigencies of pioneer life overrode the rules and usual practices of the Gallican church.

In 1663 there were close to seventy children in Montreal between the ages of five and twelve, more than half of them girls.[14] In addition, the girls may not all have left the school at the time of First Communion, for Marguerite states that Jeanne Loysel stayed until her marriage, and Marguerite Picart, who was living with her at the time of the adoption of the first Marie-des-Neiges, was fourteen when she married the following November.[15] On the other hand, Adrienne Barbier was working at the Hôtel-Dieu at the age of only eleven or twelve.[16] We can at least conclude that there were now a significant number of children to be educated and that their number was growing yearly.

Among these children can be recognized the offspring of families whose names have already become familiar in Marguerite's life. Gilbert Barbier and his wife were now the parents of a flourishing family, as were several of the women who had come with Marguerite in 1653: Michelle Artus, who had married Jean Descarie; Jeanne Rousselière; Marie Lorgeuil, who had married Toussaint Hunault, himself part of the recruitment of 1653; Catherine Hureau;[17] and Catherine Lorion, already three times married and twice widowed. Marie-Marthe Pinson, one of the very few women named in the writings of Marguerite Bourgeoys, who describes her as recruited for Montreal by de la Dauversière himself at the same time as Marie Dumesnil,[18] died in childbirth in January 1663. She left behind two children, a daughter not yet six and a son under two.[19] It is not unlikely that Marguerite cared for one or both children, at least for a time, or that with her knowledge of the families of the colony, she helped to find temporary homes for the children until their father remarried the following November. Several of her godchildren would have been pupils at the stable-school, among them Marguerite Gervaise, daughter of Anne Archambault, who had found a respectable husband in the recruitment of 1653 after the bigamous nature of her first marriage had been discovered. A younger daughter would also have been of school age during these years, and so would Agathe Saint-Père, granddaughter on her mother's side of the only family to settle in Montreal in 1642, whose father and grandfather had perished while roofing the house during the Iroquois raids of 1657. The children of Marie Dumesnil and André Charly were still too young to attend school.[20]

There is no direct information on the curriculum of the school. It is, of course, certain that the children were taught religion and prepared for what was then an act of spiritual coming of age, their First Communion. This would have involved more than simply learning what might be called catechism. It would at that time have been unthinkable in both Catholic and Protestant communities for religion to be a separate "subject" that could be presented, or not, alongside various "secular subjects"; it would rather have permeated everything taught, as it permeated every aspect of life. The world of the Catholic Reformation, in which Marguerite was formed, stressed the necessity of imparting an informed faith, an obligation that would have been taken with great seriousness in a society as devout as that of early Montreal.

The children would also, like the pupils of the Congrégation de Notre-Dame of Troyes, have learned reading and writing,[21] an immense advantage even in a pioneer society.[22] They would also have been taught various skills that would help them to earn their living and make their way in life. The Constitutions given by Pierre Fourier to his community stressed the duty of those who educate the poor to teach them how to support themselves.[23] When the poor could attend school for only a limited time, this duty superseded the responsibility to impart literacy. This was the spirit in which Marguerite had first been formed as a teacher. Many references in her surviving writings bear witness to the importance she assigned to the teaching of what she so often referred to as "honourable work." When she proposed the life of the Virgin Mary as inspiration for her sisters, she pictured a Mary who, even as a young girl in the Temple, taught her companions this honourable work.[24] By the time she established her school, she knew from personal experience the challenges faced in pioneer life, which was at best precarious. She also knew the families well. Consequently, the teaching given in her school was as practical and vitally related to the community she served as she could make it. Trudel has suggested that the school must have been satisfactory to these early Montrealers since, unlike families in Trois-Rivières, none of them at this time sent their daughters to the boarding school of the Ursulines in Quebec.[25]

To picture life in that first Montreal school as resembling life in a modern one or even in the one-room village schools that were familiar in the recent past would be quite inappropriate. The exact number of people who comprised Marguerite Bourgeoy's household at any one time is unknown since no systematic description of it exists. Marguerite Picart, who was living with her at the time of the adoption of Marie-des-Neiges, had married in November 1658.[26] When Marguerite returned from France in 1659 with her first companions, she took Marie-des-Neiges, then approaching two years old, back into her care. Marguerite Maclin, who had been entrusted to her in France, stayed with her until her marriage in October 1662.[27] Jeanne Loysel also continued to live with her until she married in 1666. This list is not inclusive; the names just cited are known because of references in Marguerite's surviving writings, and there were almost certainly others about whom no record has survived. Where, for instance, did the other young women who had come in 1659 live until their marriages? If, as Dollier wrote, Marguerite had made herself their mother from their time aboard ship, they must at least have been frequent visitors. There is direct evidence that some of them must have lived with her, for when one of them died at the hospital in October 1659, the inventory of her goods states that her box was at the house of Marguerite Bourgeoys.[28] Between October and December 1659, four of the women who had arrived that year signed their marriage contracts in the house of the Congregation, as Marguerite's house now began to be designated in official documents.[29]

There must also have been visits from the women and men she had befriended in her previous years in Ville-Marie. Perhaps women such as Madame Thibaudeau, whom she had helped aboard the *Saint-André*, came for consolation in the terrible loss she had experienced on her journey to the New World. Did she also come to confide her hope when she became pregnant and her joy when finally another child was born to her?[30] The parish registers indicate that Marguerite would have been called upon all too frequently to console bereaved parents. The care with which the names and godparents were chosen for children who lived for only a few hours contradicts the view that such losses had no great emotional significance in an age that would have been accustomed to a high rate of infant and child mortality. In August 1663 came the death of Marie-des-Neiges, her own adopted daughter, to which allusion has already been made. It is perhaps a measure of its importance, at least to her, that Dollier de Casson mentions this event in his history, for it happened years before his arrival in Montreal, and he rarely refers to a death unless it was of a prominent person or took place in the battles with the Iroquois. In fact, so blood-soaked are the pages recounting the happenings of these years that the lines about the death of this child stand out in even greater relief.[31]

It must also be remembered that this tumultuous life was all lived in a single room: the ground floor of the former stable, in which Marguerite had caused a fireplace to be installed. The loft above was used as the common sleeping area. Privacy as we know it today would not have existed, and an individual could not even have sought it in the nearby forest since to do so would have been too perilous in the early 1660s. Though the wilderness stretched to their very doors, the inhabitants of Ville-Marie in these years would have suffered a physical confinement more severe than that experienced in a teeming modern city. One must also conclude that any rule of life followed by Marguerite Bourgeoys and her companions at this time must of necessity have been very simple.

In addition, the house of the Congregation served for other public events in Montreal. The formal ceremony of signing a marriage contract, an event of considerable social significance, took place there six times between 1660 and 1663. Often, in addition to the official witnesses, large numbers of guests were invited to join the young couple – as many as thirty-one at one of the gatherings of 1659.[32] Since it was one of the few places in Ville-Marie that could hold a large gathering of people, the house was probably used on other community occasions and, according to Trudel, can at that time be considered a public building.

It must also be remembered that besides teaching the children, caring for the young members of the household, and offering encouragement to the colonists who came to them for help or advice, Marguerite and her companions also found means to support themselves so that their educational work could be offered without charge. Sister Morin writes in her *Annales* that Sister Bourgeoys and her companions worked the greater part of the night in order not to be a burden to anyone and to earn their livelihood.[33] The labour to which she alludes was needlework and laundry. In a world where all clothing was still made by hand and goods imported from the homeland were expensive, where garments were mended and patched until they could serve no more, and where men still so greatly outnumbered women,[34] the Congregation found another way of providing a necessary service to the people of the colony as well as a means of supporting themselves. The contacts made through this work would also have given them a knowledge of the male members of the colony, on which they could draw if asked for advice by the young women who had come to Montreal to marry.

Sister Morin's *Annales* bear witness to the close friendship that existed between the young Congregation de Notre-Dame and their next-door neighbours, the sisters of the Hôtel-Dieu, during these years, and indeed throughout the seventeenth century. Together they began their lives as communities in Montreal, and together they faced the many problems that beset the little colony, whether these came from the elements, the Iroquois raids, the severe poverty, or Bishop Laval. To help furnish the Hospitallers with some income, Barbe de Boullongne, widow of Louis d'Ailleboust, took up residence at the Hôtel-Dieu as a paying guest in 1661. However, her arrival also added to the work of the nuns, for their visitor would require a table separate from their own and from that of the patients in the hospital. They had lost the services of Marie Polo; the servant who had accompanied them from France had married within weeks of her arrival in Montreal.[35] Three other women from France tried out the novitiate of the Hospitallers and were loud in their praise of the sisters' devotion, but left after the briefest of stays.[36] With the advent of Madame d'Ailleboust, the sisters took into their employ Adrienne Barbier, eldest surviving child of the master carpenter, born in August 1652. This girl was so devout and she fitted into the community so well that the sisters hoped that she would join them as a lay member. However, Madame Barbier had other ideas for her daughter. After four years, according to Marie Morin, Adrienne was removed by her mother and married as quickly as possible.[37] But by that time, an aspirant from Quebec had already entered the novitiate.

The story of the dealings between Bishop Laval and the Hospitallers of St Joseph of Montreal seems to suggest that he was not always intransigent, or at least that he found it difficult to remain so in the face of passive resistance by the communities of women. At the time of their arrival in 1659, he had refused the Hospitallers permission to go to Montreal and then, within weeks, had allowed their departure, if somewhat grudgingly. Though he had at that time forbidden them to receive Canadian subjects, he allowed the thirteen-and-a-half-year-old Marie Morin to go up from Quebec to join the Hospitallers in Montreal in August 1662. He still continued to insist that he would not permit her to take the habit and begin her novitiate, but during the winter he sent a letter by one of the native people authorizing her clothing and entry into the novitiate on 19 March

1663, the feast of St Joseph and Marie's fourteenth birthday, therefore the earliest date on which that event was canonically permissible. In fact, Marie's clothing took place next day because the chapel, which also served as the parish church, was in use for the festivities of the saint who was already the patron of Canada.

The information Marie gives about her clothing ceremony underlines the friendship between the Hôtel-Dieu and the Congregation. The three hospital sisters were unable to sing, and so three sisters of the Congregation, Marguerite Bourgeoys, Anne Hioux, and Marie Raisin, sang in their stead, an event that was to forge a special bond between Marie and the Congregation.[38] When she made solemn vows in 1671, she became the first Canadian-born nun in Montreal, a second-generation Canadian on one side, for her mother, Hélène Desportes, was arguably the first white child to survive in the St Lawrence valley. Marie's older brother, Germain Morin, was the first Canadian-born priest.[39]

Bishop Laval made his first pastoral visit to Montreal in August 1660. The duties he performed during his stay included the confirmation of 107 persons, among whose number were de Maisonneuve, Jacques Le Ber, the leading merchant, and Lambert Closse. He also annulled a marriage on the grounds of non-consummation. The groom was supposed to have been cursed by a rejected suitor of the bride.[40] Laval was edified by the austere style of living he found at the house of the Congregation. Years later, Marguerite wrote: "The first visit we had was by Bishop Laval who found it good. He admitted two young women and inspected all our beds which were straw mattresses with a bolster and blankets."[41] The bishop's reaction to the beds seems to have made a considerable impression on Marguerite's mind, for it is mentioned again in her writings in a passage that indicates that the austerity of the early foundation was not an end in itself or even just a matter of necessity: its purpose was charity. Commenting on changes that had taken place in the Congregation and the colony over the years, she recalled: "When Bishop Laval made his first visit to this house, he inspected all our beds and was very pleased to find there only straw mattresses and blankets ... Whatever sheets we could get, were for lending to poor women in their need."[42]

Marguerite gives no other details about the deprivations and austerities of the early days, but some of the conditions described by Marie Morin at the Hôtel-Dieu would exist equally at the Congregation, and indeed among all the ordinary colonists. The staple food was the rough bread that they shared with their workmen. (Marguerite's expression of regret later in the century that her sisters no longer ate the same bread as their workmen implies that at the beginning, in the Congregation too, there was no such distinction.) With the bread, they had fat or lard once a day or sometimes only once in two days, eaten with the vegetables and herbs grown in their own garden and curds of skimmed milk. The price of beef put it beyond the means of the sisters at the hospital; even for the patients it was a rarity. Fresh fish, sometimes received as a gift, eggs, and even stew were feast-day fare. The only fruit served in the dining room was wild plums of such poor quality that Sister Morin says that later in the century they would have been left to rot on the ground. In the early 1660s it was too dangerous to venture out to pick the wild strawberries and raspberries that were to become a common food in later years.

Dinner consisted of "potage," the thick soup made with whatever ingredients were available, and bread, as Marguerite had promised her first companions; supper was bread and milk curds or, as a feast-day treat, pumpkin. (From the beginning, melons and pumpkins grew very plentifully and to a much greater size than in France.) In winter, the meals consisted of a little fat, preserved pumpkin, roots, peas, beans, and salted fish, either eel or sturgeon, in very small quantities during Lent and on fast days. Their only drink, winter and summer, was water from the well. To complain about food was regarded as a great failing. Marie Morin mentions the care that had to be exercised by whichever of the nuns was responsible for seeing that the food was divided equally.[43] Her writings are spoken of patronizingly by some twentieth-century scholars and are sometimes inaccurate as to names and dates, but she conveys a knowledge to social historians that is invaluable and not always to be found in the work of more scholarly commentators of the time. She provides an insight, not found elsewhere, into the concerns of women. The wives and mothers of the colony would have experienced the same difficulties as the nuns in providing meals for their households and in making sure that the food was shared fairly, which may well have meant that they themselves often went without for the sake of their families.

Besides the hardships caused by the scarcity of food and a lack of variety in its nature, the first hospital sisters also suffered severely from the cold. The cold of the region could only be understood by those who had experienced it, says Marie Morin, Canadian-born though she was. For immigrants from France, the suffering must have been intense. There were more than two hundred openings in the walls of the Hôtel-Dieu that could be penetrated by wind and snow. If those two conditions had prevailed during the night, the first task in the morning was to sweep up the snow and shovel it outside. Meals were eaten huddled over the fire so as to be able to cut the bread, which would be as hard as iron; water placed on the table for drinking froze within fifteen minutes, and even the wine kept for the poor became ice.[44] This reference to wine as something kept for the poor, like Marguerite's remarks quoted earlier about the sheets for the poor women, illustrates a point made by Elizabeth Rapley in her study of women and the church in seventeenth-century France: that women tended to keep alive the medieval sense of the poor as an *alter Christus*, another Christ, to be offered the best one could provide.[45]

Marie Morin also furnishes information about doing laundry that is definitely relevant to the lives of those first sisters of the Congregation. The accounts of the parish make it clear that one of the means by which the group earned its living was by doing not only the mending but also the laundering of the linen and vestments used in parish worship.[46] At the Hôtel-Dieu the laundry was washed in a ditch filled with rainwater or melted snow and dried in the attic. This task was performed by Sister Macé at the Hôtel-Dieu; Catherine Crolo did the laundry at the Congregation.[47]

It was a hard and demanding life, and not all of Marguerite's new companions found themselves able to sustain it. Edmée Chastel, whose father had so worried about her that he had caused her to sew gold into her underclothing as a special insurance against second thoughts, found herself unable to continue life in the house of the Congregation. But she did not use her private fund to return to France. Instead she signed a contract to become the servant or companion of the recently widowed Barbe d'Ailleboust, who guaranteed to support and care for Edmée during her own life and to pay her a pension after her death. This arrangement came about when Madame d'Ailleboust, who was also from Champagne, was taking up residence at the Hôtel-Dieu in Montreal. The agreement between the two was signed 3 April 1661, and it states that Marguerite Bourgeoys had given her consent.[48] Since Marguerite wrote that Edmée Chastel revealed the existence of the gold and gave it to her two years after their departure from France, it sounds as though this was done at the time of Edmée's leaving the stable-school and may perhaps have been an act of compensation. The decision to hand over the gold also implies that even though Edmée had not found her place in the Congregation, she was nevertheless determined to remain permanently in New France. (The donation of her goods to her godchildren would have been revoked had she returned to France.)

When Madame d'Ailleboust went to live at the Hôtel-Dieu in

Quebec, Edmée accompanied her and remained there for the rest of
her life. No criticism of the young woman has come down from
Marguerite Bourgeoys, and Marie Morin describes her as "a good
and devout woman," "virtuous," serving Madame d'Ailleboust until
the latter's death, but the annals of the Hôtel-Dieu in Quebec, where
she spent the last years of her life, paint a different picture. The gentle and saintly Madame d'Ailleboust was attended, they say, by "a
chambermaid whose disobliging manners and ill humour demanded
a continual exercise of patience on her part. This woman, even
though she loved her and admired her very much, treated her so
harshly that she sometimes refused her the most necessary of things
with the roughest reproaches."[49] Whether Edmée Chastel always had
a difficult character or was soured by time and disappointment will
probably never be known. If the description of her in the *Annales* of
the Quebec Hôtel-Dieu is at all accurate, it may even be that
Marguerite Bourgeoys and her other companions watched this first
departure from their little group with some relief. Letters written by
Edmée to her relatives and conserved well into the twentieth century might have cast light on these events. Unfortunately, they were in
all likelihood destroyed in the early 1950s.[50]

It was becoming obvious by 1662 that the stable-school and its
attached land were no longer sufficient for the needs of the
Congregation. In that year Marguerite obtained two new pieces of
property. On 6 July that year, she bought from André Charly and his
wife, Marie Dumesnil, a piece of land on which stood a house and a
small barn. The land lay diagonally opposite the school property.[51]
On 25 August she obtained the nineteen arpents that were to be the
beginning of the farm at Pointe-Saint-Charles.[52] Additional land was
needed for growing the crops and pasturing the animals that made
survival possible in the early colony. Both communities of women in
Montreal realized the necessity of setting up their own farms as soon
as possible. Sister Morin writes that when the Hospitallers received
four or five hundred *livres* from the Baron de Fancamp in 1661, they
deprived themselves of everything not absolutely necessary, even the
smallest of pleasures, in order to have farm land cleared and provide
security for their work. It was a security that the community was
enjoying by the time the annalist wrote more than thirty years later.[53]
Marguerite Bourgeoys, also, was taking steps to establish this
resource for her Congregation. Before that, however, the house on the
Charly land was to serve quite another purpose.

Marguerite's memoirs state that a few years after the journey of
1658–59 about seventeen *filles du roi* arrived in Montreal.[54] This commonly used term is extremely difficult to translate since neither

"king's wards" nor "king's girls" adequately conveys the meaning of the French. These were young women sent out from France to marry the colonists. There had earlier been some expectation that the French settlers would intermarry with the native women and produce a hardier offspring more suited to the rigours of the climate. The Ursulines in Quebec had hoped to educate native women for this role, and in 1649 Pierre Boucher, the future governor of Trois-Rivières and founder of Boucherville, had married an Ursuline-educated Huron girl. That marriage had ended with her death in childbirth late the same year, and his second marriage was to one of his own country women.[55] Hopes for finding wives for the settlers among the Amerindian women declined. Prior to 1663 the recruitment of brides for the settlers in Montreal had nothing to do with the royal court. Most of those who came were enlisted by the Société de Notre-Dame and were not therefore *filles du roi*. In his 1952 book, the first major study of the latter group, Gustave Lanctot dealt with the rumour that has reappeared at various times since the seventeenth century: that these women were prostitutes swept from the streets of French cities to the colonies. He presented evidence to show that, unlike certain other French colonies, emigrants to Canada, especially female ones, were carefully chosen, and he argues that the women called the *filles du roi* were respectable and virtuous.[56] However, the old rumour has so persistent a life that serious scholars seem to continue to believe they must address it, along with the much more likely possibility that a number of the women might have been Protestant before their departure from France.[57]

If the story of the Thibaudeau baby was rich in implications for the personality of Marguerite Bourgeoys, the passage in which she describes her response to the coming of these young women is equally rich for what it reveals about her conception of the role of the Congregation in early Montreal and the tension that sometimes existed between the founder and her first companions with regard to the interpretation of that role. "I went to meet them [the young women] at the shore," she wrote, "believing that we must open wide the doors of the Blessed Virgin's house to all young women. Our house was small. We had the little house purchased from Saint Ange put in order; and I lived with them. I had to live there because this was for the establishment of new families. I believe that I did not please the sisters and that I failed to give them the necessary instructions."[58] Marguerite is referring to the house that had been the original home of André Charly and her first "bride" protégée, Marie Dumesnil, who, with a growing family, were now able to move on to more extensive quarters. She herself seems to have taken the initiative in

the reception of the prospective brides of 1663, their need being a sufficient invitation. After the long, uncomfortable, and dangerous journey, it must have been a great relief to the new arrivals to find a friendly face and arms opened in welcome on this remote and unfamiliar shore. In the eyes of its founder, the house of the Congregation was the house of the Blessed Virgin, who had never known the inside of a cloister, and therefore a place of hospitality to all women in need.

As the stable-school was already being put to maximum use, one can sympathize with the dismay of her companions at the thought of accommodating still more inhabitants. Perhaps, too, they felt somewhat like the Ursuline who was to write unfavourably about the *filles du roi* in Quebec later in the decade. The Ursulines had been forced to rent to a group of them a little house close to the monastery, a dwelling that had originally been built for Madame de la Peltrie and then used by native boarders and later by Bishop Laval as a residence. The sister tells her correspondent: "You wouldn't believe the damage that these good creatures do, not counting the fact that they have already set the house on fire two or three times ... We are working as hard as we can to get rid of them."[59] Not everyone shared Marguerite Bourgeoys's insight into the future impact of these latest arrivals in New France. She was able to look at these perhaps not totally prepossessing newcomers and see, not disturbing nuisances, but the future of Canada.

Marguerite was as resourceful here as she was always to be while she guided the Congregation; if the stable-school was too small, the house bought from the Charlys could be adapted. The task of preparing these women for their role in the colony was so important that it required her presence in their midst to help them adjust to their new circumstances. Marguerite's openness was a gesture of human compassion towards a group of young women who must have been at least uncertain and in all probability lonely and frightened, however brash an exterior some may have presented. On their ability to adapt to life in the colony depended not only their own happiness and well-being but also that of the society in which they were to fufil so important a role as wives and mothers. In the time she spent with them, Marguerite presumably initiated them into the innumerable skills necessary to the mistress of a pioneer household, not least among them that of warming a house without burning it down. But even more important, she established a relationship with them. Whatever difficulties they later experienced, they had someone in whom they could confide. She could also introduce them to the women already in the colony who would become their neighbours and perhaps their

friends. In compensating to a degree for the loss of their extended family, she could have helped prevent some of the most serious problems encountered by immigrant women when they are isolated in a strange society.[60] Finally, by providing these women with a congenial temporary home, she relieved the pressure on them to commit themselves too hastily, to marry from the wharf, so to speak, as some of them were supposed to have done at Quebec. In a society where marriage was for life and in a situation where there were no parents to help or advise, it was important to create conditions in which the prospective spouses could make the most enlightened decision possible.

Marguerite's words suggest that initially she was not able to communicate her conviction to her companions. The conflict is similar to that over the Thibaudeau baby aboard the *Saint-André*; she is aware of the wishes of her companions and sympathetic to their difficulties, but cannot abandon her obligation to respond to an obvious human need. Again, she tries to find a way to answer the need without overburdening her companions, to whom she also has duties; she therefore arranges to live with the women in a separate house. Later there are no condemnations or recriminations. "I was not able to make them understand," Marguerite regrets. Underlying that statement is the hopeful belief that if one can make people *understand*, they will respond positively. In the end she must have been successful in convincing her companions of the value of the work, for records indicate that the Congregation continued to receive the *filles du roi* as long as they arrived in New France.

Marguerite and the Congregation were a part of another effort on behalf of the families of Ville-Marie, the organization of the Confraternity of the Holy Family in 1663. In that year, on the afternoon of 5 February, New France experienced a terrible earthquake that was felt from beyond Ville-Marie in the west to Gaspé in the east. There were two immediate aftershocks and then others that made themselves felt for the next seven months. As is often the case in natural disasters of this kind, the earthquake was perceived by many as an expression of the anger of God and a call to repentance. "On Monday at four o'clock in the afternoon," Marguerite observed, "the earthquake began and recurred nine times in nine hours; they [the shocks] were not equal either in duration or in force. Father Chaumonot encouraged [the people] saying that the devil was angry because God would be served. The first quake was so severe that the bell at our door – the only one we have – rang as fast as it could possibly be rung."[61] Records of the time describe the confusion at both Montreal and Quebec.

It seems to have been about then that Madame d'Ailleboust conceived the idea of improving family life in Montreal by promoting
devotion to the Holy Family, and she communicated her desire to
Father Chaumonot, her spiritual director. He suggested the establishment of a Confraternity and enlisted the cooperation of Abbé
Gabriel Souart, Sister Judith de Brésoles, and Marguerite Bourgeoys,
as well as Madame d'Ailleboust, for, he wrote in his biography, "We
would act together."[62] Marguerite refers to the event in her writings
and mentions one other participant, Jeanne Mance.[63] Barbe d'Ailleboust was persuaded by the Jesuits to leave the Hôtel-Dieu in
Montreal and move to Quebec to establish the devotion there.[64] The
two events, the earthquake and the establishment of the confraternity, are presented together here because they seem to be implicitly
connected in most accounts of the period, as though one was a
response to the other. The devotion to the Holy Family was to play so
important a role in French Canada that when Leo XIII extended the
celebration of the feast of the Holy Family to the universal church in
1892, it was to Marguerite Bourgeoys and Bishop Laval that he made
reference.[65]

Life in the stable-school and in Ville-Marie was, like life in all times
and places, experienced in the context of the era, a time that was, in
New France generally and in Ville-Marie in particular, extremely difficult and dangerous. The first school in Montreal, the Congrégation
de Notre-Dame of Montreal, the Hospitallers of St Joseph – all these
came into being during those so-called dreadful years. The brief
peace with the Iroquois was over, and the depredations of the first
half of the 1660s were to make life almost impossible not only in
Montreal but throughout New France. The economy, always fragile,
was on the verge of collapse. The death of de la Dauversière in bank-
ruptcy and the disappearance, through death or defection, of almost
all the early members of the Société de Notre-Dame left the future of
Montreal more and more uncertain. New France continued to be
wracked, not only by the quarrel between Laval and de Queylus, but
also by difficulties between Laval and a succession of governors.
Neither the bishop nor the governors in Quebec had much sympathy
for Montreal. It was a situation in which de Maisonneuve, struggling
to continue his mission in a world that "knew not Joseph," was finally to be destroyed.

By 1660 the Iroquois themselves were facing difficult times. No
longer able to find furs in their own territories, they were turning to
the northern regions of the Ottawa River and the area around the
Great Lakes. This expansion renewed the conflict with their long-
time enemies, now become the native allies of the French. While a

leader such as Garakontié, an Onondaga chief, believed the best future for the Iroquois lay in allying themselves with the French, his was not a view widely shared by his people. In the early days of 1660 a rumour emanated from the Hurons that the Iroquois were preparing a great army to drive the French from Canada once and for all. As such stories had circulated before, this one does not appear to have caused prolonged alarm. Then in May there took place near Montreal an event destined to become one of the great legends in the history of New France: the deaths of Adam Dollard des Ormeaux and sixteen companions at Long Sault. This group had gone out to attack Iroquois returning from their winter hunt. Instead, although later joined by some Huron and Algonquin allies, they were surprised by an overwhelming number of the enemy and perished to a man in the ruined fort in which they had taken up their position or as prisoners of the Iroquois. The event, largely forgotten for more than one hundred years, was raised to the status of heroic myth in the nineteenth century and then became a subject of the hottest and most acrimonious controversy in the twentieth.[66]

Whatever doubts may be raised about Dollard's character, the intentions of the group, and the effects of their stand, there can be none about the immediate effect on the people of Montreal. The death of 17 men in a community where the arrival of the recruitment of 1659 had brought the total number of men to only 160 was a heavy loss indeed, representing, as it did, more than 10 per cent of the male population. What is more, these were all young men, the oldest of them only thirty-one and the rest, with one exception, in their twenties like their leader. None of the men who went on this expedition was married, and so they did not leave families to mourn them, but in the tiny settlement that was Montreal in 1660, all would have been well known. Eight of them would have been very familiar to Marguerite Bourgeoys, for they had come with her in the recruitment of 1653.

The expedition had left Montreal for the last time on 20 April. According to the Jesuit *Relations* the battle began 2 May; those who were not carried off as prisoners were dead by 12 May. News of the catastrophe had certainly been carried to Montreal by escaping Hurons before 25 May, when the notary began to compile inventories of the goods of those killed. The spring of 1660 was a sad time in Montreal. Louis d'Ailleboust, who had planned its first defences and always remained its champion, was dying. His funeral took place on 1 June. On 3 June Abbé Souart drew up death certificates for the seventeen killed at Long Sault. Today it is still a striking experience, as one turns the pages of the parish register, to come upon this great

block of writing, with name after name of the young men dead, their ages at time of death inscribed after their names. Grief and fear were general thoughout the colony. But the Iroquois went off to their own country without any further attack on the French settlements. Whether they did so out of awe that so small a band of Frenchmen could resist with such heroism[67] or simply in fulfilment of their normal custom of going home at once to display their trophies and prisoners,[68] the result was respite for Montreal.

Later in the year, de Maisonneuve returned to the tactic of keeping captured Iroquois as hostages to enable the colonists to reap the harvest. With winter, however, the Iroquois returned, their arrival preceded by the sighting of omens that tell us something of the mood of the people: an earthquake at Montreal, strange voices heard at Trois-Rivières, flaming canoes in the air at Quebec, an unborn child crying in its mother's womb on the Île d'Orléans.[69] Marie de l'Incarnation wrote that in 1661 the Iroquois did more damage than in all the preceding years;[70] along the St Lawrence from Montreal in the west to Cap Tourmente in the east, more than one hundred Frenchmen were killed or captured. In Montreal, thirteen men were lost at the same time in the month of February, and in March ten more, four killed at once and six taken prisoner.[71] It became unsafe to venture away from the fortifications or to till the same field two days in a row. Before the end of the year, both the Sulpicians who had come on the *Saint-André* in 1659 were among the dead.

On 29 August Father Jacques Le Maistre, chaplain of the Hôtel-Dieu and steward of his community, was reading his breviary while he supervised a group of men working in a field at Saint-Gabriel. Suddenly, a party of Iroquois hiding at the edge of the field revealed themselves. When he attempted to defend the men with a cutlass, the Iroquois leader shot him, but the priest's action permitted all but one of his party to reach safety in the house at Saint-Gabriel. Before fleeing, the Iroquois beheaded Le Maistre and wrapped his head in a handkerchief, which they bore back with them to their people. This was the beginning of the legend about his features having become imprinted on the handkerchief.[72] They also stripped the priest of his cassock, put it on, and capered about in a parody of Christian liturgical ceremonial. At the same time, some of the attacking party are supposed to have expressed regret because they recognized in their victim the man who, as steward, had provided them with food on previous visits to Montreal.

Less than two months later, Father Guillaume Vignal was also to perish. The Sulpicians had begun to build their first Montreal residence, and on 25 October, Vignal wanted to go with a party of men to a small nearby island to gather stone. De Maisonneuve was reluctant to permit this excursion because the men had worked there the day before and to return would violate his strategy of not labouring at the same site on successive days. However, at the insistence of Vignal, he grudgingly gave his consent, but detailed Claude de Brigeac to go with the work party to offer them protection. De Brigeac was a young soldier who had come on the *Saint-André* and had been appointed de Maisonneuve's secretary. The party left so expeditiously that he was unable to catch up with them. So intent was Vignal on his purpose that, although one of the men warned him that he thought canoes had been sighted, the Sulpician insisted it must have been a moose. On landing, and contrary to the directives constantly given the colonists, the men left their firearms aside and, according to Dollier, walked about stretching their arms and legs after the cramped boat ride. When they were set upon by a party of Iroquois uttering war whoops, they scattered in confusion. In vain did de Brigeac, just landing, shout to them to rally; he was left to face the enemy alone. This he did successfully for long enough to permit many of the French to escape. As the Iroquois advanced upon him, de Brigeac shot and killed their leader, but after receiving a wound in the right arm, he himself became a captive. Father Vignal, in attempting to get into the boat of René Cuillerier, accidentally wetted his rescuer's musket, thus rendering it useless. The priest was shot several times, and both men taken prisoner.

As the Iroquois started back towards their own territory, Vignal called out in apology and encouragement to the other prisoners. The priest's condition was such that his captors decided that he would not survive the journey, so he was burned alive at once and his flesh consumed. Of de Brigeac, however, his captors took great care. He was with them for some time recovering from his wounds and was even able to get a letter to Father Simon Le Moyne, who was working among the Iroquois at this time. In it, he pleads for his own rescue and for that of Cuillerier, but says that if this does not prove possible, the two have already offered their deaths to God for the conversion of their captors.[73] After he was somewhat recovered, de Brigeac was killed at the end of a day of ritual torture, which he bore with great courage and forbearance. When Marguerite wrote of the 1660s many years later, it was this young man whose name and whose death she remembered.[74] Cuillerier was eventually to escape, reach the Dutch colony, and so get back to Montreal and tell the tale.[75]

But the most serious loss to Montreal was yet to come: on 7 February 1662 Lambert Closse, the town major, was killed. As he went to the defence of colonists who had been attacked by a party of

Iroquois, he was deserted by one of his two servants and was shot as he attempted to reload his pistols.[76] His death was a terrible blow to a colony whose most reliable defender he had been since its earliest days. He left a young widow, who had already lost both parents to the Iroquois, and one young daughter – his first child, born in 1658, had lived only a day. And still the raids continued. Peace agreements accepted by three of the five Iroquois nations would be rejected by the other two.

Again it is Marie Morin, postulant and novice at the Hôtel-Dieu during these years, who gives the most vivid account of life in Montreal at this time. At the first notice of an Iroquois attack, an alarm bell was rung to send all the able-bodied men to the support of those facing the enemy. The multiplication of areas of defence – the fact that the extremes of the settlement had now to be defended as well as the central fort – made the task more difficult than it had been before any expansion. At the Hôtel-Dieu, Sisters Marie Maillet and Catherine Macé would repair in terror to a corner of the chapel gallery to prepare themselves for death in the presence of the Blessed Sacrament. Sister Judith de Brésoles, made of sterner stuff, continued, despite her fear, to care for the sick and attend to any wounded who were brought in. (Sister Macé, and not Judith de Brésoles, had been the first choice of de la Dauversière as superior. Her replacement by Sister de Brésoles after she had insisted on her unsuitability seems, in the light of later events, to have been a wise decision.)[77] Often Marie Morin went up with Sister de Brésoles to ring the alarm so as to free another man to take part at once in the fighting. There they would sometimes stay to watch the battle from above, often fearing, if the French were hard-pressed, that their last day had really come, sometimes taking pride in the courage and generosity of their countrymen, ready to risk their lives for one another. And it was not just the men who fought. Marie says, "Even the women, like Amazons, ran out [into the fight] armed like the men."[78] In the midst of the fray the priests moved about their task, to aid the wounded and to offer whatever last rites they could to the dying.

When the fighting was finished, Marie would return to Sisters Maillet and Macé to console them and to tell them that, for this time at least, the immediate danger was over, "which restored them to life."[79] If this was the scene at the hospital, what must it have been for the children in the stable-school and for their teachers, called on to console and encourage some of them and perhaps dampen the enthusiasm of others to get into the fight? Even at night there was no safety, and the purpose of the removable ladder that led to the sleeping quarters of the stable-school becomes apparent. Frequently, says

Sister Morin, the Iroquois lay hidden in the long brush around the Hôtel-Dieu, the residence of Jeanne Mance, and the house of the Congregation next door, waiting to make short work of anyone so foolhardy as to leave any of these buildings during the hours of darkness.

Obviously, these conditions played havoc with the attempts of the colonists to carry on even subsistence farming. The harassment that prevented Montrealers from realizing even half their usual planting or harvest in 1661 brought the threat of famine the following year. Only the arrival of a shipment of grain from Quebec, paid for by Madame de la Peltrie, the Jesuits, and Bishop Laval, prevented widespread hunger.[80] De Maisonneuve introduced a special new land policy to help keep colonists in Ville-Marie.[81] He also organized in 1663 the Militia of the Blessed Virgin, mentioned by Marguerite Bourgeoys in her writings,[82] a voluntary military force that operated in groups of seven for the defence of the colony and was supported in its dedication by ceremonial acts of piety.[83]

Continual harassment by the Iroquois dealt the fragile economy of New France an even more crippling blow when it prevented the furs obtained through native allies from reaching the St Lawrence and ultimately the market in Europe. Furs were still the only commodity that could be used to obtain from the home country those goods essential to the survival of New France. In 1659 not a single canoe of furs had been able to get down the river from the Great Lakes. One result of the exploit of Dollard and his companions at Long Sault was that the diversion of the Iroquois made it possible for traders Des Groseilliers and Radisson to reach Montreal by the Ottawa River route in 1660 with furs worth 20,000 *livres*. Immediately afterwards the routes were again closed.[84] The depressed fur market in France was a cause of further economic difficulties. The Communauté des Habitants, which bought the furs and sold trade goods to the people of New France, found itself at loggerheads both with the people of the colony and with the Cent-Associés, its parent company in France. Trouble came to a head in Montreal when the Communauté des Habitants attempted to set up its own warehouse in Montreal in July 1662. The outcry was so strong that the *Journal des Jesuites* used the word *sédition* to describe the action, and one of Montreal's most prominent citizens, Jacques Le Ber, was arrested and his property seized. When de Maisonneuve attempted to go to France to remonstrate about the difficulties, he was stopped at Quebec by Governor Davaugour and ordered to return to Ville-Marie to prepare for an inquiry.[85] It was increasingly obvious that something must be done about the economic and defence problems of New France.

Montreal also faced dilemmas that were uniquely its own. The coming of the ships from France in 1660 had brought bad news: on 6 November 1659 Jérôme de la Dauversière had died at the age of sixty-three. At the time of his death his financial affairs were in considerable disorder. The 22,000 *livres* donated by Madame de Bullion for the maintenance of the hospital sisters and handed over to him for investment by Jeanne Mance before her departure for Canada the previous spring had not been separated from his own property. It was therefore seized by his creditors; the Hospitallers were without a foundation. Again they were under immense pressure to join the Hospitallers of Quebec, pressure that only the support and defence of de Maisonneuve prevented from overwhelming them.[86] But the death of de la Dauversière, following on that of Olier, also meant that the Société de Notre-Dame de Montréal had lost an indefatigable and devoted leader. Scarcely any of the earliest members now remained.[87] De Queylus, a man with considerable personal wealth, which he wished to use in the service of Ville-Marie, was still under the cloud caused by his continuing battle with Bishop Laval, for during these dangerous and anxious days for New France, the colony continued to be racked by ecclesiastical conflict.

Bishop Laval had come to New France with the intention of bringing order to the ecclesiastical affairs of the colony, with a clear vision of what he intended to accomplish, and with the will to make that vision a reality. Courageous, totally sincere, ascetic in his personal life, dedicated to the poor, he was also a man of aristocratic spirit and strong convictions, a man who had little tolerance for views and intentions that diverged from his own.[88] Marie de l'Incarnation says that Laval was "zealous and inflexible," "a man of very great piety, [who] when once he is persuaded that he is proceeding for the glory of God will never turn back."[89] Like many men of his type, the bishop may sometimes have had difficulty distinguishing the will of God from the will of François de Montmorency Laval and the glory of God from the glory of the hierarchy of the church.

Not content with routing de Queylus in 1659, Laval in February of the following year, obtained a *lettre de cachet* forbidding the Sulpician from returning to Canada. De Queylus, supported by the Société de Notre-Dame de Montréal, secured papal bulls erecting Ville-Marie into a parish independent of the vicar apostolic (Laval), the incumbent to be presented by the superior of Saint-Sulpice and appointed by the archbishop of Rouen.[90] The archbishop then appointed de Queylus parish priest of Montreal. Laval was astonished when the Sulpician appeared in Quebec with these documents on 3 August 1661. His arrival was doubly surprising because he had transferred to

a small boat at Percé and reached Quebec before the ship that had
carried him from France. In spite of the fact that Laval forbade him to
go to Montreal on pain of suspension from his priestly duties, de
Queylus slipped off there by canoe during the night of 5–6 August.
However, the arrival of a new governor in Quebec with orders from
Louis XIV for the immediate return of de Queylus to France resulted
in the departure of the Sulpician on 22 October 1661. The question of
ecclesiastical jurisdiction in New France was really over at this point.
As Archbishop Harlay of Rouen moved on to become archbishop of
Paris, his interest was transferred elsewhere. It was to be some years
before de Queylus would see Canada again.

During his first years in New France, Laval was engaged not only
in establishing claim to ecclesiastical jurisdiction but also in asserting
the role of the hierarchy of the Church in relation to the civil power.
His relationship with the governors and, after 1663, with the
Sovereign Council during the years of his mandate was more com-
plex than some recent historians have allowed.[91] Conflicts about the
placing of a prie-dieu in church, the order in which Holy
Communion might be received on feasts, the ranks in a procession –
all these matters may appear petty to a modern reader. Of course,
what was really at issue were the more important realities of which
these things were symbols. These and other quarrels like them in seventeenth-century New France show us how untypical of her time
Marguerite Bourgeoys really was when, a few decades later, she
was to insist on the equality of all the sisters in her community and
to refuse all external honours for her Congregation – special recognition in church, special sacramentals, and so on.[92] Her understanding
of Jesus' frequent admonitions to his apostles to seek the last rather
than the first place, to serve rather than lord it over others, and his
condemnation of the exhibitionism of the Pharisees was not universally shared in a society frequently obsessed with questions of prece-
dence.

In 1661 Governor d'Argenson, exhausted by quarrels within the
colony and his failure to induce the French government to send
troops for the defence of New France, asked to be recalled on the plea
of ill health. He was replaced by the Baron Pierre Dubois Davaugour,
who again was initally very friendly towards Laval and even
appointed the Jesuit Paul Ragueneau to the head of the General
Council at Quebec. Soon, however, the old conflicts arose and in this
case became especially bitter on the question of the sale or trading
of liquor with the native population. This was to be a vexed issue
for many decades to come, but one on which all the ecclesiastical
authorities agreed. Whatever else their differences, they opposed the

brandy trade, and in this were generally supported by the native chiefs. However, civil officials often saw the prohibition as giving an unfair economic advantage to the Dutch and English, who had no such scruples.

It was beginning to seem obvious, even to ecclesiastical authorities whose first priority was the evangelization of the native population, that New France needed better military defence. It was only slowly and with great regret that the Jesuits were led to accept the inevitability of a military solution.[93] Now plea after plea had been made to the home country by both civil and ecclesiastical leaders. A reader of the accounts of various battles between colonists and the Iroquois in Dollier de Casson's history finds the former professional soldier frequently castigating what he sees as the ineptitude and sometimes the cowardice of his own side. But the colonists he criticizes were not professional soldiers; they were men who came to Canada to wield the spade and the plow, not the sword and the musket. The authorities in New France, both civil and ecclesiastical, were increasingly convinced that the colony stood in need of professional soldiers, especially if the conflict with the Iroquois was ever to be resolved, rather than continue indefinitely as a defensive war of attrition. The French would themselves have to go out and guarantee the safety of their native allies. While they confined themselves simply to the defence of the French settlements, they would never win the respect of the Iroquois, especially the Mohawks. But the colony did not just need regiments; it needed a complete reorganization. On 12 August 1662 Bishop Laval and Father Ragueneau left to present its case in France. (The governor's secretary immediately followed them to protect Governor Davaugour's interests.) The results of this voyage would transform New France.

Louis XIV was just attaining his majority and beginning his direct rule. His minister, Colbert, was inclining him towards a new colonial policy. When Laval returned to Quebec in 1663, he had accomplished the recall of Governor Davaugour and was accompanied by a governor in whose selection he had himself had a voice, Augustin de Saffray de Mézy. The lands of the Cent-Associés were turned over to the king, and the fiefs they had granted abolished, and their seigneury, reunited under the crown, became a province with a dual government, a governor as the military authority and an intendant as the civil one. The Sovereign Council created to rule the province was headed by the governor and the vicar apostolic, who named the other members by mutual agreement. The king requested Rome to raise the apostolic vicariate to a bishopric.

For many years Laval was to be a centre of power in New France.

Gustav Lanctot has remarked that this is scarcely surprising in the century of Richelieu and Mazarin.[94] However, there were great differences between Laval and the two cardinals. There can be no doubt that Bishop Laval always worked for what he perceived to be the good of the church, and one cannot imagine either of the cardinals accepting the asceticism, the denial of worldly ambition, and the sacrifice of personal comfort that were characteristic of him. It must also be remembered that, in part, church leaders were often called on to play a role in the secular government of New France because they usually had considerably more experience and knowledge of the country than bureaucrats or fortune seekers who arrived from the homeland, and they were, in many cases, more capable men. During the next few years, New France was finally to move out of the state that Marcel Trudel has described as stagnation, the period when the colony had constantly lived on the verge of military and economic ruin. Laval also brought back the promise of a regiment for the defence of New France, a new state policy to encourage settlement, and the revitalization of trade through the creation of a new commercial organization.[95] But the new provisions for the colony destroyed the earlier autonomy of Montreal, which was now integrated into the general structure. Nor was this the only profound change in the status of Montreal.

Jeanne Mance had left for France a little over a month after Laval to attend to the financial affairs of the Hospitallers. Because de Maisonneuve had been prevented from making the voyage, it was also her responsibility to speak for the welfare of the whole of Ville-Marie. On her arrival in Paris she found that, apart from the Sulpicians, there were only two of the original members of the Société de Notre-Dame de Montréal left in France. The financial affairs of the group were in such a sorry state that she did not feel herself able to press for funds for the Hospitallers in Montreal. The solution to the problems of the debt-laden association seemed to lie in the transference of responsibility for the little colony from the almost defunct society to the Sulpician community, whose late founder had been one of the originators of the project and whose members had from the beginning played a vital part. A number of the first Sulpicians had been men of considerable inherited wealth. The members of the community did not renounce their goods by a vow of poverty, but instead many of them devoted their personal fortunes to the support of projects in which the community was engaged. The remaining members of the Société de Notre-Dame unanimously consented to cede the island of Montreal to the Messieurs de Saint-Sulpice. Jeanne Mance and de Maisonneuve were among the remaining members who acceded to this change, which suggests that they had discussed this possibility before Jeanne's departure from Canada.

The act of cession was signed on 9 March 1663.[96] But for some weeks the fate of Montreal still hung in the balance. To assume such a heavy responsibility, to take on a colony already so laden with debt, would place considerable strain on the resources of a community founded as recently as was the Messieurs de Saint-Sulpice. It was a responsibility the Sulpicians were hesitant to assume if they could not count on the presence in Montreal of the Abbé de Queylus, whose fortune and organizing abilities they saw as essential to the survival and maintenance of the Canadian colony. Approaches were made to Bishop Laval, but he proved intransigent in the face of all overtures and pleas. Only after prolonged prayer did the Sulpicians finally accept Montreal at the end of the month.[97] On 18 August of the same year they took formal possession of the island.[98] The Sulpicians became seigneurs of the island of Montreal in an agreement that guaranteed for life the positions of both Jeanne Mance and de Maisonneuve.

In Canada, however, the fate of Montreal was now largely in the hands of a governor and a bishop who regarded the colony with some suspicion, if not hostility. From the beginning, Montreal had inspired little sympathy in Quebec, where it was perceived as, at best, a drain on resources from the centre and, at worst, a dangerous rival whose location gave it an advantage in the fur trade. For Laval, Montreal was associated with his quarrel with de Queylus. Two of its founders, de Maisonneuve and Jeanne Mance, lay people though they were, were protecting the Hospitallers, whom he wished to unite with the Quebec hospital sisters.[99] In the Sulpicians, the Jesuits saw a negation of their monopoly on the Canadian missions. When the Sulpicians took over as seigneurs of Montreal, they were denied the customary right already exercised there of administering seigneurial justice.[100] Instead, at the end of September 1663 Governor de Mézy and Bishop Laval set up a system of royal justice in Montreal, naming a judge, a procurator, and a notary. Their decision was confirmed in October by the Sovereign Council in Quebec, which they had appointed. The Montrealers saw this action as a violation of the rights conferred from the beginning on the Société de Notre-Dame de Montréal and transmitted to the new seigneurs. Its consequence was, of course, the undermining of the authority of de Maisonneuve as governor of Montreal.

From the point of view of Montrealers, worse was yet to come. When Souart and de Maisonneuve went to Quebec to object to the proceedings just described, de Mézy signed a document acknowl-

edging de Maisonneuve's valour, experience, and wisdom and naming him governor of Montreal as long as he, de Mézy, judged him
useful to the king's service.[101] The implication of such a document
was, of course, that the governor of Quebec and not the Sulpicians
had the right to name the governor of Montreal. When the Sulpicians
protested these violations of their rights, they were ordered to present their documentation to the Sovereign Council. After the
unavoidable delay occasioned by the necessity of applying to France,
copies of the required documents were presented to the Council, but
it now demanded the originals. De Bretonvilliers, unwilling to
entrust such precious documents to the perils of the sea, had to resort
to court in France to compel the Sovereign Council to accept notarized copies, and the dispute dragged on until the autumn of 1666. By
that time, de Mézy would be dead and de Maisonneuve forever gone
from New France, so that it was simply the supression of the royal
court at Montreal that was requested and received.[102] In the mean-
time, what Montrealers saw as a campaign of harassment, the next
step was for de Mézy to assume the right to appoint an interim com-
mandant in Montreal in the event of the absence of de Maisonneuve.
He then apparently attempted to bring about his absence, though
without success.[103]

Besides the attacks on de Maisonneuve, Montreal saw itself as
undermined in other ways. When the king sent out new colonists in
the autumn of 1663, only ten were allotted to Montreal. More serious
and direct economic damage was threatened when, in July the following year, the Sovereign Council forbade all merchants from
France from transporting any of their goods out of Quebec for thirty
days beginning eight days after their arrival. Even then, they were
not allowed to take more than one-quarter of their wares to Montreal
or Trois-Rivières. Montrealers could come to Quebec to buy, but must
furnish the Council with declarations as to the nature and quantity of
any purchases. Again, this regulation was a violation of a royal right
granted to the Société de Notre-Dame de Montréal, that of importing
goods from France directly without interference from Quebec. The
tendency of the measure was to give Quebec the opportunity to
remove all the choicest merchandise and even to establish a quasi-
monopoly on certain goods.

In 1664 Bishop Laval arrived in Montreal on his second pastoral
visit. Auditing the accounts of the Hôtel-Dieu, he demanded restitution of the 22,000 *livres* donated by Madame de Bullion and given by
Jeanne Mance to de Maisonneuve to help finance the recruitment that
had saved the colony from extinction in 1653. Laval demanded to see
the consent of Madame de Bullion to this transaction in writing and

said that, since he did not regard the land grant given in exchange as having equal value, the land and the money should be returned. As Madame de Bullion had never allowed her name to be used in connection with her bounty to Montreal, it was impossible to produce anything from the past in writing, nor could she be applied to because she had died on 3 July 1664. Both de Maisonneuve and Jeanne Mance affirmed their integrity in the matter and pointed to the essential use to which the money had been put, but the bishop continued to demand the restitution of the 22,000 *livres*. Even after the King's Council in Paris had ruled against the bishop's claim in 1667, he continued to pursue it. The fact that the matter was not set to rest until it was dismissed by Laval's successor in 1695, long after the deaths of both de Maisonneuve and Jeanne Mance, is convincing evidence of the implacability of Bishop Laval on this question.[104]

This was the period described by Marie Morin in her *Annales* when de Maisonneuve came so often to Marguerite Bourgeoys, Judith de Brésoles, and the Abbé Souart, the parish priest, to seek relief from his trials in laughter.[105] It is not to be supposed that the usual worries of the colony were suspended at this time. Even though the Iroquois, with the exception of the Mohawks, were beginning to sue for peace, this was still a time when any man working outside the fort was at risk. In the summer of 1665 Charles Le Moyne himself was taken prisoner and carried off by the Mohicans, and there was little hope of his safe return.[106] In these last trying years, as he had done in the fracas over his name-day in 1642, de Maisonneuve donned the armour of comradeship and laughter. It is refreshing to see these first Montrealers joyful in the face of adversity and to know that if they often sowed in tears, they sowed in mirth too. Marie Morin tells another anecdote about this period. De Maisonneuve, she says, asked to examine a habit belonging to one of the Hospitallers, themselves so desperately poor at this time, and made the whole group laugh at the fact that the garment was so mended that it was impossible to determine the original material.[107] But it was no longer 1642, and this time, Montrealers would not remain masters of their place.

In 1664, as had been the case with former governors, difficulties arose between de Mézy and other members of the Sovereign Council, including Laval. The bishop and de Mézy were only reconciled when the latter became dangerously ill. The governor died in May 1665, before the ships from France could arrive with orders for his recall to undergo investigation in the home country, and his private papers, which might have presented his side of the dispute with Laval, were destroyed. In June there arrived at Quebec General de Tracy with the long-awaited French troops who were to deliver New France from fear of the Iroquois. They were to achieve this largely by their very presence in Canada and with scarcely any bloodshed on either side. De Tracy was received with all possible pomp and honour by Bishop Laval, to whom he appears to have given complete confidence in the fulfilment of a mission to regulate the ecclesiastical disputes in Canada.

These events marked the end of the career of Paul de Chomedey de Maisonneuve. He was "permitted" to return to France "to settle his personal affairs." In his biography, Lanctot interprets this directive as an order to go and attend to the matter of the 22,000 *livres* and sees Bishop Laval as the moving force behind it.[108] Desrosiers sees it, rather, as the work of all the elements in Quebec hostile to Montreal.[109] The many historians whose sympathies are not particularly involved with Montreal view it simply as an inevitable development in the growth and organization of New France. When he sailed from Quebec in October 1665, de Maisonneuve had given twenty-five years of his life to Montreal, twenty-four since its foundation. He was never to return to New France, though he remained nominal governor until 1668.

The people he left behind in Montreal seem to have had a presentiment of the fact that this was his final departure, for his going was a source of great grief in the settlement and of deep indignation that a man who had served the colony so selflessly should receive such shabby treatment. Dollier de Casson says that the more clear-sighted felt a great deal of bitterness "when they saw their father and most dear governor, M. de Maisonneuve, leave them this time for good, and leave them in the hands of others from whom they could not expect the same disinterestedness, the same affection and the same regard for the exclusion of vices which have, in fact, risen and grown here since that time, along with many other troubles and misfortunes which had not up to that time made their appearance here."[110] Marie Morin says that de Maisonneuve was removed from his post of governor as incapable, something she could not have believed had she not been told so by Marguerite Bourgeoys herself.[111] Lanctot and Desrosiers both reject the idea that the governor was officially removed. Lanctot believed that Sister Morin must have misunderstood Marguerite Bourgeoys; after all, de Maisonneuve continued as governor until his voluntary resignation, and only after that was a new governor named. But if Marie Morin is wrong about the official facts, she is faithful to the underlying implications and to the feelings of Marguerite and probably de Maisonneuve himself about the circumstances of his departure. After this, Marguerite can have retained few illusions about either ecclesiastical or civil authority.

Because it coincided with events that permanently altered the course of the city's history, the departure of de Maisonneuve closed what used to be called the heroic era of Montreal. He left behind a permanent achievement. As Lanctot points out in his summary of the governor's accomplishments, by 1665 Montreal contained all the institutions necessary to an autonomous, growing community: civil and military government with a garrison and militia, popular representation in the persons of an elected syndic and police judges,[112] a parish church and secular clergy, a seigneural court and land registry, a public school and hospital.[113] Unlike many other colonial administrators in New France, de Maisonneuve did not reward himself materially at the expense of the colony. Dollier was to comment ironically about the departure in 1668 of the soldiers who had arrived three years earlier: "After having been here three years against the Iroquois, part of them went back home loaded with their spoils, which since then they have exchanged for good louis d'or and silver which have not the odour of furs, a transmutation which M. de Maisonneuve was never able to learn."[114] The governor's parting gesture was to make over to the Hôtel-Dieu 6,000 *livres* owed him at the store.[115] His last thoughts would be of Montreal. In his will, dictated on 8 September 1676, the day before his death, the first and largest legatee was Marguerite Bourgeoys and her Congrégation de Notre-Dame of Montréal and the second largest, the Hospitallers of St Joseph of Montreal.[116]

Although she remained in Montreal, the active role of Jeanne Mance in its history was now largely over. Her health would be poor during the eight years of life that remained to her, years spent in the shadow of the affair of the 22,000 *livres*, in which she had played a major role. There was, of course, no place for her in the administration of the new Montreal, although Dollier de Casson makes it clear that she continued to be highly respected by at least some of the Sulpicians. Yet her actions had helped ensure the survival of the little settlement in some of its most difficult moments, and she had succeeded in establishing the sisters from the community founded by Jérôme de la Dauversière at the Hôtel-Dieu. If, in the end, she had jeopardized their financial stability, they were demonstrating that they could cope for themselves.

By 1665 Marguerite Bourgeoys, too, had accomplished the purposes for which she had come to Montreal. The first of these was to establish a school for the children. This she had done, and although the stable-school would eventually be replaced by larger and more commodious quarters, it was always to have the first place in her heart and in her memory. She had also laid the foundations of what would be a long-term commitment on the part of her community to preparing women for their role in pioneer society and offering them support in the fulfilment of that role. She had made provision for the continuance and stability of these services to Montreal by finding the means to finance them and creating a group of women committed to carrying them on, so that their survival did not depend on her alone. She had also fulfilled the dream that was more tenuous when she left France: that of gathering together a group of women who would live in community in the midst of society, without cloister, wimple, or veil, taking as their inspiration the life of the Virgin Mary, especially her activity in the post-Resurrection church. Unlike the two women with whom she had earlier attempted to found such a community in Troyes, the three who remained from 1659 were there to stay.[117] Official legal recognition of this group was still several years in the future,[118] and eccesiastical approbation would not come until the end of the century (1698). But the people of Montreal recognized its existence; from June 1662 on, "la Congrégation" figures regularly in civil and religious documents.[119]

It is deeply ironic that the missionary work for which Montreal had been founded, in which so little progress had been made before 1665, was to become possible just when the role of the settlement was altering profoundly. The Carignan-Salières regiment brought about peace with the Iroquois. However, the members who stayed on in Montreal as settlers were part of a new influx of population that had no connection with the recruiting efforts of the now-defunct Société de Notre-Dame de Montréal. The peace that made feasible the evangelization of the native people also encouraged the development of the fur trade on a scale not possible in the earlier period. The location of Montreal at the confluence of the St Lawrence and Ottawa rivers, chosen originally for its missionary possiblities, was to make it the economic centre of Canada. From the island, explorers would soon venture as far as the Gulf of Mexico. The Montreal that had had its roots in faith and sacrifice was to be an exciting place in later decades of the seventeenth century, but it was not to be the place its founders had envisaged.

Of course, the efforts of the founders were not wasted or futile. Marguerite Bourgeoys was the only one of the Montreal leaders from the period before 1665 to remain active in the later decades of the seventeenth century. During these early years, she had experienced the kind of friendship that can only come from the sharing of a great dream. Now she would transform that dream.

The human vision of helping to create an ideal society is perennial, though it manifests itself much more powerfully in some eras than in others. Inevitably, the dreamer must eventually contemplate the apparent failure of that dream. On the other side of the Atlantic in the 1660s, another man whose vision of an ideal Christian society and the means of achieving that end were quite different from those of the founders of Montreal was also trying to come to terms with apparent failure: out of his experience of frustration and disappointment, John Milton was composing his great epics. But temperamentally and philosophically, Marguerite Bourgeoys would have had more in common with another Englishman who, more than a century earlier, had reflected on the possibility of an ideal society. In the first book of his *Utopia* Thomas More had written:

If evil opinions cannot be quite rooted out, and if you cannot correct habitual attitudes as you wish, you must not therefore abandon the commonwealth. Don't give up the ship in a storm, because you cannot control the winds. And do not force unheard-of advice upon people, when you know that their minds are different from yours. You must strive to guide policy indirectly, so that you make the best of things, and what you cannot turn to good, you can at least make less bad. For it is impossible to do all things well unless all men are good, and this I do not expect to see for a long time.[120]

Just so; Marguerite Bourgeoys would not abandon Montreal but would adapt herself to different conditions, needs, and minds as the century progressed. Though she was never to diminish her commitment to Montreal, she would respond to the educational demands of a changing and expanding New France.[121] And if the ideal of the primitive Christian church that Montreal had been intended to embody could not be preserved for the whole of society, there was one place where Marguerite would try to keep the flame alive. That place was among the sisters of her Congregation, to whom in later years she addressed these words, testimony to her continued fidelity to the vision that had inspired the founding of Montreal: "O my dear sisters, let us revive at least among ourselves the true spirit of cordiality and love which formed the glory and beatitude of the first Christians."[122]

Notes

AA   Archives de l'Aube (France)

ACMB   Archives du Centre Marguerite-Bourgeoys

ACND   Archives de la Congrégation de Notre-Dame de Montréal

AHDM   Archives de l'Hôtel-Dieu de Montréal

AJM   Archives Judiciaires de Montréal

CMB   *Courrier Marguerite-Bourgeoys*

DCB   *Dictionary of Canadian Biography*

DdeC   Dollier de Casson, *A History of Montreal*, trans. and ed. Ralph Flenley

EMB   *Les écrits de Mère Bourgeoys*, ed. S.S. Damase-de-Rome

HCND   Sainte-Henriette, *Histoire de la Congrégation de Notre-Dame*

HSV   M. Morin, *Histoire simple et véritable*, ed. Legendre

JR   *The Jesuit Relations and Allied Documents*, ed. Thwaites

RAPQ   *Rapport des Archives de la province de Québec*

RHAF   *Revue d'histoire de l'Amérique française*

RND   Registers of Notre-Dame Parish, Montréal

SCHEC   Société Canadienne de l'Histoire de l'Église Catholique (reports)

WMB   *The writings of Marguerite Bourgeoys*, trans. M.V. Cotter

INTRODUCTION

1 Born in Ville-Marie in 1669 to two of the town's most prominent families (his mother was a Le Moyne), Pierre Le Ber was teaching painting there in the 1690s. Where he obtained his training is unknown. Women religious were not generally depicted during their lifetime since having one's portrait painted was regarded as a mark of vanity; hence the custom of recording their likeness after death. The restoration of the por-

trait of Marguerite Bourgeoys was widely covered in the Montreal
press and in art journals at the time in 1964 and continues to inspire
comment, most recently in Karch, *Les ateliers du pouvoir*, 53-6.

2 Both the Le Ber portrait and the copy in oil by Jori Smith Palardy of the
painting that had overlaid it are conserved at the Centre Marguerite-
Bourgeoys in Montreal, as are copies of the correspondence between
Korany and the Congrégation de Notre-Dame.

3 Since 1942 many other books, articles, and theological studies of
Marguerite Bourgeoys have appeared, some of them excellent. A number of these are cited in my text and included in the bibliography. The
decade after her beatification in 1950 and the years after her canonization in 1982 were particularly rich in this respect. None of these publi-
cations, however, was intended as a full-length, documented retelling
of her life. In fact, though undocumented biographies of Marguerite
Bourgeoys in the English language began to appear in the nineteenth
century, Faillon and Jamet were never translated, and there has never
been a documented biography in that language.

4 Dodd, *The Founder of Christianity*, 27-8.

CHAPTER ONE

1 *WMB*, 163 (234). Reference will usually be made to the English translation, followed by a cross-reference in parentheses to the original French
EMB.

2 "I am setting my repugnance aside, to inform you ..." Ibid., 141 (203).

3 Ibid. In fact, it was the year in which the island of Montreal was bought
by the Société de Notre-Dame de Montréal.

4 Ibid., 141 (203–4).

5 Described in the *JR*, 24: 225–7.

6 *WMB*, 19 (37–8). The connection between these two events, Marguerite's
conversion of 1640 and the foundation of Montreal, was noted by her
first scholarly biographer, Étienne-Michel Faillon, whose account of her
life is shaped by his perception of Montreal as a project inspired by
providence for the preservation of Roman Catholicism in North
America. In the introduction to his work, he says, "Sister Bourgeoys'
vocation was intimately intertwined with the founding of Ville-Marie,"
and later, "Sister Marguerite's vocation was closely connected with the
plan of God for the new Christianity of Ville-Marie." Faillon, *Vie de la
Soeur Bourgeoys*, 1: ix, x.

7 Chabroux, *Troyes – Marguerite Bourgeoys*, 23.

8 DdeC, 188. Dollier de Casson, a Sulpician who arrived in Montreal in
1666, composed his history in 1672–1673, drawing on the memories of
the first Montrealers, especially Jeanne Mance, and is therefore one of

the most important contemporary sources for the history of that period. Although a new critical edition of this work appeared in 1992, references to the Flenley edition are retained because it provides the reader with a page by page English translation. References to odd-numbered pages are to the English translation, and those to even-numbered pages to the French text in the few cases when I have found it preferable to make my own translation. The introduction to the Trudel-Baboyant edition contains a discussion of the reliability of Dollier de Casson as a historian (22–7).

9   Trudel, *Montréal, la formation d'une société*, 41.

10 Desrosiers, *Les dialogues de Marthe et de Marie*.

11 Toynbee. *Towards the Holy Spirit*, 38 (emphasis in original).

12 DdeC. Letters written by the prime minister of Canada and the premier of Quebec at the time of Marguerite's canonization on 31 October 1982 separate these two aspects of Marguerite's personality. Pierre Trudeau's letter speaks of the founding of Ville-Marie as one of the events of the religious past that "defy explanation," stating that "the origins of Montreal are steeped in a strange and mystical atmosphere, and the lives of Marguerite Bourgeoys, Jeanne Mance, Jean Jacques Olier and de Maisonneuve, remain unfathomable if we ignore the role of the Spirit in the history of mankind." The letter from the office of René Lévesque praises the active and innovative Marguerite, who "at a time when only boys were given an opportunity for formal schooling ... was adamant in the expression of her conviction that Christian education should be made available to girls as well ... and ... made the dangerous voyage between France and Quebec, not once but several times, in order to ensure the application of those views which she had energetically defended." *Saint Marguerite Bourgeoys: Canonization*, 74–5.

13 J. Roserot de Melin, *Le Diocèse de Troyes*, 65. In a city in which women were to play a significant role, the existence of such a legend is of some interest. The monastery was destroyed at the time of the Revolution. At that time too, a statue of Louis XIV over the entrance to the city hall, built in the lifetime of Marguerite Bourgeoys, was seriously damaged. Later, this statue was saved by being transformed into one of the goddess Minerva.

14 Scott, "Transformation." See also Roserot de Melin, *Le Diocèse de Troyes*.

15 The first invasion and destruction of the church took place about the end of May 1266. A second shortly afterwards resulted in the issuing of the bull *Per execrabilem insolentiam* by the successor of Urban IV, who had died in 1264. Roserot, *Troyes, son histoire*, 87–8.

16 Ibid.

17 Rouquet, *Troyes à travers les âges*, 25.

18 Instituted by Count Hugues (1093–1125); ibid., 9.

19 Schwarzfuchs, *Rachi de Troyes*, 7.

20 Roserot, *Troyes, son histoire*, 38.

21 Haughton, *The Catholic Thing*, 96.

22 Villehardouin, marshall of Champagne, wrote *Histoire de la conquête de Constantinople* (1198–1207); Joinville, *seneschal* and then grand master to Thibault IV, was the historian of St Louis, whom he accompanied on a crusade.

23 Crubellier and Juillard, *Histoire de la Champagne*, 38–9.

24 Originally an element in pagan Celtic folklore and mythology and introduced into Arthurian legend by Chrétien de Troyes, the Grail became in the romances emanating from the Cistercian monasteries one of the most important Christian mystical symbols. The influence of Bernard's doctrine regarding grace on some of the Grail romances was pointed out by Étienne Gilson. See Jean Frappier, "The Vulgate Cycle," in *Arthurian Literature in the Middle Ages*, ed. Loomis, 293–318.

25 Rouquet, *Troyes à travers les âges*, 29.

26 Crubellier and Juillard, *Histoire de la Champagne*, 47.

27 Ibid., 50.

28 The best published account of the family of Marguerite Bourgeoys is *Marguerite Bourgeoys et sa famille d'après des documents inédits*, by J.C. Niel, which makes use of documents unknown to previous biographers and corrects several of their errors. Three important documents, of which Niel was the first to make use, were the marriage contract and marriage act of Abraham Bourgeoys and Guillemette Garnier and the exceedingly valuable inventory made at the time of Guillemette's death, all discovered in the 1940s. However, since 1950 the invaluable and patient research of Alfred Morin in the ecclesiastical and municipal archives of Troyes has shown some of the dates in even the Niel work to be incorrect and have added several other pieces of information to our knowledge of the Bourgeoys family. Lucienne Plante continues research into the family in France.

29 Niel, *Marguerite Bourgeoys et sa famille*, [3].

30 AA 2 E10, Dépôt Nicolas Claude Bourgeois, 43. This important document will be discussed below.

31 An article in *L'Evangeline*, 20 November 1950, claimed that Marie Bourgeoys Semilliard was the daughter of Daniel Bourgeoys, the brother of Abraham, Marguerite's father. This claim was based on the marriage contract of Louise Sommillard and François Fortin. However, the appearance of a Marie among the Bourgeoys offspring in the inventory made on the death of their mother, the mention of a Marie, wife of Orson Semilliard, in the inventory made on the death of Abraham Bourgeoys, and a contract made by Marguerite Bourgeoys in favour of

the children of this couple in 1659 all seem to support the traditional view that she was Marguerite's sister.

32 A. de Barthélemy, "Les monnayers de Troyes au xvi siècle," *Rev de Champ. et de Brie* 3 (1877): 100–5, cited in Niel, *Marguerite Bourgeoys et sa famille*, [8].

33 Chabroux, *Troyes – Marguerite Bourgeoys*, 25–6.

34 Ibid., 27.

35 The name of the proprietor was Memgin or Mangin Bertrand. Niel explains the process in which ancient tax roles were used to determine the location of the house in question.

36 The inventory of 1639 proceeding, as it does, room by room, gives a good idea of how the house was laid out. By our own standards, it would have been very tiny for such a large family, but people then required much less space.

37 AA 2 E 10, Dépôt Nicolas Claude Bourgeois, 43. This document, which was not discovered until 1949, is significant for several reasons. Among them are the following: (1) it fixes the date of Marguerite's mother's death, an event that earlier biographers had tended to place several years earlier in Marguerite's life; (2) it fixes the number and relative ages of the nine Bourgeoys children alive at the time of their mother's death: the three eldest were over twenty-five, and two of them were married; the next three were aged between eighteen and twenty-five; the youngest three were under eighteen; three whose baptismal records exist were dead; Claude, Anne, and Marie, whose baptismal records have never been found, were unknown until this time; (3) it lists important family documents such as the marriage contracts of the two eldest children, Claude and Sirette; (4) by a reference to the rent owing for the house, it made possible its identification; (5) it provides valuable evidence about the economic position of the Bourgeoys family.

38 As noted above, no record of his baptism has been discovered. As in the case of his sisters Marie and Anne, his date of birth was determined by reference to his position in the family according to the inventory of 1639.

39 Niel, *Marguerite Bourgeoys et sa famille*, [20]. This fact raises the possibility that a connection between the two families might have been of help to Marguerite Bourgeoys in her later dealings with the court.

40 Jamet, *Marguerite Bourgeoys*, 1: 19. Boutiot gives a horrifying account of famine, civil unrest, and repression in Troyes in the second half of the 1620s in his Histoire de la ville de Troyes, 4: 341–8.

41 WMB, 23 (43).

42 Marguerite herself relates an incident from the early days of Ville-Marie in which the grave of three men killed by the Iroquois was repeatedly

uncovered by dogs, and "this caused terror among the people, leading them to believe that it was a punishment from God." *WMB*, 21 (41).

43 It has been suggested that infant death was so common in the seventeenth century that it had little emotional impact on the parents: "The family was scarcely disturbed, the dead baby was replaced in less than two years! A terrible tragedy today, [the death of an infant] appeared then like a mishap of the almanac, less serious than a big storm or a devastating hail or the death of a horse" (Chabroux, *Troyes – Marguerite Bourgeoys*, 23, quoting P. Goubert, *Louis XIV, ou vingt millions de français*). It would perhaps be truer to say that infant death was less surprising to parents than it would be in a developed country today. The infant mortality rate did not fall significantly until well into the twentieth century, but epitaphs written for children from the early seventeenth century on, whether the sophisticated efforts of poets or the pathetic verses to be found in all older cemeteries, testify that grief at the loss of a child is not an exclusively twentieth-century phenomenon.

44 AA, 15 G 207, fo. 37 (1638–39), registres de compte de la fabrique de Saint-Jean-du-Marché. Alfred Morin discusses his discovery of these documents in *Du nouveau sur Marguerite Bourgeoys*.

45 Glandelet, *La vie de la soeur Marguerite Bourgeoys*, 33.

46 *WMB*, 200 (282).

47 *WMB*, 162–3 (233).

48 Marie-Emmanuel Chabot, "Simon de Longpré, Marie-Catherine de," in *DCB*, 1: 607.

49 Faillon, *Vie de la Soeur Bourgeoys*, 1: 2–3.

50 The records now indicate that in his opening paragraphs Glandelet was in error as to the size of the Bourgeoys family and Marguerite's position in it, as well as about her age at the time of her mother's death.

51 Faillon, *Vie de la Soeur Bourgeoys*, 1: 5. His source is *Gallia christiana*, 12: col. 521. Roserot says that they began to make approaches in 1626 but were not established until 1628 (see *Troyes: son histoire*, 45). Rapley has described the circumstances of the foundation in "Life and Death of a Community," 5–20.

52 Jamet, *Marguerite Bourgeoys*, 1: 16. So far, research has been unable to discover any information about such schools in Troyes.

53 Desrosiers, *Les dialogues de Marthe et de Marie*, 18.

54 A group of young laywomen associated with the sisters and trained by them as a kind of "outreach" group. They will be dealt with at greater length in the next chapter.

55 *Les vraies constitutions*.

56 Roserot de Melin, *Le Diocèse de Troyes*, 158.

57 *WMB*, 163 (234).

58 Glandelet, *La vie de la soeur Marguerite Bourgeoys*, 36.

59 Jamet, *Marguerite Bourgeoys*, 1: 18.

60 *WMB*, 163 (234).

61 The considerable value put on these objects by the appraiser is another indication of the substance of the family.

62 *WMB*, 141 (203–4).

63 Chabroux, *Troyes – Marguerite Bourgeoys*, 16–17.

64 The extent to which Marguerite had kept this moment fresh is an example of what Abraham Heschel meant when he wrote, "Prayer revives and keeps alive the rare greatness of some past experience in which things glowed with meaning and blessing." Heschel, *Man's Quest for God*, 8.

65 Nearly two hundred years later, in a very different milieu, an eighty-four-year-old John Henry Newman wrote in similar terms of his own "conversion" some seventy years earlier: "I should say that it is difficult to realise or imagine the identity of the boy before and after August 1816 ... I can look back at the end of seventy years as if on another person." Newman, *Apologia pro vita sua*, 24 n.2.

66 *WMB*, 143 (206).

67 The prefecture now stands on the site of the ancient abbey.

68 Each statue may not have been returned to the same church from which it had been taken, but the old churches of Troyes are so close together that all of them would have been known to the populace in general.

69 As is generally the case, exceptions to this rule can be found, but they are the exceptions, not the rule.

70 For the best recent account of apocryphal works on Mary, see Hervieux, the *New Testament Apocrypha*. There is a somewhat more sympathetic comment in Marina Warner's *Alone of All Her Sex*, 25–33.

71 Assigning Mary an elderly widower as a husband seems to have made her perpetual virginity more plausible to the authors of this work, and the existence of Joseph's sons from a previous marriage would account for the references in the canonical scriptures to the brethren of the Lord.

72 This is not the only pose in which Anne and the young Virgin can be depicted. Notre-Dame cathedral in Paris, for example, contains a group in which Anne instructs Mary holding, not a book, but a distaff.

73 *WMB*, 56 (91), 67 (108); Marguerite probably got this idea from the Congrégation de Notre-Dame of Troyes. Alix Le Clerc, the co-founder of that community, wrote that Mary in the Temple "worked like the other young girls, performing ordinary actions with them." Gelson, "May God Be Your Whole Love," 21.

74 Glandelet, *La vie de la soeur Marguerite Bourgeoys*, 36.

75 *WMB*, 59 (95).

CHAPTER TWO

1 *WMB*, 141–2 (204–5).

2 Ibid., 163 (234). The reference is to Marie-Nicolas Desguerrois, who died in 1676 at the age of almost one hundred. His sermons occupy nearly two thousand pages in three manuscript volumes, and he also collected the lives of saints of the area. As penitentiary of the parish of Saint-Jean-au-Marché he was empowered by the bishop to deal with certain cases of conscience reserved to the latter. See A. Morin, ACMB, "Marie Nicolas Desguerrois."

3 The five women who were the original members of this congregation participated in a form of ceremony at Christmas 1597, but did not leave their families and begin to live together until the eve of Corpus Christi 1598.

4 Rapley points out the relationship between this development and the desire to counteract the spread of Protestantism from mother to daughter. See *The Dévotes*, 42–3.

5 Jamet, *Marguerite Bourgeoys*, 1: 32. The convent did, however, enjoy some encouragement from the nobility: the queen, Anne of Austria, conferred their veils on its first professed members in 1630, and during the outbreak of plague in 1633, the members of the community took refuge with the marquise de Blaigny. For the cause of the financial problems of the convent, see Rapley, "Life and Death of a Community."

6 Even in the seventeenth century, for example, the observance of the rule of cloister was non-existent at Notre-Dame-aux-Nonnains.

7 Derréal, *Un missionaire de la Contre-Réforme*, 221–2.

8 Glandelet, *La vie de la soeur Marguerite Bourgeoys*, 37.

9 Jamet, *Marguerite Bourgeoys*, 1: 32. In this period, the suburbs were not a desirable place to live. Those who could afford the taxes, such as Marguerite's own family, lived in the city. The poor were forced to live further out.

10 Faillon, *Vie de la Soeur Bourgeoys*, 1: 5. The source that he cites is *La conduite de la Providence dans l'établissement de la Congrégation*.

11 Faillon, *Vie de la Soeur Bourgeoys*, 1: 5.

12 DdeC, 188.

13 "It is a great weakness ... to wish to be singled out ... because of particular clothing or some visible mark." *WMB*, 69 (111).

14 Faillon, *Vie de la Soeur Bourgeoys*, 1: 5.

15 Glandelet, *La vie de la soeur Marguerite Bourgeoys*, 37.

16 DdeC, 188.

17 Faillon, *La vie de la soeur Bourgeoys*, 1: 5.

18 DdeC, 188. It is difficult to imagine that Marguerite was the source of this information. By the time that Dollier wrote, there were in Montreal other former members of the extern congregation, including Catherine

Crolo. Coming in the context that it does, it may very well have been a statement made by Louise de Chomedey in recommending Marguerite to her brother.

19 Jamet, *Marguerite Bourgeoys*, 1: 33.

20 Glandelet, *La vie de la soeur Marguerite Bourgeoys*, 39.

21 Jamet, *Marguerite Bourgeoys*, 1: 30.

22 That laughter continued in Marguerite's life is made evident in the writings of the annalist of the Montreal Hôtel-Dieu, to be considered in a later chapter.

23 *WMB*, 91–2 (140–4).

24 Jamet, *Marguerite Bourgeoys*, 1: 29.

25 *Les vraies constitutions*, from part 3, "De l'instruction des filles seculières," 2. For an account of changing attitudes towards children, see Aries, *Centuries of Childhood*, especially 100–33.

26 For an account of the backlash against women educators, see Rapley, *The Dévotes*, 23–73.

27 *Les vraies constitutions*, part 16: 77-8.

28 Like all prohibitions, they imply the existence of these reprehensible practices, or at least tendencies.

29 *Les vraies constitutions*, part 16: 72, 77–8.

30 Derréal, *Un missionaire de la Contre-Réforme*, 101–15.

31 A life of Alix Le Clerc quotes this early-seventeenth-century comment on Pierre Fourier: "The Reverend Father would have preferred that his daughters remain without cloister rather than give up the free tuition to externs because of the marvelous results that were being produced everywhere, and of which the poor as well as the rich could have the benefit." See "A Fertile Vine."

32 *Les vraies constitutions*, part 3: 3.

33 Glandelet, *La vie de la soeur Marguerite Bourgeoys*, 39.

34 Chabroux, *Troyes – Marguerite Bourgeoys*, 33–6. She cites as a principal source *Les cahiers de doléances du baillage de Troyes, pour les États généraux de 1614*, by Y. Durand (1966).

35 AA, 2 E 6/37, [13], minutes Claude Bourgeois, dépôt Nicolas.

36 Chabroux, *Troyes – Marguerite Bourgeoys*, 41–8.

37 Glandelet, *La vie de la soeur Marguerite Bourgeoys*, 43.

38 Faillon says, "This woman is said to have been Miss Crolo, who attached herself to Sister Marguerite from that moment and followed her a few years later to Canada" (Faillon, *Vie de la Soeur Bourgeoys*, 1: 20). He cites as his source the first published biography of Marguerite Bourgeoys, Michel-François Ransonet's *La vie de la Soeur Marguerite Bourgeois*. Ransonet's version of the story is much more dramatic than that found in Glandelet, but makes no attempt to identify the victim of the incident.

39 The letter describing the event is, of course, one of the documents that

have perished. Thus all we know of its contents is what Glandelet quotes.

40 Jamet, *Marguerite Bourgeoys*, 1: 34.

41 Ibid., 35–6.

42 ACMB, A. Morin, "Antoine Gendret." Morin points out that he always signed "Gendret" and not "Jendret."

43 WMB, 164 (235).

44 DdeC, 188.

45 Faillon, *Vie de la Soeur Bourgeoys*, 1: 14.

46 Glandelet, *La vie de la soeur Marguerite Bourgeoys*, 39–40.

47 This would have been one reason why she never sought entry into the Benedictines at Notre-Dame-aux-Nonnains, whose members were usually drawn from the greatest families, according to Roserot de Melin in *Le Diocèse de Troyes*, 65.

48 Even in Canada in the seventeenth and eighteenth centuries, the dowry that a parent was expected to pay for a daughter entering religious life was several times that offered for one entering marriage. Research indicates, however, that the full amount of the religious dowry was seldom paid. See D'Allaire, *Les dots des religieuses au Canada français*, 100–3.

49 Research by Mary Anne Foley in the "Registre des professions, vêtures et sépultures" of the Carmelite convent of Notre-Dame de Pitié at Troyes (AA, 25 H 1) revealed that there were no professions from 1642 to 1653. See Foley, "Uncloistered Apostolic Life for Women," 30; citing AA, 25 H 1, registre des professions, vêtures et sépultures, Carmelites.

50 Quoted by Vinot in an unpublished paper, ACMB, "Notes de lecture sur la bienheureuse Marguerite Bourgeoys et quelques monastères de la ville de Troyes dans la première moitié du 17ième siècle." He cites AA, MS A, Carmelites, p. 58.

51 WMB, 164 (235).

52 Lewis, *The Splendid Century*, 114–19.

53 Ibid., 115.

54 Glandelet, *La vie de la soeur Marguerite Bourgeoys*, 41.

55 Jamet, *Marguerite Bourgeoys*, 1: 37.

56 WMB, 169 (243).

57 Glandelet, *La vie de la soeur Marguerite Bourgeoys*, 40.

58 WMB, 161, 173 (231, 250); Glandelet, *La vie de la soeur Marguerite Bourgeoys*, 40; Faillon, *Vie de la Soeur Bourgeoys*, 15.

59 WMB, 173 (250).

60 Ibid., 141–2 (204–5).

61 Jamet, *Marguerite Bourgeoys*, 1: 39.

62 For example, WMB, 77 (121). Although current scriptural scholarship sees Mary Magdalen and Mary of Bethany as two different women, they were for many centuries perceived to be the same person.

63 Jamet, *Marguerite Bourgeoys*, 1: 39.

64 Glandelet, *La vie de la soeur Marguerite Bourgeoys*, 41.

65 *WMB*, 88 (136).

66 Graef, *Mary: A History of Doctrine and Devotion*, 1: 51.

67 Brown, *Mary in the New Testament*, 105–77.

68 Luke 1:42–5; 11:27–8.

69 Luke 1:12–14.

70 *WMB* 72 (114-15). See also 48–9, 50–1, 67, 71, 73, 77 (79–80, 80–1, 107–8, 114, 116, 121–2).

71 Ibid., 167 (240).

72 Glandelet, *La vie de la soeur Marguerite Bourgeoys*, 42.

73 Ibid.

74 Though this arrangement calls to mind Fourier's plan for "double houses," one of cloistered and the other of secular women, the fact that Marguerite's projected community was to follow a Rule drawn up by Father Gendret indicates a separation from the Congrégation de Notre-Dame of Troyes.

75 Niel, *Marguerite Bourgeoys et sa famille*, [20–2]. Rumilly makes the identification in *Marguerite Bourgeoys*, 15.

76 A. Morin, *Du nouveau sur Marguerite Bourgeoys*.

77 Niel, *Marguerite Bourgeoys et sa famille*, [21]. See also chapter 4, especially note 82.

78 *WMB*, 201 (284).

79 Ibid., 78 (122). The painting now hangs in that part of the mother house of the Congregation that sees to the needs of sisters on the overseas missions.

80 Desrosiers related Marguerite's use of the metaphor of the blood of Christ to Alix Le Clerc's "Little souls, without equal, reddened with the blood of Jesus Christ, I love you above all else" (Desrosiers, *Les dialogues de Marthe et de Marie*, 17). Describing the vocation of Madame de la Peltrie to New France, Marie de l'Incarnation attributed it to a passage in the Jesuit *Relations*: "Ah, can some good and virtuous lady not be found who is willing to come to this country to gather up the blood of Jesus Christ in teaching the little Indian girls?" (Marie de l'Incarnation, *Correspondance*, 904, referring to the *Relation* of 1635).

81 *WMB*, 164 (236).

82 AA, 2 E 6/37, [15], minutes Claude Bourgeois, dépôt Nicholas.

83 Ibid.

84 Using the price of a milk cow in 1650 and in 1995 as a basis, Lucienne Plante has estimated that Marguerite's share of the family inheritance (550 *livres*) would be equivalent to between $29,000 and $30,000 Canadian today. See Plante, "The Family of Marguerite Bourgeoys," 31.

85 A. Morin made use of the parish account registers of Saint-Jean-au-

Marché to determine that Anne Bourgeoys took up the collection in the parish church on 12 January 1643 (during Marguerite's twenty-third year) but that, as in her mother's case, she died during the following week (AA, 15 G 213, fo. 32 and 8, 1642–43 registres de compte de la fabrique de Saint-Jean-au-Marché). She had apparently never married, perhaps in part because of the responsibilities she assumed on the death of her mother, and she would not, at the time of her death, have attained the age of thirty-two.

86 See Plante, "The Family of Marguerite Bourgeoys," for information about the later lives of these brothers and sisters of Marguerite.

87 More than two pages of this inventory are in the handwriting of Marguerite Bourgeoys herself. Among other things, she lists fifty-eight debtors for her father's daybook. This is the only specimen of her handwriting ever found in her native city, except for a few signatures on notarial acts.

88 WMB, 164 (236). There is no other information on how the projected community was to be financed.

89 Glandelet, La vie de la soeur Marguerite Bourgeoys, 44.

90 HSV, 63. She also says that he was from Troyes, which was not true.

91 DdeC, 70.

92 WMB, 164 (236). Other references give the same impression. When, for example, Marguerite writes about the picture given to de Maisonneuve by his sister, she says, "I knew nothing of all this" (19); she seems to be speaking of the entire situation, not just of events in Montreal.

93 Ibid., 19 (37–8). Quoting La conduite de la Providence dans l'établissement de la congrégation (1732), Faillon, in accordance with conventional hagiography, says that Louise de Chomedey, like Teresa of Avila, early desired to find martyrdom bringing the faith to pagans. When she heard about the Montreal project, she was immediately touched with compassion for the native people and considered it a special indication of providence that her own brother had been made governor (Faillon, Vie de la Soeur Bourgeoys, 1: 25–6). It is much more likely that she heard about the project through her brother's involvement with it.

94 WMB, 141 (204).

95 Georges Viard has suggested that sisters in the various houses of the Congrégation de Notre-Dame may sometimes have been ready to embark on projects that Pierre Fourier, their founder, would have considered imprudent. Certainly, Montreal exhibited none of the conditions that he had described as necessary for the foundation of a monastery: "A location truly and peacefully theirs, and not just any place or house, but a monastery fully built and complete with all its rooms, church, cemetery, dormitory, refectory, kitchen, root cellar, pantry, yard, wardrobe or vestry, laundry, garden. And not just that, but endowed with sufficient income to support the nuns, the vestments or

sacristy, the buildings, the chaplain." "L'installaticn de la congrégation de Notre-Dame en Champagne et Saint Pierre Fourier," in *Saint Pierre Fourier en ses temps*, ed. Taveneaux, 117, citing Fourier, *Sa Correspondance*, 2: 101.

96 Glandelet, *La vie de la soeur Marguerite Bourgeoys*, 45.

97 Except when she gives dates. Then she always makes reference to saints' festivals, rather than the month and day.

98 *WMB*, 142 (205). This statement seems to contradict Glandelet's claim that Marguerite "had, however, in coming to Canada, no plan of establishing a community here, as she herself admits in one of her writings" (*La vie de la soeur Marguerite Bourgeoys*, 34). Perhaps some of the contradictions arise from different meanings to be attached to the word "community." Certainly, Marguerite had no intention of founding a community like those she already knew in France, but among the very few possessions she brought with her to Canada was the Rule designed by Father Gendret for the community that she had already attempted to found. Marguerite never proceeded from a set of abstract ideas. Her work, and eventually the Congregation that she would found in Montreal, developed in response to the real needs that she perceived around her.

99 *WMB*, 142 (205); also 165 (237). See also Dollier's account of de Maisonneuve's insistence on founding his settlement on the island of Montreal (DdeC, 90).

100 *WMB*, 142, 165 (205, 238).

101 Glandelet says it was 6 or 8 February. See, *La vie de la soeur Marguerite Bourgeoys*, 49.

102 Identified by Glandelet as M. Cossard (ibid., 49). This would have been Blaise Cossard, husband of Marguerite Garnier, who was a sister of Marguerite's mother, Guillemette Garnier.

103 She brought no luggage. She says, "I left, without a stitch, without a penny, with only a little package that I could carry under my arm." *WMB*, 143 (206).

104 Ibid., 166 (239).

105 Ibid., 33 (58).

106 DdeC, 191. Again, tradition has identified Catherine Crolo as the other member of the extern congregation.

107 Glandelet identified her as the sister of M. Delbo, canon of the Sainte-Chapelle. See *La vie de la soeur Marguerite Bourgeoys*, 49. Jamet identified a Canon Dolbeau who had a sister in Paris. This family came from Langres and were first cousins of Jeanne Mance. See Jamet, *Marguerite Bourgeoys*, 1: 58, note.

108 *WMB*, 143 (206).

109 Glandelet, *La vie de la soeur Marguerite Bourgeoys*, 49.

110 *WMB*, 143 (206).

111 See chapter 3 of this book.

112 *EMB*, 59. The French phrasing here is more effective than any English translation.

113 *WMB*, 34 (59).

114 Ibid.

115 Jamet, *Marguerite Bourgeoys*, 1: 72.

116 Glandelet, *La vie de la soeur Marguerite Bourgeoys*, 52.

117 *WMB*, 25 (45–6).

118 Glandelet, *La vie de la soeur Marguerite Bourgeoys*, 54.

119 Jamet, *Marguerite Bourgeoys*, 1: 72.

120 Ibid., 73.

121 *WMB*, 143 (207). A similar passage occurs at 166–7 (239–40).

122 Glandelet, *La vie de la soeur Marguerite Bourgeoys*, 44.

123 *WMB*, 165–6 (238).

124 Sister Scott wrote in an unpublished paper,"Departure," now in the ACMB, "The visual quality of the narrative is important and convincing ... Even at such a solemn moment she is aware of texture. Perhaps we should recall that her maternal grandfather had been a master-weaver ... Marguerite's ability to create a strong visual impression comes to us as we read."

125 *WMB*, 174 (251).

126 Ibid., 142–3 (206). Sister Scott, on the other hand, was convinced that this event took place in Paris or Nantes; see ACMB, "Departure," 4.

127 Her account of the miraculous manifestations surrounding the deaths of some of the colonists at the hands of the Iroquois would indicate this. See *WMB*, 20–1 (39–40).

128 *Actes de Belliotte, notaire à Saint-Nazaire, 20 juin, 1653, Archives du séminaire de Villemarie, engagements de 1653; quoted in Faillon, Vie de la Soeur Bourgeoys*, 1: 62.

129 Ransonet, *La vie de la soeur Bourgeois*, 44.

130 Ibid., 46–52.

131 *WMB*, 24 (45). About the number of passengers on the *Saint-Nicholas*, Jamet says, "Le rôle des colons de 1653 and Belmont's *Histoire du Canada* give different counts ... It became a tradition in Montreal to call the recruitment of 1653, the recruitment of the hundred men. At the end of the century Sister Morin will not say otherwise in her *Annales*." Jamet, *Marguerite Bourgeoys*, 1: 83.

132 *WMB*, 25 (46). This story is confirmed by Dollier de Casson: "M. de Maisonneuve [on arrival in Quebec] ... went to pay his respects to M. de Lauson to whom he told the mishaps of his voyage, amongst other things that his delay had been due to a leak which had made them put back into port three weeks after their departure." DdeC, 183.

133 *WMB*, 25 (46).

134 Glandelet, *La vie de la soeur Marguerite Bourgeoys*, 54–5. The origins of a belief in France that colonists to Canada, especially women, were from the dregs of French society is discussed by Gustave Lanctot in his *Filles de joie ou filles du roi*.
135 *WMB*, 25 (46).

CHAPTER THREE

1 The French is "avec soumission." The word *soumission* had the sense in the seventeenth century of placing one's self under someone's authority or of the disposition to obey. See *Dictionnaire historique de la langue française*, 2: 1991. The sense is that the native people who would come would do so willingly, because they wanted to, unlike the forced "conversions" imposed on the natives in some of the Spanish domains in the Americas.
2 *WMB*, 19(37).
3 The approach to the founding of Montreal followed here, that is, recognition of the primary role played by Jérôme le Royer de la Dauversière, is that of Daveluy, who was the leading expert on the Société de Montréal. Her book *La Société de Notre-Dame de Montréal* is an indispensible source for anyone working on the subject.
4 Mullet's *The Counter-Reformation and the Catholic Reformation in Early Modern Europe*, 37–45, provides an interesting brief discussion of this aspect of early modern religious history.
5 Verrazano called the Atlantic coast Nova Gallia and gave the name Arcadia to the territory eventually to become Virginia. The name survived in the more northern territory, which became Acadia.
6 Since 1992 the site of an archeological and historical museum.
7 The name Montreal became official only in the documents ceding it to Jean de Lauson in 1636. According to Lanctot, the island received the name that Jacques Cartier had given the mountain, but in the form Mont-Réale, which recalled its origin, the Montreale of Sicily (see *Montréal sous Maisonneuve*, 21–2), but this claim continues to be disputed. A recent article on the subject examines the various theories and reaches the conclusion: "Among the hypotheses concerning the origin of Montréal's name, the most acceptable to Toponomy is the one that finds it to be a variant of *mont Royal*" (Poirier, "Origine du nom de la ville de Montréal," 37–44).
8 This was the first of a series of companies that in return for a monopoly on the fur trade were to fulfil certain obligations, among them the recruitment and settlement of colonists. It was followed by the Compagnie des Cents-Associés and the Communauté des Habitants.
9 See, for example, Trudel, *The Beginnings of New France*, 37.

10   Lucien Campeau, "Du Thet, Gilbert," DCB, 1: 299.
11   One of the few surviving examples of the original 1643 edition, now
     preserved in the Huntington Library, San Marino, California, is repro-
     duced in Daveluy's *La Société de Notre-Dame de Montréal*. The document,
     which appeared without reference to place or author, was attributed in
     the late nineteenth century to Jean-Jacques Olier by Hospice-Anthelme
     Verreau. Since then it has been credited by Jamet to Gaston de Renty,
     secretary to the Société de Notre-Dame de Montréal, but is perceived
     by Daveluy as a collective effort written in part by Olier, in part by de
     la Dauversière, and in part by other members of the society (19). Oury
     has presented what he believes are definitive arguments for the author-
     ship of Jean-Jacques Olier in "Le rédacteur des 'Véritables motifs': M.
     Olier?" 211–24. Tallon believes that a large role was played by Elie
     Laisné de la Marguerie. See "La Compagnie du Saint-Sacrement et la
     fondation de Montréal," *Les origines de Montréal*, ed. Brault, 39–62.
12   The role played by women in the early church was of great importance
     to Marguerite Bourgeoys. Her idea of that role, however, was to be
     much more dynamic than the one presented in *Les Véritables Motifs*,
     where they are perceived as the sweeteners of life, those who bring a
     civilizing and gracious note into human existence. Earlier in the centu-
     ry, the poet and adventurer Marc Lescarbot had lamented the absence
     of European women in Acadia on the occasion of the death of several
     cows introduced into the colony: "Which shows how necessary a
     woman is in a house ... For my part, I shall always believe that, in any
     settlement whatsoever, nothing will be accomplished without the pres-
     ence of women. Without them life is sad, sickness comes, and we die
     uncared for." *JR*, 1: 101–3.
13   *Les Véritables Motifs*, 29. De Maisonneuve and Jeanne Mance are also
     treated together and as equals in DdeC (65–79) in a passage that makes
     apparent Dollier's great affection and admiration for Jeanne Mance.
14   Jacques Rousseau and George W. Brown, in DCB, 1: 9.
15   *Les Veritables Motifs*, 1–18.
16   Oury in *L'homme qui a conçu Montréal*, 31–4, examines the question of
     the number of children and provides what is known about five of them.
17   His grandson, Joseph-Jérôme Le Royer, composed a short memoir of
     Jérôme Le Royer de la Dauversière, "Mémoires de quelques particular-
     ités arrivées en l'établissement des Filles de Saint-Joseph de La Flèche,"
     of which a 1715 manuscript copy is in the archives of the Hospitaller of
     La Flèche. Oury suggests that this memoir may have incorporated pas-
     sages from the grandfather's notebooks put into the possession of the
     family by the Baron de Fancamp before the latter's death in 1692. See
     L'homme qui a conçu Montréal, 44. References in Dollier's history to a
     work entitled "Le dessein de Montréal," composed by de la

Dauversière in the spring of 1641 at the request of Jeanne Mance, led Daveluy to hope that some copy of this document might yet come to light. See *La Société de Notre-Dame de Montréal*, 97.

18 Oury situates de la Dauversière's devotion to the Holy Family in the context of the development of this observance from the fifteenth century on, as traced in iconography. See *L'homme qui a conçue Montréal*, 69–77. The works of art to which he makes reference are similar to those already described in the discussion of what Marguerite Bourgeoys saw in her native Troyes.

19 HSV, 109. As the original of this letter no longer exists, one must rely on Morin's transcription. The sisters referred to are the Hospitallers, the order that he founded. An anecdote in this letter demonstrates that de la Dauversière was not inordinately impressed with clerical authority. On one occasion, his confessor had submitted an account of his penitent's mystical experiences to a "holy" fellow priest, who suggested that they manifested too much "nature" intermingled with "grace." When this verdict was made known to de la Dauversière, he took up the matter with the Lord in prayer and was assured, "The priest is a man like any other ... in eight days you will see that he will change his mind." This change, of course, came about just as predicted.

20 Daveluy accepts the date 1633, as suggested by Fancamp's letter. See *La Sociéte de Notre-Dame de Montréal*, 96.

21 The *Véritables Motifs* of 1643 puts this event "seven or eight" years earlier. It seems unlikely that this section could have been written by de la Dauversière himself since it refers to him as "a virtuous man" (26).

22 Ibid.

23 Daveluy, *La Société de Notre-Dame de Montréal*, 63.

24 Daveluy presents and evaluates the information available about Fancamp in *La Société de Notre-Dame de Montréal*, 103–8.

25 It has been suggested that Olier's devotion to Mary the mother of the Lord increased with his growing estrangement from his own mother, who had reportedly treated him with harshness even when he was a child. See Poinsenet, *France religieuse de XVIIe siècle*, 204.

26 Tallon situates the founding of Montreal within the missionary impulse of the Compagnie in "La Compagnie du Saint-Sacrement et la fondation de Montréal," in *Les origines de Montréal*, ed. Brault, 39–62.

27 Poinsenet, *France religieuse du XVIIe siècle*, 242–53. This book devotes a chapter to what is, on the whole, a balanced account of the Compagnie. If it errs on the side of sympathy, it provides a useful corrective to the usually hostile accounts.

28 He and his wife soon afterwards dedicated themselves to celibacy, she in a Carmelite convent and he in the world, causing some commentators to describe him as a religious fanatic.

29 Poinsenet, *France religieuse du* xviie *siècle*, 244.

30 Ibid.

31 Since each religious community already had a proper spirituality.

32 One of their members wrote: "Most of the priests hang about with their arms folded. God must raise up laypeople, cutlers, and haberdashers, to achieve the work of do-nothing priests." See Poinsenet, *France religieuse de* xviie *siècle*, 244.

33 The Recollets, a Franciscan community, were the first missionaries in Quebec where they arrived in May 1615. They pursued their work there and among the Hurons until the capture of Quebec by the Kirkes in 1629. Their attempts to return and continue their work after the colony was handed back to France in 1632 were frustrated by the Jesuits, who were convinced that missionary work in New France would be more effective if entrusted to a single religious community – their own, of course.

34 J. Monet, "Lauson, Jean de, Sr" in *DCB*, 1: 428.

35 Trudel comments on the difficulty of knowing the "real" de Maisonneuve because the main seventeenth-century sources cast him in an idealized and romantic light, which has influenced later biographers; see "Paul de Chomedey de Maisonneuve pour un renouvellement de la question," in *Les origines de Montréal*, ed. Brault, 105–12.

36 Desrosiers, *Paul de Chomedey*, 36.

37 DdeC, 71.

38 Desrosiers, *Paul de Chomedey*, 37.

39 *Les Véritables Motifs*, 30.

40 Roussel, *Le lieu de naissance et la famille de Jeanne Mance* (Langres, 1932), cited in Daveluy, *Jeanne Mance*, 20.

41 HSV, 39.

42 Daveluy, *Jeanne Mance*, 23.

43 Ibid., 27.

44 Ibid.

45 Deroy-Pineau, *Jeanne Mance*, 95–6.

46 HSV, 39.

47 Catholic children responded to stories from the lives of the saints, Protestant children to Biblical stories such as the calling of Samuel.

48 Daveluy, *Jeanne Mance*, 25. Faillon says, "She ... dedicated herself to all the practices of a perfect life ... without experiencing any attraction towards life in a cloister" (*Vie de Mademoiselle Mance*, 1: 4).

49 HSV, 42.

50 Daveluy, *Jeanne Mance*, 25.

51 DdeC, 75.

52 Although the identity of Jeanne's director in Langres is unknown, biographers conclude that he must have been a Jesuit.

53 Daveluy, *Jeanne Mance*, 30.

54 This mission was on the Isle of Miskou, or Miscou. At the end of 1642 Jean Dolebeau became ill, probably because of the harsh climate of the island, which few of the Jesuits were able to endure. The ship on which he had been placed for the return to France in the summmer of 1643 was attacked by three frigates. During the pillaging of the captive ship, the powder magazine blew up and Father Dolebeau was thrown into the ocean and drowned. Accounts from the *Relations des Jésuites* for 1643 and 1647 are cited by Daveluy, *Jeanne Mance*, 31; see also Lucien Campeau, "Dolebeau, Jean" in *DCB*, 1: 266.

55 Charles Dolebeau, the Carmelite provincial who offered Marguerite a place in Carmel in 1653, was another member of this family. See Daveluy, *Jeanne Mance*, 32.

56 DdeC, 77.

57 *HSV*, 40.

58 DdeC, 79.

59 *HSV*, 46.

60 Daveluy, *Jeanne Mance*, 42–3.

61 It is also the version presented by Mondoux in the modern history of the Hôtel-Dieu of Montreal, *L'Hôtel-Dieu, premier hôpital de Montréal*.

62 *HSV*, 39.

63 Couanier de Launay, *Notions*, 226–8, cited in Daveluy, *Jeanne Mance*, 45, n12.

64 *HSV*, 42–3.

65 DdeC, 81.

66 Jeanne's health made the journey arduous, but otherwise it seems to have been much easier than that taken by Marguerite Bourgeoys in 1653, when she had so much difficulty finding a place even to spend the night. "God so disposed people on her behalf that she was always well received, and after treating her so well they would scarcely take her money when she departed from the inns." DdeC, 83.

67 Ibid., 81.

68 *HSV*, 46.

69 *Les Véritables Motifs*, 30.

70 *HSV*, 46.

71 DdeC, 87. This is the document that Daveluy hoped would one day turn up.

72 Ibid., 89. The ships regularly left France for Canada in the spring and returned in the autumn. Dollier's accounts always stretch from the departure of the ships from Canada in one year to their departure the following autumn.

73 It has been argued that Eurocentric historians have erred in attributing the hostility between the Iroquois and the French to economic motives

when in fact the psychology and motivation of the Iroquois derived from their own traditional values. In this view, the French alliance with the Hurons was the principal cause of attack by the Iroquois. See Dickinson, "Annaohata et Dollard vus de l'autre côté de la palissade."

74 Ironically, it was the contact between the French and their allies that was the cause of these epidemics, when the native peoples were exposed to diseases against which they had developed no immunity. The Iroquois were spared this misfortune because they had minimal contact with the Dutch. It is now believed that disease, far more than the Iroquois, was responsible for the disappearance of the Hurons.

75 DdeC, 91, and Desrosiers, *Paul de Chomedey*, 45–6.

76 Daveluy, *Jeanne Mance*, 73, n4. This baptismal record has led Daveluy to suppose that de Maisonneuve's arrival took place about 20 September. Early accounts range as wide as 20 August (DdeC, 89) and October (*HSV*, 49).

77 DdeC, 91–3.

78 Ibid., 93.

79 Lanctot, *Montréal sous Maisonneuve*, 37; Trudel, *Montréal, la formation d'une société*, 13.

80 *JR*, 22: 211.

81 Desrosiers, *Paul de Chomedey*, 47.

82 DdeC, 93.

83 The account of the whole incident is in Faillon, *Histoire de la colonie française au Canada*, 1: 430–4.

84 Oury says that she saw in the Montreal expedition a better way to work for the evangelization of the native people, the reason that she had come to New France, than in the restricted life of a monastery. See *Madame de la Peltrie*, 88.

85 Ibid., 96–7. Oury says that she had joined the expedition to Montreal in the belief that doing so would enable her to live among the native people. Disappointed when she was not immediately able to do so, she contemplated going off into Huron country with the Jesuit missionaries. In view of the problems that they believed such action would create, as well as the desperate situation of the Ursulines in Quebec, the Jesuits of Quebec, Montreal, and the Huron mission all lent their efforts to persuading her to return to Quebec.

86 Marie de L'Incarnation described the life and inspiration of Madame de la Peltrie in the letter to Father Poncet of 25 October 1670 already cited. See Marie de l'Incarnation, *Correspondance*, 904.

87 DdeC, 243–5.

88 Daveluy, *Jeanne Mance*, 83.

89 DdeC, 97.

90 *HSV*, 52.

91 Trudel, *Montréal, la formation d'une société*, 14. I have accepted the age assigned to Mathurine, the youngest child, in *HCND*, 2: 131, which states that she was thirty-five when she died in childbirth on 12 November 1672. This age corresponds best with other known dates connected with the family. The source of the information might well have been one of Mathurine's three daughters, who were to enter Marguerite's Congregation.

92 DdeC, 99; *HSV*, 52.

93 DdeC, 99.

94 *JR*, 22: 207.

95 Ibid., 213.

96 DdeC, 101. Passages such as this and the earlier comment of Jeanne Mance about her first journey up the St Lawrence appear to disprove the argument that the earliest European settlers were aware only of the harshness and not of the natural beauty of the land to which they had come.

97 *JR*, 22: 209.

98 DdeC, 103.

99 There is still a candlelight procession in Old Montreal after the offices of the feast of the Assumption.

100 *JR*, 22: 215.

101 Ibid., 217.

102 Ibid., 24: 221–3. The word *pays*, translated in this passage as "countries," would be better rendered "regions." The statement is another reminder of the power of regional loyalties and differences in seventeenth-century France.

103 DdeC, 123–5.

104 *JR*, 24: 225–7.

105 The exact spot at which the first cross stood is uncertain. Marguerite Bourgeoys locates it on the site of the mountain fort constructed by the Sulpicians in the 1670s: "None of these people ever saw the result of their prayers. But this was the first place the Indians came to be instructed; even the girls, by the sisters of the Congregation" (*WMB*, 19 [37]). The most likely original site was probably somewhat higher than the intersection of the present-day Sherbrooke Street and Atwater Avenue. This spot is also at the distance designated by Marguerite Bourgeoys: a league, or about three miles, from the first fort.

106 DdeC, 123. Trudel says in his edition of Dollier de Casson that the author was in error in stating that this was the first wheat grown in Canada, that the Jesuits had grown wheat in Quebec some years before. See Dollier de Casson, *Histoire de Montréal*, 99, n11.

107 Dollier de Casson wrote that de Puiseaux "had spent this long life in incredible labours, both in New Spain where he had amassed his for-

tune, and in New France where he had spent it. That he used up such a fortune here is not to be wondered at, indeed he could not fail to do so in such large enterprises, since everything was extravagantly dear then and there was no supply from the country either in food or clothing." DdeC, 115.

108 In view of the continuing controversy among Canadians about the benefits of "free trade," it is of interest to note that in 1647 d'Ailleboust was involved in unsuccessful negotiations with the colonies of New England, the object of which was a treaty of offensive and defensive alliance and commercial union. According to Daveluy, "M. d'Ailleboust's prudence remains praiseworthy. He was only too justified in suspecting the intentions of a neighbour whose commercial designs were not exempt from egoism." (Marie-Claire Daveluy, "Ailleboust de Coulonge et d'Argentenay, Louis d'," in *DCB*, 1: 45.)

109 Trudel, *Montréal, la formation d'une société*, 22. Trudel provides a list of the numbers of new arrivals in the various years and also attempts some suggestions about why the birth rate was so low.

110 *Journal des Jesuites*, October 1646, 68.

111 Marie-Claire Daveluy, "Chomedey de Maisonneuve, Paul," in *DCB*, 1: 218.

112 DdeC, 151–3.

113 Ibid., 107–11, also a brief mention in *JR*, 25: 193.

114 DdeC, 119. Pilotte is given immortality not only by Dollier but also in the *JR*, 32: 27. As well, she is commemorated on the monument in Place d'Armes.

115 DdeC, 121–3.

116 Ibid., 155–7, also Marie de l'Incarnation, *Correspondance*, 416.

117 DdeC, 165–7.

118 Ibid., 151.

119 Letter of 30 August 1650, in Marie de l'Incarnation, *Correspondance*, 394.

120 DdeC, 159.

CHAPTER FOUR

1 *WMB*, 23, 26 (43, 47).

2 Daveluy, *La Société de Notre-Dame de Montréal*, 29.

3 Faillon, *Vie de la Soeur Bourgeoys*, 1: xxxvi, citing the Archives du Séminaire de Paris.

4 Maland, *Culture and Society in Seventeenth-Century France*, 177.

5 Daniel-Rops, *Monsieur Vincent*, 40. Marguerite Bourgeoys may have met Vincent de Paul in Paris in 1653, for he wrote in 1658: "About five years ago a lady came to see me to tell me about her wish to go to Canada. At

first I found it difficult, given the quality of the person; but seeing, through her perseverance, that her vocation was from God, I advised her to follow it. She went and is still there where she bears much fruit." See *Correspondance*, 10: 508. Is he describing someone of higher rank than Marguerite Bourgeoys? Why does she not mention him among those whom she consulted in 1653? On the other hand, who else could this lady have been? I am grateful to Elizabeth Rapley for drawing my attention to this passage.

6 Ibid.

7 Ibid., 41.

8 *WMB*, 72, 56, 68 (115, 91, 109).

9 The best source of information about the colonists of 1653 is *La Grande Recrue de 1653* by Roland-J. Auger. The author incorporates the findings of previous studies, including Mondoux's "Les 'Hommes' de Montréal."

10 DdeC, 185–9.

11 *WMB*, 25 (46). Auger estimates the number at about 125.

12 DdeC, 191.

13 *WMB*, 24 (45); Dollier de Casson says 27 September (DdeC, 183).

14 *HSV*, 72.

15 Ibid., 68.

16 Ibid., 69.

17 Desrosiers suggests that it may have been the perception of this grow-ing friendship that made some of the colonists initially suspicious about the nature of the relationship between the two (*Paul de Chomedey*, 152). The understanding between them was such that by the time that Marie Morin knew them in the early 1660s, she thought they had been acquainted since childhood and was only corrected in this opinion in the course of the composition of her *Annales*, almost certainly by Marguerite Bourgeoys herself (*HSV* 75, 84).

18 For this reason, Trudel discounts Dollier's portrayal of the enthusiasm of de Maisonneuve's welcome (Dollier de Casson, *Histoire de Montréal*, ed. Trudel and Baboyant, 155 n42). However, he does not seem to account for the place that this recruitment was to hold in the memory of the colony.

19 DdeC, 177.

20 Desrosiers, *Paul de Chomedey*, 153.

21 This was, of course, the same Jean de Lauson from whom the Société de Notre-Dame had purchased the island of Montreal. His governorship was not perceived as advantageous to Montreal. With heavy sarcasm, Dollier de Casson wrote: "The new governor, anxious to show to the gentlemen of the company of Montreal the good will he had towards

them and the generous treatment that they might expect therefrom, deducted 1,000 livres of salary that the gentlemen of the General Company allowed to M. de Maisonneuve both for himself as Governor of Montreal and for his garrison." DdeC, 163.

22 Ibid., 189.

23 *WMB*, 25–6 (47). She means that they were dressed in homespun rather than the white habits they would have worn in France. Mother Juchereau says that the Hospitallers had been obliged to substitute the grey habits because they could not keep their white ones clean when they were caring for patients in the huts of the Amerindians. See *Les annales de l'Hôtel-Dieu de Québec*, 41. This is a reminder that the strict rule of cloister could not be followed in Canada.

24 Lauson was himself a member of the Société de Notre-Dame de Montréal, but his governorship was perceived as hostile to Montreal not only by Dollier de Casson, but also by historians Lanctot in *Montréal sous Maisonneuve* and Desrosiers in *Paul de Chomedey*. The former sees him as a tool of the Jesuits, who had become disaffected with Montreal; the latter as a cowardly, indecisive, and self-serving governor.

25 *WMB*, 24 (45).

26 Ibid., 72 (115).

27 Ibid., 24 (45).

28 Ibid.

29 Ibid., 22 (42).

30 Desrosiers, *Paul de Chomedey*, 153.

31 *WMB*, 170 (245).

32 Boucher, *Histoire véritable*, 17.

33 *WMB*, 26 (47).

34 This document is preserved at McGill University. Trudel discusses its authenticity in *Montréal, la formation d'une société*, xxvii–xxviii.

35 *HSV*, 73.

36 Ibid., 68, 71.

37 *WMB*, 56 (91).

38 Desrosiers's biographies are well researched and written with considerable sympathetic insight, but unfortunately, they lack explicit documentation.

39 Desrosiers, *Paul de Chomedey*, 180. The theory that he expressed here does not seem to have occurred to Desrosiers when he was writing his biography of Marguerite Bourgeoys a decade earlier, but rather to have been the fruit of his research on de Maisonneuve. The fact that he himself was a married layman may have inclined him to view events differently from earlier clerical, commentators.

40 *HSV*, 66.

41 In an index in *Montréal, la formation d'une société*, 269–81, Trudel pre-

sents a list of the marriages in Montreal in the years 1642–62, including the date of baptism of the first child, compiled from the earliest church registers.

42 *WMB*, 23 (43–4).

43 Two of the marriages were solemnized at Quebec, thirteen at Montreal.

44 DdeC, 163.

45 *HCND*, 1: 44–5.

46 Desrosiers, *Paul de Chomedey*, 167. Desrosiers also draws attention to the custom of providing for the offspring of those men who had fallen in the service of the colony in the marriage contracts of second marriages made by their mothers.

47 DdeC, 195. Anne Archambault's parents had left Quebec and settled in Montreal. Her father, Jacques Archambault, is honoured as the digger of the first well in Montreal, close to the monument to the founders of Montreal near Pointe-à-Callière.

48 Five-year-old Catherine André in Pointe-Saint-Charles in 1673.

49 *WMB*, 178 (257).

50 Desrosiers, *Paul de Chomedey*, 167.

51 The primary sources of information about the colonization of Montreal in this period are to be found in the Archives de Saint-Sulpice in Paris and Montreal. Copies and microfilms of relevant documents can be found in the National Archives of Canada. See Lanctot, *Montréal sous Maisonneuve*, 94–5, and Desrosiers, *Paul de Chomedey*, 162–4.

52 Desrosiers, *Paul de Chomedey*, 166.

53 DdeC, 199–201.

54 Ibid., 221–3.

55 *WMB*, 20 (39).

56 Ibid.

57 One can see in Marguerite's account of a later marvel connected with the killing of one of the Sulpicians, the conflict between a charitable respect for the word of those who attest to such wonders and a natural scepticism, or at least a desire for convincing evidence. The image of the dead priest was supposed to have been imprinted on his kerchief, which was born off by his killers. She says: "As I was getting ready to go to France, I happened to think of what I might say if anyone should ask me whether this was true. I went to find Lavigne who was also brought back from this territory ... He told me that it was true, not because he had heard it said, but because he had seen it. He had promised them [the Iroquois] everything he could in exchange for it, assuring them that when he was back in Montreal where they had promised to bring him, he would not fail to satisfy them. But they would not accept this, saying that it was a flag for going to war." See *WMB*, 21 (40).

58 *HCND*, 1: 44.

59 DdeC, 73. Trudel suggests that the tailor might have been Louis
    Delaporte. See Dollier de Casson, *Histoire de Montréal*, ed. Trudel and
    Baboyant, 69 n41.

60 *WMB*, 19 (38).

61 Ibid., 19, 141 (37–8, 203).

62 As Marguerite Bourgeoys arrived in Montreal in mid-November 1653,
    the most likely date for the re-erection of the cross, involving, as it did,
    camping out on the mountain, would have been the following spring.

63 Marie Morin describes the importance the chapel had assumed in the
    life of the New France by the end of the century. See *HSV*, 74.

64 Ibid., 72.

65 Jamet, *Marguerite Bourgeoys*, 1: 160.

66 *WMB*, 32 (56).

67 Ibid., 32, 113 (56, 171).

68 Glandelet, *La vie de la soeur Marguerite Bourgeoys*, 55–6.

69 Rumilly, *Marguerite Bourgeoys*, 43.

70 RND.

71 AHDM, 4A/3. Marguerite wrote that she had her copy of the grant of
    the stable with her in France in 1659. She says that she showed it to the
    father of Edmée Chastel; See *WMB*, 28 (51).

72 *WMB*, 113 (171).

73 AHDM, 4A/3.

74 The verb she uses in this context is *curer*, which has connotations of
    cleaning out harbours, sewers, etc. (*EMB*, 47). The English translation
    should read: "The children cleaned it ... (26).

75 By happy coincidence, this beginning of formal education in Montreal
    occurred on the feast of a saint who is one of only two women declared
    doctors (teachers) of the church.

76 *WMB*, 26 (47).

77 DdeC, 209.

78 Dollier himself, who is very careful and discreet in the statements he
    makes about this and subsequent events; Daveluy in her article on de
    Maisonneuve in the *DCB* and other works on the events and persons of
    this period; Desrosiers in his biography of de Maisonneuve.

79 Lanctot, *Montréal sous Maisonneuve*, 106. As Lanctot also observes, the
    many references in documents of the period to the maintenance and
    promotion of harmony between Quebec and Montreal is a certain sign
    of its absence.

80 Léon Pouliot, "Ragueneau, Paul," *DCB*, 1: 561–2.

81 Rochemonteix, *Les Jésuites de la Nouvelle France*; quoted in *DCB*, 1: 562.

82 Desrosiers, *Paul de Chomedey*, 189. Desrosiers provides the most com-
    plete information about the unhappy fate of both Jacqueline de
    Chevilly and her husband; drawn from the Archives de l'Aube. On the

settlement of a prolonged and complicated dispute about an inheritance, Guillaume de Rouxel, Sieur de Défan de Medavie, the husband of a cousin of Jacqueline, shot her husband, François Bouvot, to death in 1651 and then disappeared. The same man shot and killed Jacqueline herself in August 1655, and then again escaped being brought to justice. Although he was known and condemned, he was never punished, possibly through the assistance and protection of fellow members of the league.

83 Blain, "L'archevêque de Rouen, l'église de Canada et les historiens" and "Les structures de l'église et la conjoncture coloniale en Nouvelle-France."

84 Blain says that the archbishop of Rouen became involved with New France through the presence in Quebec of Hospitallers from Dieppe, who were undoubtedly under his jurisdiction. The problem arose when there was question about religious profession by the Ursulines in Quebec because they came from different regions of France, as did the secular colonists, whose marriages might also be in question.

85 Blain suggests that the secrecy was probably to avoid conflict with other French bishops, who might also advance claims for jurisdiction because colonists came from their dioceses. See "L'Archeveque de Rouen," 214.

86 DdeC, 217.

87 Desrosiers, *Paul de Chomedey*, 208.

88 Jean de Lauson had returned to France in 1656, entrusting his office to his son, but the latter also chose to return there the following summer, and Louis d'Ailleboust was once more exercising the office of governor until another could be appointed.

89 Dr Marcel Cadotte has attempted a diagnosis in "Jeanne Mance: un diagnostic médical après trois cents ans," in *Les origines de Montréal*, ed. Brault, 149–59.

90 *WMB*, 26 (48).

91 Marguerite Picart was about fourteen years old at this time. She was married at the end of 1658 to Nicolas Godé, son of the first Montreal family, whose father and brother-in-law had been killed by the Iroquois the previous year.

92 *WMB*, 26–7 (48–9).

93 A letter written by Louis Tronson in 1686 and cited in Faillon, *Vie de la Soeur Bourgeoys*, 1: 287, urges that Marguerite Bourgeoys must be reassured about the efforts to Europeanize the Indian children, which is, in any case, a policy on which the court is determined.

94 *WMB*, 27 (48). The English translation should read, "the little Lacroix woman" rather than "the Lacroix child," "petite" serving as familiar diminutive here.

95 Trudel, *Montréal, la formation d'une société*, 271.

96 *WMB*, 27 (49).

97 DdeC, 293.

98 *WMB*, 26 (48).

99 Daveluy, *Jeanne Mance*, 160.

100 DdeC, 227.

101 *HSV*, 97.

102 DdeC, 213–15.

CHAPTER FIVE

1 *WMB*, 174, 35 (251, 61).

2 Ibid., 30 (53–4).

3 ACMB, Scott, "The Stable Foundation," 6.

4 Faillon, *Vie de Mademoiselle Mance*, 1: 101. In these days of greater religious tolerance, biographers have more difficulty in interpreting the incident.

5 The group known as the Aa was, like the Compagnie du Saint-Sacrement, a secret association. Its members, drawn from the great Marian associations, were committed to the strict observance of the rules of these groups, to common prayer and penance, and to the practice of works of charity under the protection of the Blessed Virgin. The beginnings were in La Flèche, but the principal Aa was that of Paris, founded in 1643 and commonly known as the Société des Bons Amis. Demers, in "Nomination et sacre de Mgr Laval," 15 n8, 9, provides a bibliography.

6 Ibid., 17, citing the correspondence of St Vincent de Paul.

7 *HSV*, 81.

8 *WMB*, 28 (50). Both were writing long after the event. Sister Jumeau, who was later to come to Montreal, was the superior at Baugé when Jeanne Mance and Marguerite Bourgeoys stopped there. It is possible that the memory of the arrival for Christmas midnight mass was hers. It is quite plausible that the two travellers stayed at Baugé for several days, giving Jeanne a chance to brace herself for the second part of her painful journey.

9 DdeC, 233.

10 *HSV*, 81.

11 *WMB*, 33 (57).

12 AA, 2 E 6/45, Claude Bourgeois II. This document is concerned with the share of these children in the estate of the late Abraham Bourgeoys and Guillemette Garnier, further indication that this Marie was indeed Marguerite's sister. The research to date on Marie Bourgeoys is summarized in Plante, "The Family of Marguerite Bourgeoys," *CMB* 52: 25–6.

13 Jamet, Marguerite Bourgeoys, 1: 201.

14 2 E 6/45, Claude Bourgeois II. This formal renunciation was made on the afternoon of 31 March 1659. Neither Madeleine nor Pierre was present, their uncle Cossard accepting for them. This fact seems to call into question her statement that she made this renunciation in the presence of a notary in Paris before her original departure in 1653, unless some kind of provisional settlement was drawn up at that time. See WMB, 166 (239).

15 WMB, 28 (51).

16 ACMB, A. Morin, "Antoine Gendret," citing AA, fonds Saint-Nizier, 18 G liasse 12.

17 It was later to happen to the bodies of both Jeanne herself and Marguerite Bourgeoys.

18 Faillon, *Vie de Mademoiselle Mance*, 1: 109.

19 *Attestation authentique de miracles attribués à M. Olier, déclaration de Mlle Mance*, 51; cited in Faillon, *Vie de Mademoiselle Mance*, 1: 110.

20 Ibid.

21 DdeC, 237.

22 HSV, 83.

23 For a discussion of medical and psychological aspects of the cure, see Marcel Cadotte, "Jeanne Mance: un diagnostique médical après trois cents ans," in *Les Origines de Montréal*, ed. Brault, 15–48.

24 Faillon, *Vie de Mademoiselle Mance*, 1: 115, 116. This volume contains a facsimile of the opening phrases of the official attestation.

25 WMB, 28 (50).

26 Ibid., 174 (251).

27 Jamet, *Marguerite Bourgeoys*, 1: 202–3.

28 WMB, 64 (103–4). To the reader of today, the comparison, which continues, "fit to receive all kinds of rubbish and incapable of refreshing," may imply a disconcertingly low opinion of human nature. However, in Glandelet's *Vray esprit*, the passage goes on: "unless it [the life of the sisters] is joined to its source. I do not find any more suitable means of achieving this than to follow the Blessed Virgin, to imitate the course of her life in all things and to go to God through her as the Eternal Father gave us His Son through her" (70). Marguerite lived at a time when there was a much greater consciousness of the corruption that was the result of original sin than is now the case – a century that produced the Jansenist movement in the Catholic Church. Also, as she makes her claim for her sisters here, as when she compares them with the apostles, she is well aware of the criticism and objections that may be raised and is concerned to deflect them.

29 Ibid., 81 (125). Marguerite is comparing her community with the college of apostles as noted above.

30 Ibid., 50 (82).

31   Ibid., 90 (139).
32   Ibid., 28 (51).
33   HCND, 2: 281.
34   HSV, 74–5.
35   WMB, 35 (61). Edmée Chastel was the only one of the four women who joined Marguerite in 1659 not to become a permanent member of the community.
36   Ibid., 28 (51). This is one of the passages which indicates that Marguerite had with her her own copy of the deed to the stable, a document that later disappeared.
37   AA, 2 E 7/174, notaire royal Vinot.
38   WMB, 28–9 (51–2).
39   L. Morin, *Deux familles troyennnes de musiciens et de comédiens*, 11–12. Morin suggests that the genesis of Marie's vocation may be found in the presence of several priests in the family, at least one of whom possibly belonged to the Compagnie du Saint-Sacrement. He also remarks on the frequent and apparently spontaneous appearance in the families of Troyes connected with the tailoring occupation of artists, writers, and thinkers. He asks: "Does this occupation, peaceful, often solitary, where one has the leisure to reflect as one plies the needle, have an influence on the minds developing around the paternal workbench?"
40   WMB, 29 (52).
41   Ibid., 29–30 (52–3).
42   Ibid., 36 (62).
43   Ibid., 30 (53).
44   HCND, 1: 341. As Bishop Laval sailed from La Rochelle for Quebec on 13 April 1659, there would indeed have been very little time for Marguerite and her companions to have seen him before his departure.
45   WMB, 33 (57).
46   AJM, 248, 14 October 1662, Basset.
47   Godbout, Les passagers du Saint-André, 38.
48   WMB, 29 (52). The identity of this young man is not known. Godbout mentions a Richard Pajot, who appears on the roll of passengers on the *Saint-André*, but of whom there is no later trace in the colony (*Les passagers du Saint-André*, 41). No name can be suggested from among the deaths recorded at Ville-Marie two years later. There were to be other such *donnés* attached to the Congregation, as there were to other religious communities. They pledged their services for varying lengths of time and in return were supported by the community to which they had attached themselves.
49   WMB, 33 (57).
50   Ibid., 29–30 (53).
51   HSV, 80.

52 According to Sister Morin, Madame de Bullion also paid all Jeanne Mance's travelling expenses and entrusted her with sums of money for the relief of the poor families of Montreal. See *HSV*, 84.

53 Faillon, *Vie de Mademoiselle Mance*, 1: 122.

54 *HSV*, 100. Lapointe-Roy places the work of Judith de Brésoles as apothecary within its historical context in "L'apothicairerie française au XVIIe siècle et son implantation à Ville-Marie par Mère de Brésoles, r.h.s.j," in *Les origines de Montréal*, ed. Brault, 251–68.

55 *HSV*, 136–7.

56 Daveluy, *Jeanne Mance*, 185–7. As it happened, both these prospective postulants were to marry in New France, but this community, which encountered so many obstacles to its foundation, was soon to have among its members the first Canadian-born nun, Marie Morin, who came from her native Quebec to join the hospital sisters in Montreal in 1662.

57 DdeC, 247.

58 Oury, *L'homme qui a conçu Montréal*, 197–9.

59 DdeC, 241–3. The fact that Dollier draws attention to one of the words used in the letter would suggest that he was familiar with the specific content of at least part of it and not just with the sense of the contents.

60 Ibid., 243. Dollier gives their number as thirty-two, but some twentieth-century estimates are lower.

61 Ibid., 243–5.

62 In the hope that within the year he would have the sisters from Quebec established at Montreal.

63 *WMB*, 35 (61–2).

64 Ibid., 30 (53). In French, *très honnête capitaine.*

65 Ibid., 35 (62). "Lad" or "young fellow" might be a better translation of *garçon* here.

66 A transcript of this contract is included in Daveluy's *Jeanne Mance*, 262–5.

67 Sister Scott's correction is in her papers at ACMB. The note in question is to be found in *EMB*, 47 (*WMB*, 26).

68 See Malo and Sévigny, *Participation of Associates in the Charism of the Congregation*, 10–13. Because they were not cloistered, the sisters of the Congrégation de Notre-Dame of Montreal would not have needed the assistance of such an association in quite the same way as the cloistered Congrégation de Notre-Dame of Troyes, though they seem to have had assistance at times when numbers were not sufficient to send two sisters on a mission.

69 *HCND*, 2: 86–9.

70 Godbout, *Les passagers du Saint-André*, 7–11. E.Z. Massicotte, in an article included in this study (1–5), estimates that other passengers on the

ship destined for Montreal or Quebec probably brought the number up
to about two hundred, not counting the crew.

71 *Voyages et passagers de jadis*, by Georges Lenôtre; quoted in Godbout, *Les
passagers du Saint-André*, 3.

72 DdeC, 249.

73 WMB, 31 (54).

74 DdeC, 249.

75 HSV, 90.

76 Marguerite never mentions her own sickness in her account of the voyage, but it is alluded to by Marie Morin in her narrative, which is obviously derived from the founders of her community in Montreal (HSV,
91).

77 Ibid., 90–1.

78 DdeC, 249.

79 Godbout, *Les passagers du Saint-André*, 46.

80 WMB, 31 (54).

81 Trudel, *Montréal, la formation d'une société*, 266.

82 WMB, 31 (54).

83 The Thibaudeaus did have another child, Marie-Marthe, born in 1661,
who married Jean Boursier in 1673 and whose descendants are still
extant.

84 The first church was begun in 1658. Archaeological exploration has
revealed that it stood northwest of the present basilica. In later years,
ships customarily fired a salute as they passed. See Gagné and Asselin,
Saint Anne de Beaupré, 6, 16.

85 WMB, 31 (55).

CHAPTER SIX

1 WMB, 63, 81 (101–2, 125).

2 DdeC, 231.

3 WMB, 113 (172).

4 HSV, 92. See also Daveluy, *Jeanne Mance*, 193.

5 Lanctot, *Montréal sous Maisonneuve*, 136.

6 HSV, 174.

7 Faillon, *Vie de Mademoiselle Mance*, 1: 156.

8 Ibid., 158–9, citing a MS. found in the library of the Louvre, in-fol. 32,
fol. 72.

9 Trudel, *Montréal, la formation d'une société*, 237–67.

10 Ibid., 84.

11 WMB, 23 (43–4). There is no information as to why Jeanne Loysel should
have continued to live with Marguerite for so many years. When she
was four and a half her mother would have had another daughter not

quite a year old, and a son was born in November 1654. Perhaps the mother was not in good health and the situation, once initiated, became permanent. Perhaps it was a symbolic offering of the "first fruits." Marguerite was godmother to a Loysel boy born in June 1658, who survived less than a month. See RND.

12 *WMB*, 23 (43–4).

13 Faillon says: "In the beginnings when they were still few in number, she raised all the children of Villemarie without distinction, until at last, the population becoming more considerable, she confined herself to the education of the girls, the priests of the seminary being then charged with the care of instructing and forming the boys themselves." *Vie de la Soeur Bourgeoys*, 1: 181.

14 Trudel, *Montréal: la formation d'une société*, 240–67.

15 Ibid., 277.

16 *HSV*, 122.

17 Marguerite Bourgeoys had twice acted as godmother to daughters of Catherine Hureau and her husband, Jean Lemercher. The first Marguerite Lemercher, born in 1655, lived less than a year, but a second, born in 1657, survived. See RND.

18 *WMB*, 24 (45).

19 RND. Marie-Marthe Pinson, Madame Milot, was buried on 23 January 1663. A daughter, Françoise, had been baptized on the previous day and was buried on 29 January at the age of seven days. In all, Marie-Marthe bore six children between 1655 and 1663; four of whom died within a few days of their birth. Among their godparents were the most illustrious persons in the community: de Maisonneuve, Jeanne Mance, Lambert Closse, Catherine Primot. Marie-Marthe had also been the victim of an attempted rape. In 1657 Louis de la Saudraye, found guilty of this crime, was sentenced by de Maisonneuve to the confiscation of his land, half to go for the benefit of the parish church and half to the children of the injured woman. See Lanctot, *Montréal sous Maisonneuve*, 207.

20 The couple were married nearly five years before the birth of their first child. This pattern, repeated in several other marriages, would suggest that in some cases the bride had not yet attained puberty at the time of marriage.

21 Marie Morin wrote that Marguerite had sought companions in France in 1658–59 "in order to bring up the children of their sex in the fear and the love of the Lord in teaching them to read and write." *HSV*, 74.

22 Trudel calls attention to the fact that the early civil administration of New France was drawn from the ranks of the military and suggests that this was due to the higher degree of literacy prevailing among the former officers, which greatly increased their social mobility. See *The Beginnings of New France*, 265.

23 *Les vraies constitutions*, 17, 18.

24 *WMB*, 56, 68 (91, 109). As noted before, this respect for work was part of the spirit of her native city, Troyes.

25 Trudel, *Montréal, la formation d'une société*, 84.

26 She married Nicolas Godé, eldest son of the only family to come to Montreal in 1642, on the same day on which his widowed sister, Mathurine, married Jacques Le Moyne.

27 She married the Jean Chicot who had survived scalping by the Iroquois in 1651. See RND.

28 Inventaire des biens meubles de deffunte Magdelaine Fabre, AJM, 116, 16 novembre 1659, Basset.

29 Trudel, *Montréal, la formation d'une société*, 110.

30 RND. Marie-Marthe, baptized 21 February 1661, was named after her godmother, Marie-Marthe Pinson.

31 DdeC, 293. In the custom of choosing names for children who would soon die can be seen further evidence of grief at their early death. When Toussaint, ten-year-old son of Toussaint Hunault and Marie Lorgeuil, died in April 1673, a nephew born the day of the funeral was promptly given his name, though he also died within the week. The same pages of the RND record the death on 29 April of another Marie-des-Neiges at the Congregation.

32 The signing of the marriage contract of Pierre Raguideau and Marguerite Rebours on 15 November 1659. See Trudel, *Montréal, la formation d'une société*, 118.

33 *HSV*, 75.

34 In June 1663, 62.9 per cent of the total population of New France was male. The number of marriageable men outnumbered even the most generous estimate of marriageable women by more than seven to one. See Trudel, *The Beginnings of New France*, 261–2.

35 To Daniel Panier. Their marriage contract was signed at the house of Marguerite Bourgeoys on 23 October 1659. See Trudel, *Montréal, la formation d'une société*, 110.

36 *HSV*, 119.

37 Ibid., 122–3. Adrienne was married 16 January 1667 to Étienne Truteau. He, like her father, was a carpenter, and he had arrived in the recruitment of 1659. The two had a large family and, according to Godbout, were the ancestors of all the Trudeau families in Canada (*Les passagers du Saint-André*, 47). The little carpenter of those first days in Ville-Marie was to number a prime minister among his twentieth-century descendants.

38 *HSV*, 130.

39 Ethel M.G. Bennet, "Desportes, Hélène," in *DCB*, 1: 264; Honorius Provost, "Morin, Germain," in *DCB*, 2: 489.

40 This affair is the subject of the first chapter of Robert-Louis Seguin's *La sorcellerie au Canada français du xviie au xixe siècles*, 9–21. Both parties later remarried and had offspring.

41 *WMB*, 174 (251–2).

42 Ibid., 171 (247).

43 *HSV*, 139.

44 Ibid., 104–5.

45 Rapley, *The Dévotes*, 77. Rapley distinguishes between this attitude and that which tends rather to perceive the poor as a social problem.

46 There is evidence of this activity in the sums listed as paid to Marguerite Bourgeoys for such work in Archives de la Fabrique, Paroisse Notre-Dame, Comptes-rendus des marguilliers, premier registres.

47 *HSV*, 99–100, 75.

48 *AJM*, 195, 3 avril 1661, Basset.

49 *HSV*, 119; Juchereau, *Les annales de l'Hôtel-Dieu de Québec*, 211. The ambiguity about who loved and admired whom is in the French.

50 In December 1964 Alfred Morin reported that Madame Hubert Lamotte, née Defert, daughter of a former notary of Troyes, told him that she remembered, as a child, being read passages from letters, written by Edmée Chastel to her relatives, that were then in the possession of Madame Defert's father, a much later successor of the Chastel notaries. Morin's research led to the sad conclusion that, if these letters had existed, they had been pulped at least ten years earlier. A full account of his report appears in "A Lost Treasure?"

51 *AJM*, 238, 6 juillet 1662, Basset. The property measures half an arpent or French acre. The French acre was the equivalent of one and a half English acres.

52 A complete study of the history of the Congregation land in Pointe-Saint-Charles is to be found in Chicoine, *La métairie de Marguerite Bourgeoys à la Pointe-Saint-Charles*.

53 *HSV*, 123.

54 *WMB*, 178 (257).

55 Raymond Douville, "Boucher, Pierre," *DCB*, 2: 86.

56 Lanctot, *Filles de joie ou filles du roi*, passim.

57 Landry, *Orphelines en France pionnières au Canada*, 19–33.

58 *WMB*, 178 (257).

59 Mère Marie de S. André to the assistant of the Ursuline Convent in Magny, 29 October 1668; in Marie de l'Incarnation, *Correspondance*, 1007.

60 Marguerite did the work now undertaken by family-support groups organized by some immigrants. Much physical abuse of wives among immigrants has been attributed to the fact that husbands vent their frustration on their wives because of the absence of the support and

counselling that would be available through the extended family in their native land. Marguerite Bourgeoys's work should have helped make the situation of these women less miserable than that described by Louise Dechêne in *Habitants and Merchants in Seventeenth Century Montreal*, 37.

61 *WMB*, 23 (43). Father Pierre-Joseph-Marie Chaumonot was a Jesuit whose presence in Montreal will be explained later in this chapter. The earthquake is mentioned in all the contemporary sources, with the most vivid and detailed description having been written by Marie de l'Incarnation in letters to her son in the late summer. See her *Correspondance*, 686–93.

62 Faillon, *Histoire de la colonie française en Canada*, 3: 55. In the excerpt from Chaumonot's biography quoted by Faillon, Chaumonot speaks of the mother superior of the Hôtel-Dieu and then refers to Marguerite Bourgeoys by name, describing her as superior of the Congregation. The biography was not written until 1688, but can perhaps still give a valid impression as to how Marguerite and her companions were seen at the time of the organization of the Confraternity, that is, as a group that could be paralleled with the *réligieuses* at the Hôtel-Dieu.

63 *WMB*, 23 (43). As is noted, this could only have been possible if Jeanne Mance signed on her return from France in 1664.

64 *HSV*, 120–1. This meant, of course, that the Quebec institution, rather than the one in Montreal, received the remainder of Barbe d'Ailleboust's estate when she died.

65 Devotion to the Holy Family "was implanted in America, in the region of Canada where it flourished, thanks largely to the solicitude and activity of Venerable François de Montmorency Laval, first bishop of Quebec and of the venerable servant of God, Marguerite Bourgeoys." Brief of 14 June 1892.

66 The best evaluation of the primary sources relating to this event and description of the controversy is in André Vachon's article on Dollard in *DCB*, 1: 266–74. See also Lanctot, *Montréal sous Maisonneuve*, 135–55; Desrosiers, *Paul de Chomedey*, 222–30; and articles cited in bibliography.

67 Dollier de Casson attributes to the Iroquois the following statement: "If seventeen Frenchmen dealt with us in that fashion when they were in such a wretched hole, how shall we be treated when we have to attack a strong building in which are collected a number of such people? We mustn't be so mad as to go any farther, to do so would mean death to us all. Let us go home." DdeC, 267.

68 André Vachon, "Dollard des Ormeaux, Adam," in *DCB*, 1: 273. Vachon says that Dollier de Casson did not understand the native people.

69 Trudel, *The Beginnings of New France*, 271. This was a smaller earthquake than that of 1663.

70 Letter to her son, September 1661, in Marie de l'Incarnation, *Correspondance*, 665.

71 DdeC, 271.

72 Marguerite Bourgeoys's reference to this story has already been cited (*WMB*, 21), and there are references in all the standard contemporary documents. Like her, others – in particular, the Jesuit Simon Le Moyne – attempted to verify the authenticity of this event, but without success. The fact that the death and decapitation of Le Maistre took place just after he had celebrated the mass and while he was reciting the office of the feast of the Decapitation of St John the Baptist was regarded as an especially striking circumstance. See DdeC, 277.

73 *JR*, 47: 176–8. The Jesuit account of this incident is less gory than that of Dollier de Casson. It says that the Sulpician was killed at once because he was incapable of travelling and that de Brigeac was killed because his captors did not want to be burdened with a cripple. No details of the deaths are given.

74 Marguerite Bourgeoys appears to confuse this incident with that at Long Sault, and it was Faillon's use of the reference in her writings, with the suppression of the name of de Brigeac, that helped make Dollard a Christian martyr. "M. Brisar [*sic*] assembled 16 or 17 of the most generous men to go to war and attack the Indians; they were ready to give up their lives if it was God's will. But they were betrayed and all were killed with various kinds of suffering. M. Brisar encouraged them to endure well. The Indians left him for last to torture him at will. This they did with all the cruelty that they could imagine. But his patience and the love of God for whose sake he showed joy in suffering won the admiration of the Indians as well as that of other Frenchmen who had been captured previously." *WMB* 21–2 (41).

75 DdeC, 281–7.

76 Ibid., 287.

77 It is fortunate too that it was Judith de Brésoles who was involved in another incident described by Marie Morin. De Maisonneuve was our friend, says Marie, but still he sent wounded Iroquois to be cared for in the infirmary of the Hôtel-Dieu, a proceeding that she perceived as involving considerable danger for the sisters and their other patients. Some of these Iroquois were well enough to attack one of the sisters before anyone was the wiser. One day an Iroquois patient tried to smother Judith de Brésoles by crushing her between a door and a cupboard. She was rescued because Marie Morin happened to pass by and, seeing what was taking place, summoned the other able-bodied patients to her help. See *HSV*, 136.

78 Ibid., 135. Dollier de Casson describes an incident in February 1661 in which Barbe Poisson DuClos saved a group of colonists, including

Charles Le Moyne, who had been surprised without their weapons by a group of Iroquois. She saw their situation, and since there was no man in her house to send to help them, "she herself took a load of muskets on her shoulders and, fearless of a swarm of Iroquois whom she saw rush from every direction towards her house, she ran to our Frenchmen." (DdeC, 273). Mme Duclos would have had children in the stable-school in the 1660s. It is not surprising that some of these women, called upon to play traditionally masculine roles, should also have emulated men in other ways; de Maisonneuve had several times to officiate at the trials of women accused of physical assault, in some cases on men (See Lanctot, *Montréal sous Maisonneuve*, 204).

79 *HSV*, 134. The description cited here is found on 134–5.

80 Lanctot suggests that the arrival of Father Chaumonot to distribute the grain and other supplies from Quebec was an attempt on the part of the Jesuits and the bishop to bring Montreal back under Jesuit influence. He expresses surprise that Souart received Chaumonot so warmly and that the Sulpicians even gave him a pension during his stay (*Montréal sous Maisonneuve*, 178–9). The evidence seems to indicate that the power struggles undoubtedly taking place in the colony did not prevent the participants from practising elementary humanity and Christian charity and that the rivalries among those in authority did not necessarily extend to other members of their communities. Abbé Souart, deprived of the help of the two Sulpicians killed by the Iroquois and of the presence of de Queylus, seems to have been glad to accept the assistance of Father Chaumonot who even became his spiritual director during the Jesuit's stay in Montreal.

81 Ibid., 179.

82 *WMB*, 22–3 (42).

83 *Montréal sous Maisonneuve*, 186.

84 Trudel, *The Beginnings of New France*, 272.

85 See Trudel, *The Beginnings of New France*, 271–4, for a summary of the economic problems.

86 Daveluy discusses the implications of the contemporary statements, in a letter written by Baron de Fancamp and in the *Annales* of Sister Morin, about the disappearance of the 20,000 *livres*. See *Jeanne Mance*, 198.

87 The Compagnie du Saint-Sacrement had been suppressed in 1660.

88 Among twentieth-century Canadian historians, English-language scholars such as W.J. Eccles, biographer of Frontenac, Laval's long-time nemesis, treat the bishop with more sympathy than do French-language historians such as Gustav Lanctot and Marcel Trudel.

89 From letters of 13 October 1660, when the bishop was interfering in the Ursulines' manner of selecting a novice mistress, and of 13 September

1661, when he was attempting to alter their Constitutions. See Marie de l'Incarnation, *Correspondance*, 643, 652–3.

90 André Vachon, "Thubières de Levy de Queylus, Gabriel," in *DCB*, 1: 646.

91 Campeau has presented a more balanced view in an article that also situates the conflicts which arose in the context of differing philosophies in seventeenth-century France about the relationship between secular and ecclesiastical power; see "Mgr de Laval et le Conseil souverain 1659–1684."

92 *WMB*, 171–2, 191–2 (246–8, 271–2).

93 Marie de l'Incarnation discusses this issue in a letter to her son in November 1660. He appears to have reproached her for not favouring the conversion of the Iroquois rather than military domination. She replies that both the Jesuits and Bishop Laval had previously shared his opinion, but the futility of their efforts had led them to accept the opinion of "all the wise people of this country." Marie de l'Incarnation, *Correspondance*, 649.

94 Lanctot, *Montréal sous Maisonneuve*, 192.

95 Trudel, *The Beginnings of New France*, 279.

96 The terms of the document are to be found in Daveluy, *La Société de Notre-Dame de Montréal*, 38–43.

97 Daveluy, *Jeanne Mance*, 212–14; citing Faillon, *Histoire de la colonie française en Canada*, 3: 60–2.

98 DdeC, 295.

99 Marie Morin makes explicit de Maisonneuve's support of her community at this time. See *HSV*, 126–7.

100 DdeC, 295.

101 Lanctot, *Montréal sous Maisonneuve*, 197.

102 Ibid., 200.

103 Ibid., 198–9.

104 De Maisonneuve on 1 May 1673, wrote a memorandum responding to these charges. A handwritten copy of this document is preserved in AHDM and the contents are printed in Daveluy, *Jeanne Mance*, 268–70.

105 *HSV*, 69.

106 DdeC, 299.

107 *HSV*, 140.

108 Lanctot, *Montréal sous Maisonneuve*, 224.

109 Desrosiers, *Paul de Chomedey*, 288.

110 DdeC, 301.

111 *HSV*, 70.

112 Lanctot also signals the fact that against the seventeenth-century orientation towards autocratic centralization, there was in Montreal under de Maisonneuve a tendency towards popular representation in the public domain. See *Montréal sous Maisonneuve*, 237.

113 Ibid., 238.

114 DdeC, 329.

115 *HSV*, 71.

116 Le Blant, "Les derniers jours de Maisonneuve et Philippe de Turmenyes."

117 A brief sojourn with the Ursulines in 1666 was simply to confirm Marie Raisin in her commitment to the Congregation.

118 Letters patent were issued in 1671.

119 In an inventory of the goods of the late Simon LeRoy, Marguerite is still styled simply "l'honneste fille" AJM, 233, 17 mars 1662, Basset), but three months later, in an inventory of the goods of the late Michel Louvard, she is "l'honneste fille Marguerite Bourgeoys de la Congrégation" (AJM, 235, 29 juin 1662, Basset), and when a marriage contract is signed between Pierre Maillet and Marie Anne Hardy less than two weeks later, it is signed "en la maison des filles de la Congrégation" (AJM, 239, 9 juillet 1662, Basset). See also the marriage contract between François Roy and Elisabeth Haguin (AJM, 244, 6 septembre 1662, Basset).

120 More, *Utopia*, trans. and ed. H.S.V. Ogden (New York: Appleton-Century-Crofts 1949), 23.

121 The census of 1666 already shows Marie Raisin teaching (temporarily) in Trois-Rivières.

122 *WMB*, 187 (267).

Bibliography

ARCHIVAL SOURCES

Archives de l'Archevêché de Montréal
Charles de Glandelet. "Vie de la Soeur Bourgeoys." In Procès *ne pereant*,
139e session, 13 avril 1889, 3184–3299

Archives de l'Aube (AA)
    2 E 10, dépôt Nicolas Claude Bourgeois, 43
    2 E 6 37, minutes Claude Bourgeois, dépôt Nicolas
    G 3545
    2 E 7 174, notaire royal Vinot
    2 E 6 45, notaire Claude Bourgeois II
    15 G 207, fo. 37 (1638–39), registres des comptes de la fabrique de Saint-
    Jean-au-Marché
    15 G 213 fo. 8 and 32, 1642–43, registres des comptes de la fabrique de
    Saint-Jean-au-Marché
    25 H 1, registres des professions, vêtures et sépultures, Carmelites

Archives du Centre Marguerite-Bourgeoys (ACMB)
M. Eileen Scott. Correspondence with Edward Korany and Alfred Morin;
    miscellaneous unpublished articles, essays, and notes
Mary Aline Gelson. "May God Be Your Whole Love." Unpublished paper
    translated from H. Derréal, *La bienheureuse Alix Leclerc et ses écrits* (Nancy
    1947)
Alfred Morin. "Antoine Gendret, George Proffit, Marie Nicolas
    Desguerrois"
André Vinot. "Notes de lecture sur la bienheureuse Marguerite Bourgeoys
    et quelques monastères de la ville de Troyes dans la première moitié du
    17ième siècle"

Archives de la Congrégation de Notre-Dame de Montréal (ACND)
Because of the fires that destroyed the mother house of the Congrégation
  de Notre-Dame in 1768 and 1893, the Archives have few original seventeenth-century documents. However, they do contain certified copies of
  most known documents pertaining to the life of Marguerite Bourgeoys
  and the beginnings of her Congregation.

Archives de l'Hôtel-Dieu de Montréal (AHDM)
The oldest extant copy of the deed for Montreal's first school is in the
  archives of the Hôtel-Dieu (4A2/3)

Archives judiciaires de Montréal (AJM)
  116, 16 novembre 1659, Basset
  195, 3 avril 1661, Basset
  233, 17 mars 1662, Basset
  235, 29 juin 1662, Basset
  238, 6 juillet 1662, Basset
  239, 9 juillet 1662, Basset
  244, 6 septembre 1662, Basset
  249, 14 octobre 1662, Basset

Archives de la Paroisse Notre-Dame de Montréal
Registres de l'église Notre-Dame de Montréal (RND). A facsimile of the old-
  est parts of the registers of baptism, marriage, and burial was published
  by the Société des Dix in 1961 under the title *Premier registre de l'église
  Notre-Dame de Montreal*. This work reproduces the entries from 1642 to
  1681. The originals are conserved at the Paroisse Notre-Dame in
  Montreal.
"Délibérations des assemblées des marguilliers" (beginning 1657)
"Comptes rendus par les marguilliers" (beginning 1658)

Archives du Séminaire de Québec
Charles de Glandelet. "Vie de la soeur Marie Barbier"

Registres de catholicité de Troyes
Registres de la paroisse Saint-Jean-au-Marché
Registres de la paroisse Saint-Rémi

School Sisters of Notre Dame, Wilton, Conn.
"A Fertile Vine: Life of the Blessed Alix Leclerc, CoFoundress of the
  Congregation of Notre Dame." Translation of an unpublished manuscript
  in library of the School Sisters of Notre Dame

PRINTED SOURCES

Allard, Michel, Robert Lahaise, et al. *L'Hôtel-Dieu de Montréal, 1642–1973*.
Montreal: Hurtubise 1973
Aries, Philippe. *Centuries of Childhood: A Social History of Family Life*. Trans.
Robert Balcick. New York: Vintage Books 1962
Ashley, Maurice. *The Age of Absolutism, 1648–1675*. Springfield, Mass.:
Merriam 1974
Audet, Louis-Philippe. "L'éducation au temps de Mgr de Laval," SCHEC 25
(1957–58): 59-78
– "L'instruction de dix mille colons, nos ancêtres," *Cahiers des Dix* 37 (1972):
9–49
Auger, Roland-J. *La grande recrue de 1653*. Société généalogique, no. 1.
Montreal, 1955
Baboyant, Marie. "Dollier de Casson," CMB, no. 55 (1995)
Baillargeon, Noel. *Le Séminaire de Quebec sous l'épiscopat de Mgr de Laval*.
Québec: Université de Laval 1972
Beaudoin, Marie-Louise. *Les premières et les filles du roi à Ville-Marie*.
Montréal: Maison Saint-Gabriel 1996
Béchard, Henri. *Jerôme de la Dauversière – His Friends and Enemies*.
Bloomingdale, Ohio: AFC 1991
Belin, Christian. "Écriture et oraison au XVIIe siècle." *La vie spirituelle*, no.
715 (mai–juin 1995): 281–92
Belmont, François Vachon de. *Éloges de quelques personnes morte en odeur de
sainteté à Montréal, 1722*. RAPQ, no. 10 (1929–30): 144–89
Blain, Jean. "L'archevêque de Rouen, l'église du Canada et les historiens: un
exemple de déformation historique." RHAF 21, no. 2 (septembre 1967):
199–216
– "Les structures de l'église et la conjoncture coloniale en Nouvelle-France,
1632–1674." RHAF 21, no. 4 (mars 1968): 749–56
Boland (S.S. Marguerite of the Sacred Heart). *The Pearl of Troyes*. Montreal:
Canada Printing Company 1878
Boucher, Pierre. *Histoire véritable et naturelle des moeurs et productions du pays
de la Nouvelle-France vulgairement dite le Canada 1664*. Société historique de
Boucherville 1964
Boulenger, Jacques. *The Seventeenth Century in France*. New York: Capricorn
Books 1963
Bourgeoys, Marguerite. *Les écrits de Mère Bourgeoys: autobiographie et testa-
ment spirituel*. Classés et annotés par S.S. Damase-de-Rome. Montréal:
Congrégation de Notre-Dame 1964. Published in English as *The Writings
of Marguerite Bourgeoys: Autobiography and Spiritual Testament*, trans. M.V.
Cotter (Montréal: Congrégation de Notre-Dame 1976)

Boutiot, T. *Histoire de la ville de Troyes et de la Champagne méridionale*. Vol. 4.
    Troyes: Dufey-Robert, 1874

Brault, Jean-Rémi, ed. *Les origines de Montréal*. Montreal: Leméac 1993

Breton, Bernadette. *Marguerite Bourgeoys and the Native People*. Trans.
    Patricia Landry. CND, Heritage no. 4. Montreal, 1992

Brown, Raymond, et al., eds. *Mary in the New Testament: A Collaborative
    Assessment by Protestant and Roman Catholic Scholars*. Toronto: Paulist
    Press 1978

Burgess, Joanne, Louise Dechêne, et al. *Clés pour l'histoire de Montréal: bibli-
    ographie*. Montreal: Boréal 1992

Butler, Elizabeth. *The Life of Venerable Marguerite Bourgeoys*. New York, P.J.
    Kenedy & Sons 1932

Campeau, Lucien. "Mgr de Laval et le Conseil souverain 1659–1684." RHAF
    27, no. 3 (décembre 1973): 323–59

Carré, Gustave. *Histoire populaire de Troyes et du département de l'Aube*.
    Troyes: Lacroix 1881

Caza, Lorraine. *La vie voyagère, conversante avec le prochain Marguerite
    Bourgeoys*. Montreal: Bellarmin; Paris: Cerf 1982

Chabroux, Evelyne. *Troyes – Marguerite Bourgeoys: la rencontre d'une cité et
    d'une sainte*. Troyes: Renaissance 1984

Charbonneau, Hubert, et al. *Naissance d'une population: les Français établis au
    Canada au XVIIe siècle*. Montreal: Presses de l'Université de Montréal 1987

Charron, Yvon. *Mother Bourgeoys*. Trans. S.S. Godeliva. Montreal:
    Beauchemin 1950

Chaumonot, Pierre-Joseph-Marie. *Un missionnaire des Hurons: autobiographie
    du Père Chaumonot de la Compagnie de Jésus et son complément*. Ed. Felix
    Martin. Paris: Oudin 1885

Chicoine, Émilia. *La métairie de Marguerite Bourgeoys à la Pointe-Saint-Charles*.
    Montreal: Fides 1986

Cliche, Marie-Aimée. *Les pratiques de dévotion en Nouvelle-France*. Québec:
    Université de Laval 1988

Crubellier, Maurice, and Charles Juillard. *Histoire de la Champagne*. Paris:
    Presse universitaire de France 1969

D'Allaire, Micheline. *Les dots des religieuses au Canada français, 1639-1800:
    étude économique et sociale*. Cahiers du Québec collection histoire.
    Montreal: Hurtibise HMH 1986

Daniel-Rops, Henri. *Monsieur Vincent: The Story of Saint Vincent de Paul*.
    Trans. Julie Kernan. New York: Hawthorn 1961

Daveluy, Marie-Claire. *Jeanne Mance (1606–1673)*. Montréal: Fides 1962
– *La Société de Notre-Dame de Montréal (1639–1663)*. Montréal: Fides 1965

Dechêne, Louise. *Habitants and Merchants in Seventeenth-Century Montreal*.
    Trans. Liana Vardi. Montreal: McGill-Queen's University Press 1992

Demers, Georges-Edouard. "Nomination et sacre de Mgr de Laval." SCHEC 24 (1957): 13–32

Deroy-Pineau, Françoise. *Jeanne Mance: de Langres à Montréal, la passion de soigner.* Montréal: Bellarmin 1995

Derréal, H. *Une grande figure lorraine du XVIIe siècle: saint Pierre Fourier, humaniste et épistolier.* Paris: Berger-Levrault 1942

– *Un missionnaire de la Contre-Réforme: saint Pierre Fourier et l'institution de la Congrégation de Notre-Dame.* Paris: Plon 1964

Desrosiers, Léo-Paul. *Dans le nid d'Aiglons, la Colombe: vie de Jeanne Leber, la recluse.* Montréal: Fides 1963

– *Les dialogues de Marthe et de Marie.* Montréal: Fides 1957

– *Paul de Chomedey, Sieur de Maisonneuve.* Montréal: Fides 1967

Dickenson, John A. "Annaotaha et Dollard vus de l'autre côté de la palissade." RHAF 35, no. 2 (1981): 163–78

Dictionary of Canadian Biography. Ed. Brown, Trudel, and Vachon. Vols. 1 (1966), 2 (1969). Toronto and Quebec: Universities of Toronto Press and Les Presses d'université Laval.

Dodd, C.H. *The Founder of Christianity.* New York: Macmillan 1970

Dollier de Casson, François. *Histoire de Montréal.* Nouvelle éd. critique par Marcel Trudel et Marie Baboyant. Montréal: Hurtubise 1992

– *A History of Montreal, 1640–1672.* Trans. Ralph Flenley. Toronto: Dent 1928

Doyle, Sister Saint Ignatius. *Marguerite Bourgeoys and Her Congregation.* Gardenvale: Garden City Press 1940

Drummond, Margaret Mary. *The Life and Times of Marguerite Bourgeoys.* Boston: Angel Guardian Press 1907

Eccles, W.J. *Canada under Louis XIV, 1663–1701.* Toronto: McClelland and Stewart 1964

L'exploit du Long-Sault: les témoignages des contemporains. Présenté par Adrien Pouliot and Silvio Dumas. Québec, Société historique 1960

Fabre-Surveyer, Édouard. "La justice à Montréal sous Maisonneuve." in *Cahiers de l'Académie canadienne-française* 8 (1964): 164–70

Faillon, Étienne-Michel. *Histoire de la colonie française en Canada.* 3 vols. Montréal: Bibliothèque paroissiale 1865

– *Vie de la Soeur Bourgeoys, fondatrice de la Congrégation de Notre-Dame de Ville-Marie en Canada, suivie de l'histoire de cet institut jusqu'à ce jour.* 2 vols. Villemarie: Congrégation de Notre-Dame 1853

– *Vie de Mademoiselle Mance et histoire de l'Hôtel-Dieu de Villemarie en Canada.* 2 vols. In *Mémoires particuliers pour servir à l'histoire de l'église de l'Amérique du Nord.* Paris: Périsse Frères 1854

– *Vie de M. Olier, fondateur du Séminaire de Saint-Sulpice.* Paris: Poussielgue-Rusand 1843

Foley, Mary Anne. "Uncloistered Apostolic Life for Women: Marguerite

Bourgeoys's Experiment in Ville Marie." Dissertation, Yale University 1991

Fourier, Pierre. *Sa correspondance 1598–1640*. 5 vols. Nancy: Presses universitaires de Nancy 1986–91

Gagné, Lucien, and Jean-Pierre Asselin. *Saint Anne de Beaupré: Pilgrim's Goal for Three Hundred Years*. Trans. Eric W. Gosling. Saint Anne de Beaupré 1984

Gauthier, Henri. *Sulpitiana*. Montréal: Oeuvres paroissiales de St.-Jacques 1926

Gauthier, Jean. *Ces Messieurs de Saint-Sulpice*. Paris: Fayard 1957

Gauthier, Roland. *La dévotion à la Sainte Famille en Nouvelle-France au XVIIe siècle*. Lumière sur la Montagne 3 Montréal: Oratoire Saint-Joseph 1996

Gies, Joseph, and Frances Gies. *Life in a Medieval City*. New York: Thomas Crowell 1969

Glandelet, Charles de. *La vie de la soeur Marguerite Bourgeoys*. Ed. Hélène Tremblay. Montréal: CND 1993

– *Le vray esprit de l'institut des soeurs seculières de la Congrégation de Notre-Dame établi à Ville- Marie en l'Isle de Montréal en Canada*. Notes rédigées par l'abbé Charles de Glandelet, 1700–01. Ed. Hélène Tremblay. Montréal: Congrégation de Notre-Dame 1976. Published in English as *The True Spirit of the Institute of the Secular Sisters of the Congregation de Notre Dame*, trans. Frances McCann (Montreal: Congrégation de Notre-Dame 1977)

Godbout, Archange. *Les passagers du Saint-André: la recrue de 1659*. Société généalogique canadienne-française, no. 4. Montréal 1964

Gosselin, Amédée. *L'instruction au Canada sous le régime français (1635–1760)*. Québec: Typ. Laflamme et Proulx 1911

Gosselin, Auguste. *Vie de Monseigneur de Laval*. 2 vols. Québec: L.J. Demers et Frères 1830

Graef, Hilda. *Mary: A History of Doctrine and Devotion*. 2 vols. London: Sheed and Ward 1963

Hale, Horatio. *The Iroquois Book of Rites*. Toronto: University of Toronto Press 1963

Haughton, Rosemary. *The Catholic Thing*. Springfield, Ill.: Templegate 1979

– *The Recreation of Eve*. Springfield, Ill.: Templegate 1985

Hervieux, Jacques. *The New Testament Apocrypha*. Trans. Wulstan Hibberd. Twentieth century encyclopedia of Catholicism, 72. New York: Hawthorne Books 1960

Heschel, Abraham. *Man's Quest for God*. New York: Charles Scribner's Sons 1954

Hunt, George T. *The Wars of the Iroquois*. Madison: University of Wisconsin Press 1960

Hurtubise, Pierre. "Ni janséniste, ni gallican, ni ultramontaine: François de Laval." RHAF 28, no. 1 (juin 1974): 3–26

Jamet, Albert. *Marguerite Bourgeoys, 1620–1700.* 2 vols. Montréal: La Presse catholique panaméricaine 1942

The Jesuit Relations and Allied Documents: Travels and Explorations of the Jesuit Missionaries in New France, 1610–1791. Ed. Reuben Gold Thwaites. 73 vols. New York: Pageant Books 1959

Le Journal des Jésuites, publié d'après le manuscrit original conservé aux Archives du Séminaire de Québec. Ed. Laverdière et Casgrain. Montréal 1892

Juchereau de la Ferté, Jeanne-Françoise de Saint-Ignace, et Marie- Andrée Duplessis de Sainte-Hélène. *Les annales de l'Hôtel- Dieu de Québec, 1636–1716.* Ed. Albert Jamet. Québec et Montréal 1939

Jugements et délibérations du Conseil souverain de la Nouvelle- France. Vol. 1. Québec: A. Coté et Cie 1885

Karch, Pierre. *Les ateliers du pouvoir.* Collection documents. Montreal: XYZ 1995

La Flèche et Montréal, ou l'extraordinaire entreprise canadienne du fléchois Jérôme le Royer de la Dauversière. La Flèche: Éditions fléchoises 1947

Lambert, Thérèse. *Marguerite Bourgeoys, éducatrice, mère d'un pays et d'une église.* Montréal: Bellarmin 1982

Lamontagne, Sophie-Laurence. *L'hiver dans la culture québécoise (XVIIe–XIXe siècles).* Montréal: Institut québécois de recherche sur la culture 1983

Lanctot, Gustave. *Filles de joie ou filles du roi: etude sur l'émigration féminine en Nouvelle-France.* Montréal: Chantecler 1952

– *Montréal sous Maisonneuve.* Montréal: Beauchemin 1966

Landry, Yves. *Orphelines en France pionnières au Canada: les filles du roi au XVIIe siècle.* Montréal: Leméac 1992

Le Blant, Robert. "Les derniers jours de Maisonneuve et Philippe de Turmenyes." *RHAF* 13 (1959): 262–80. This article includes copies of de Maisonneuve's statement in support of Marguerite Bourgeoys's application for letters patent for the Congrégation de Notre-Dame of Montreal and his last will and testament.

Lefebvre, Esther. *Marie Morin, premier historien canadien de Villemarie.* Montréal: Fides 1959

Leleu, J.-M. *Histoire de Notre-Dame de Bon-Secours à Montréal.* Montréal: Cadieux & Derome 1900

Lemieux, Denise. *Les petits innocents: l'enfance en Nouvelle- France.* Québec: Institut québécois de recherche sur la culture 1985

Lewis, W.H. *The Splendid Century.* London: William Sloane Associates 1953

Loomis, Roger Sherman, ed. *Arthurian Literature in the Middle Ages: A Collaborative History.* Oxford: Clarendon Press 1959

Marie Odile, Soeur Sainte. "Bibliographie critique de la vénérable Marguerite Bourgeoys." Dissertation, Université de Montréal 1949

Maland, David. *Culture and Society in Seventeenth Century France.* London: Batsford 1970

Malo, Denise, and Jeannine Sévigny. *Participation of Associates in the Charism of the Congregation of Notre Dame: A Heritage Rediscovered.* Trans. Patricia Landry CND, Heritage no. 22. Montreal 1995

Marchal, Léon. *Les origines de Montréal: Ville-Marie, 1642–1665.* Montréal: Beauchemin 1942

Marie de l'Incarnation. *Correspondance.* Ed. Guy Oury. Solesmes: Abbaye de Saint-Pierre 1972

– *Word from New France: The Selected Letters of Marie de l'Incarnation.* Trans. and ed. Joyce Marshall. Toronto: Oxford University Press 1967

Marsat, André. *La cathédrale de Troyes.* Paris: La Goélette [n.d.]

Massicotte, E.-Z. "Où demeura M. de Maisonneuve?" *Cahiers des Dix* 10 (1940): 178–81

Mitford, Nancy. *The Sun King: Louis XIV at Versailles.* London: Hamish Hamilton 1966

Molette, Charles. "La dévotion à Marie au XVIIe et XVIIIe siècle dans les congrégations féminines." Communication donnée le mardi 13 septembre 1983 au 9e Congrès mariologique international tenu à Malte, 8–15 septembre 1983

Mondoux, Maria. "Les 'hommes' de Montréal." *RHAF* 2, no. 1 (juin 1948): 59–80

– *L'Hôtel-Dieu, premier hôpital de Montréal.* Montréal: Hôtel-Dieu 1942

Mongolfier, Étienne. *The Life of Venerable Sister Margaret Bourgeois, Foundress of the Sisters of the Congregation de Notre Dame, Established at Montreal, Canada, 1659.* Trans. by a religious. New York: D. & J. Sadlier & Co. 1880

– *La vie de la vénérable Soeur Marguerite Bourgeoys dite du Saint Sacrement.* Ville Marie: William Gray 1818

Monier, Frédéric. *Vie de Jean-Jacques Olier.* Paris: Ancienne Librairie Poussielgue 1914

Morin, Alfred. *Du nouveau sur Marguerite Bourgeoys.* Troyes: Renaissance 1964

– "A Lost Treasure?" *CMB* 56 (Spring 1996): 6

Morin, Louis. *Deux familles troyennes de musiciens et de comédiens, les Siret et les Raisin.* Troyes: Paton 1927

Morin, Marie. *Histoire simple et véritable: annales de l'Hôtel-Dieu de Montréal, 1659–1725.* Ed. Ghislaine Legendre. Montreal: Université de Montréal 1979

Mullet, Michael. *The Counter-Reformation and the Catholic Reformation in Early Modern Europe.* London: Methuen 1984

Newman, John Henry. *Apologia pro vita sua.* Ed. A. Dwight Culler. Boston: Houghton Mifflin Company 1956

Niel, J.C. *Marguerite Bourgeoys et sa famille d'après des documents inédits.* Troyes: Renaissance 1950

Nitray, A. de. *Une éducatrice au xviie siècle.* Paris: Gabriel Beauchesne 1919

Oury, Guy-Marie. *L'homme qui a conçu Montréal, Jérôme Le Royer, Sieur de la Dauversière.* Montréal: Méridien 1991

– *Jeanne Mance et le rêve de M. de la Dauversière.* Chambray: C.L.D. 1983

– *Madame de la Peltrie et ses fondations canadiennes.* Perché: Amis du Perché 1974

– "Le rédacteur des 'Véritables motifs': M. Olier?" *Église et théologie* 21 (1990): 211–24

Paris, Charles B. *Marriage in xviith Century Catholicism.* Montreal: Bellarmin 1975

Pellus, Daniel. *Femmes célèbres de Champagne.* Amiens: Martelle 1992

Pitaud, Bernard. *Petite vie de Jean-Jacques Olier.* Paris: Desclée de Brouwer, 1996

Plante, Lucienne. "The Family of Marguerite Bourgeoys" *CMB.* 52 (spring 1994): 25–6, 53 (autumn 1994): 25–7, 54 (spring 1995): 29–31, 55 (autumn 1995): 29–31

Poinsenet, M.D. *France religieuse du xviie siècle.* Paris: Casterman 1954

Poirier, Jean. "Origine du nom de la ville de Montréal." *RHAF* 46, no.1 (1992): 37–44

Poissant, Simone. *Marguerite Bourgeoys, 1620–1700.* Trans. Frances Kirwan. Montreal: Bellarmin 1993

Porter, Fernand. *L'institution catéchistique au Canada français, 1633–1833.* Montréal: Les Éditions franciscaines 1949

Quigley, Florence. *In the Company of Marguerite Bourgeoys.* Montreal: Novalis 1982

Ransonet, Michel-François. *La vie de la Soeur Marguerite Bourgeois.* Liège: Barnabé 1728

Rapley, Eizabeth. *The Dévotes: Women and Culture in Seventeenth- Century France.* Montreal: McGill-Queen's University Press 1990

– "Life and Death of a Community: The Congrégation de Notre-Dame of Troyes, 1628–1762." Canadian Catholic Historical Association, *Historical Studies* 58 (1991): 5–29

Remiremont, A. de. *Mère Alix LeClerc, 1576–1662.* Paris: Congrégation de Notre-Dame 1946

Renault, J. *Le idées pédagogiques de saint Pierre Fourier.* Paris, P. Lethielleux [n.d.]

Robert, Jean-Claude. *Atlas historique de Montréal.* Montréal: Art Global Libre Expression 1994

Rochemonteix, Camille de. *Les Jésuites et la Nouvelle France au xviie siècle.* Paris: Letouzey et Ané 1890

Roserot, Alphonse. *Dictionnaire historique de la Champagne méridionale (Aube) des origines à 1790.* Angers: Éditions de l'Ouest 1948

– *Troyes: son histoire, ses monuments des origines à 1790.* Troyes: Paton 1948

Roserot de Melin, Joseph. *Le Diocèse de Troyes des origines à nos jours (IIIe siècle – 1955).* Troyes: Renaissance 1957

Rouquet, Chantal. *Troyes à travers les âges.* Troyes: CNDP 1985

Rousseau, François. *La croix et le scalpel: histoire des Augustines et de l'Hôtel-Dieu de Québec. Vol. 1, 1639–1892.* Québec: Septentrion 1989

Rousseau, Jacques. "Les premiers Canadiens." *Cahiers des Dix* 25 (1960): 9–64

Roy, Pierre Georges. *Inventaire des greffes des notaires du régime français.* Vol. 1. Archives de la province de Québec, 1: Québec 1943

Rumilly, Robert. *Histoire de Montréal.* Vol. 1. Montréal: Fides 1970

– *Marguerite Bourgeoys.* Paris: Spes 1936

– *Marie Barbier: mystique canadienne.* Montréal: Albert Levesque 1935

Sainte-Henriette, Sister. *Histoire de la Congrégation de Notre-Dame.* Vols. 1–4. Montréal: Congrégation de Notre-Dame 1941

Saint Marguerite Bourgeoys: Canonization. Montreal: Congrégation de Notre-Dame 1982

Sales, Francis de. *Introduction to the Devout Life.* Trans. and ed. John K. Royan. New York: Harper and Brothers 1950

– and Jane de Chantal. *Letters of Spiritual Direction.* Trans. Peronne Marie Thibert. Selected and introduced by Wendy M. Wright and Joseph F. Power. New York: Paulist Press 1988

Schwarzfuchs, Simon. *Rachi de Troyes.* Paris: Albin Michel 1991

Scott, Mary Eileen. "The Constant Heart." Play first produced by the Genesian Players at the Gésu Theatre, Montreal 1951

– "Religious Attitudes in New France and Their Political and Social Grounds." Lecture delivered at the Thomas More Institute, Montreal, Spring 1976

– "Spirit, Purpose and Some Charisms of Mother Bourgeoys." Paper circulated in Congrégation de Notre-Dame, June 1968

– "The Spiritual Legacy of Montreal." Lecture delivered at Mass Rally for Christ, Montreal Forum, 8 March 1971

– *A Spirituality of Compassion.* Montreal: Congrégation de Notre-Dame 1979

– "The Stable Foundation." ACMB

– "Transformation." ACMB

Sedgwick, Alexander. *Jansenism in Seventeenth-Century France: Voices from the Wilderness.* Charlottesville: University of Virginia Press 1977

Seguin, Robert-Lionel. *La civilisation traditionnelle de l'"habitant" aux 17e et 18e siècles.* Montréal: Fides 1967

– *La sorcellerie au Canada français du XVIIe au XIXe siècle.* Montréal: Ducharme 1961

Sévigny, Jeannine. *Social and Religious Context of Marguerite Bourgeoys's*

Mission as Educator. Trans. Patricia Landry. CND, Heritage no. 9. Montreal 1993

Taveneaux, Réné, ed. *Saint Pierre Fourier en son temps.* Nancy: Presses universitaires 1992

Tooker, Elisabeth. *An Ethnography of the Huron Indians, 1615–1649.* Midland, Ont.: Huronia Historical Development Council 1967

Toynbee, Philip. *Towards the Holy Spirit.* London: SCM Press Ltd 1982

Tremblay, Hélène. "Historiographie de Marguerite Bourgeoys aux XVIIe et XVIIIe siècles." Dissertation, Université de Montréal 1967

– *Marguerite Bourgeoys and the Education of Women.* Trans. Elizabeth Jane Fraser. CND, Heritage no. 12. Montreal 1993

Trigger, Bruce G. *The Huron: Farmers of the North.* Montreal: Holt, Rinehart and Winston 1969

Trudel, Marcel. *The Beginnings of New France, 1524–1663.* Trans. Patricia Claxton. Toronto: McClelland and Stewart 1973

– *Montréal, la formation d'une société, 1642–1663.* Montreal: Fides 1976

– *La population du Canada en 1666: recensement constitué.* Sillery: Septentrion 1995

– *Le terrier du Saint-Laurent en 1663.* Ottawa: University of Ottawa 1973

Vachon, André. "L'affaire du Long Sault: valeurs des sources huronne." *Revue de l'université Laval* 18, no. 6 (1964): 495–515

– "Valeurs des sources iroquoises et françaises." *Cahiers des Dix* 40 (1975): 197–222.

Les Véritables Motifs de Messieurs et Dames de la Société de Nostre Dame de Monréal pour la Conversion des Sauvages de la nouvelle France. S.l. [Paris] 1643. Copy in the Huntington Library, San Marino, Calif., reproduced in Daveluy, *La Société de Notre-Dame de Montréal.*

Vie intime de la Vénérable Mère Alix Le Clerc. Gembloux: Duculot 1923

Vincent de Paul, Saint. *Correspondance, entretiens, documents.* Ed. Pierre Coste. 14 vols. Paris : Librairie Lecoffre, J. Gabalda 1920–25

Les vraies constitutions des religieuses de la Congregation de Nostre Dame; Faites par le venerable serviteur de Dieu Pierre Fourier leur instituteur, et chanoines reguliers de la Congregation de nôtre Sauveur, approuvées par nôtre saint pere le Pape Innocent X. 2d éd. Toul, 1694

Vuillemin, Jean-Baptiste. *La vie de la Vénérable Alix Le Clerc.* Paris: Société Saint-Augustin, Desclée, De Brouwer et Cie 1910

Walsh, H.H. *The Church in the French Era.* Toronto: Ryerson 1966

Warner, Marina. *Alone of All her Sex: The Myth and Cult of the Virgin Mary.* New York: Knopf 1976

Index